AWA UPSHOT PRESENTS

PRIMOS

STORY BY AL MADRIGAL & FELIPE FLORES

AL MADRIGAL
WRITER

CARLO BARBERI
ARTIST

BRIAN REBER
COLORIST

ANDWORLD DESIGN
LETTERER

DAVE JOHNSON
COVER ARTIST

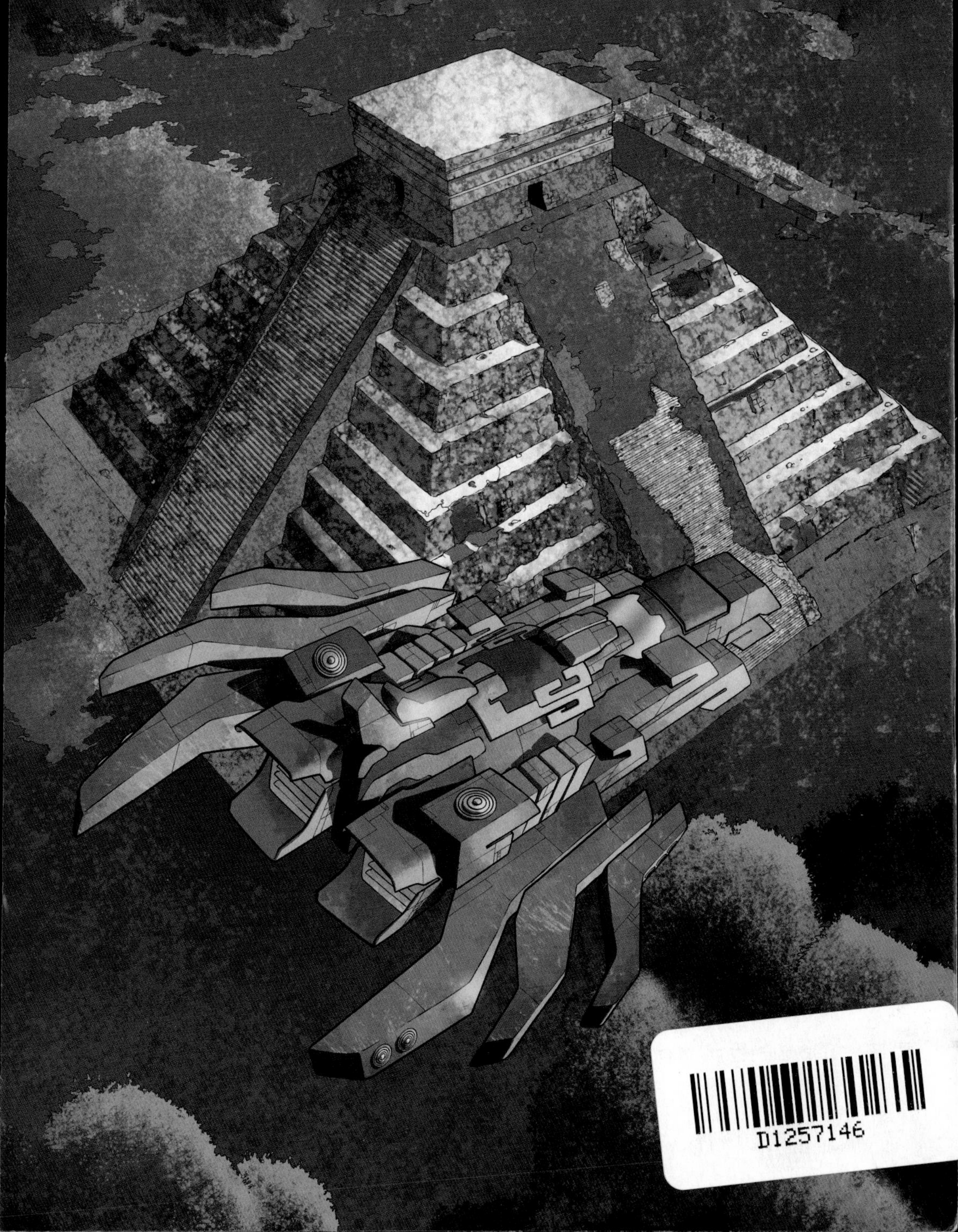

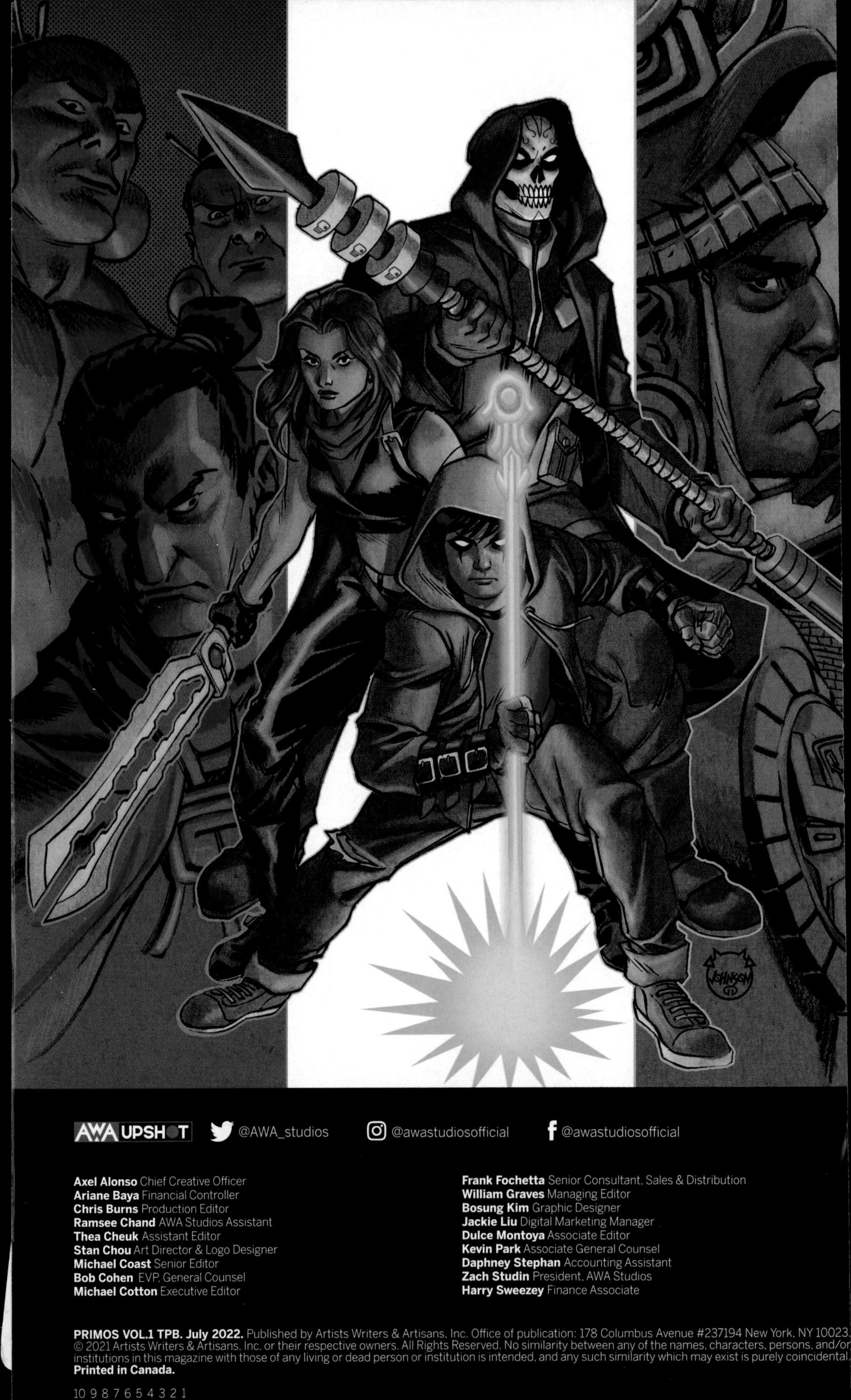

AWA UPSHOT @AWA_studios @awastudiosofficial @awastudiosofficial

Axel Alonso Chief Creative Officer
Ariane Baya Financial Controller
Chris Burns Production Editor
Ramsee Chand AWA Studios Assistant
Thea Cheuk Assistant Editor
Stan Chou Art Director & Logo Designer
Michael Coast Senior Editor
Bob Cohen EVP, General Counsel
Michael Cotton Executive Editor
Frank Fochetta Senior Consultant, Sales & Distribution
William Graves Managing Editor
Bosung Kim Graphic Designer
Jackie Liu Digital Marketing Manager
Dulce Montoya Associate Editor
Kevin Park Associate General Counsel
Daphney Stephan Accounting Assistant
Zach Studin President, AWA Studios
Harry Sweezey Finance Associate

PRIMOS VOL.1 TPB. July 2022. Published by Artists Writers & Artisans, Inc. Office of publication: 178 Columbus Avenue #237194 New York, NY 10023.

Printed in Canada.

10 9 8 7 6 5 4 3 2 1

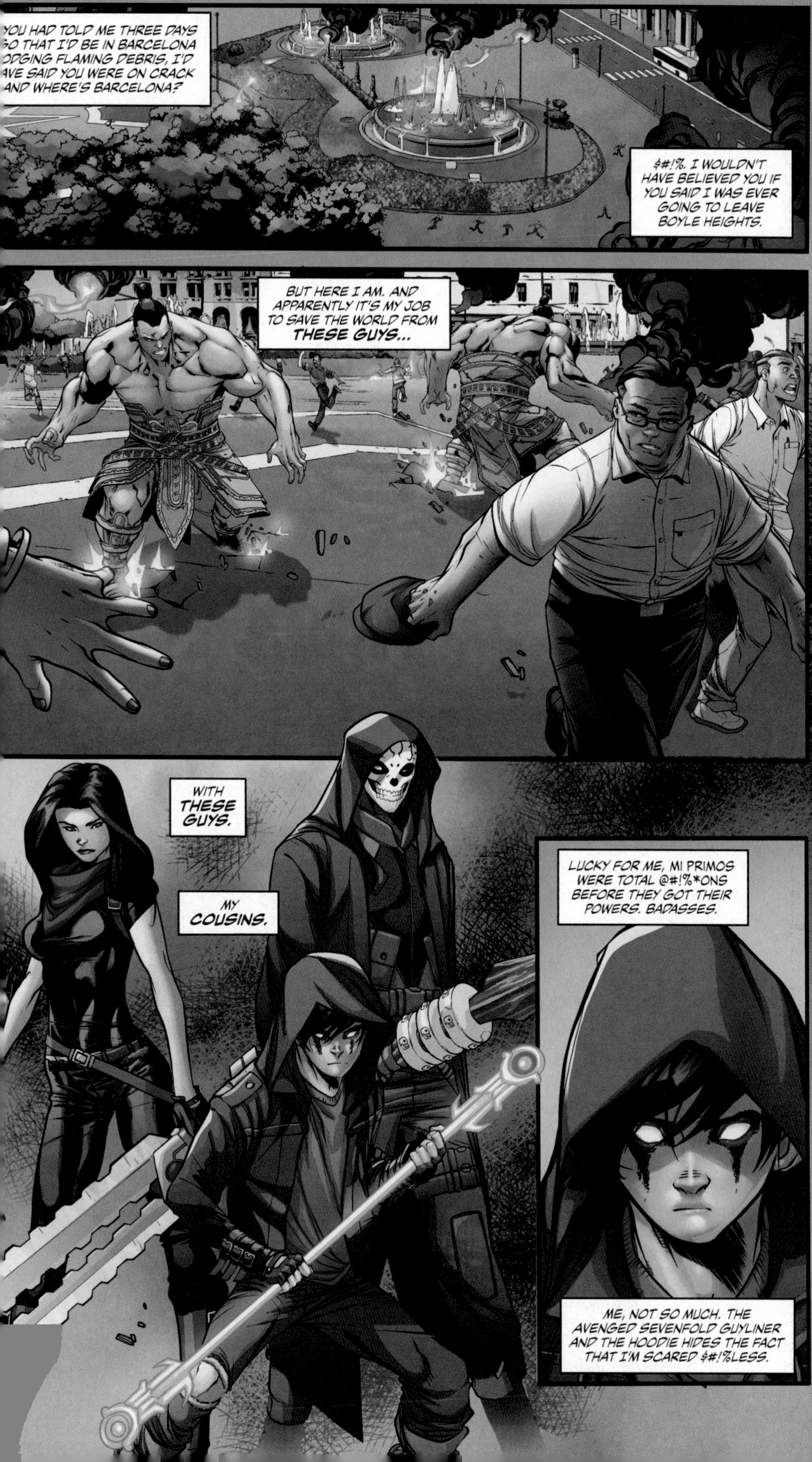
YOU HAD TOLD ME THREE DAYS GO THAT I'D BE IN BARCELONA ODGING FLAMING DEBRIS, I'D AVE SAID YOU WERE ON CRACK AND WHERE'S BARCELONA?
$#!%. I WOULDN'T HAVE BELIEVED YOU IF YOU SAID I WAS EVER GOING TO LEAVE BOYLE HEIGHTS.
BUT HERE I AM. AND APPARENTLY IT'S MY JOB TO SAVE THE WORLD FROM THESE GUYS...
WITH THESE GUYS.
MY COUSINS.
LUCKY FOR ME, MI PRIMOS WERE TOTAL @#!%*ONS BEFORE THEY GOT THEIR POWERS. BADASSES.
ME, NOT SO MUCH. THE AVENGED SEVENFOLD GUYLINER AND THE HOODIE HIDES THE FACT THAT I'M SCARED $#!%LESS.

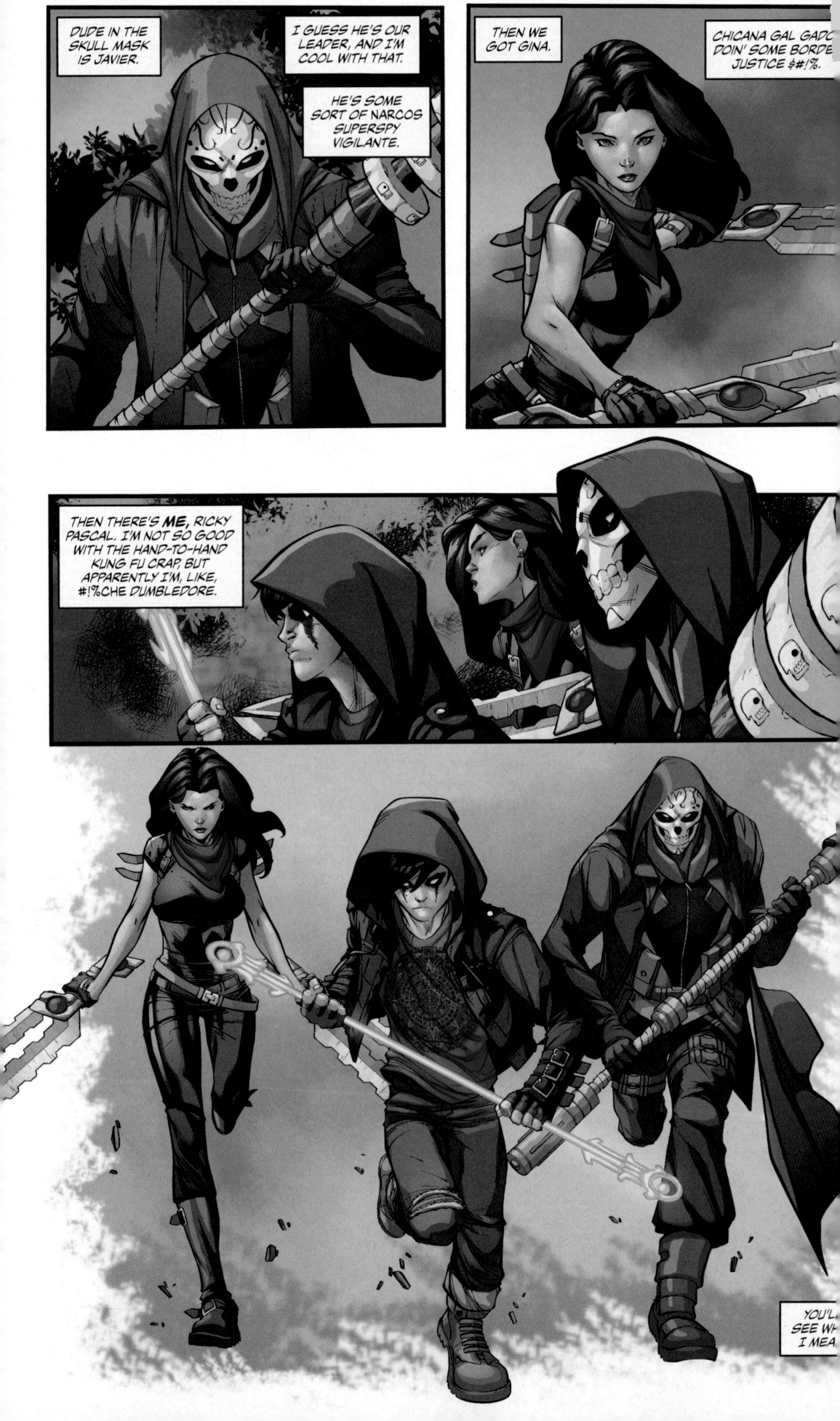
DUDE IN THE SKULL MASK IS JAVIER.
I GUESS HE'S OUR LEADER, AND I'M COOL WITH THAT.
HE'S SOME SORT OF NARCOS SUPERSPY VIGILANTE.
THEN WE GOT GINA.
CHICANA GAL GADO DOIN' SOME BORDE JUSTICE $#!%.
THEN THERE'S ME, RICKY PASCAL. I'M NOT SO GOOD WITH THE HAND-TO-HAND KUNG FU CRAP, BUT APPARENTLY I'M, LIKE, #!%CHE DUMBLEDORE.
YOU'L SEE WH I MEA

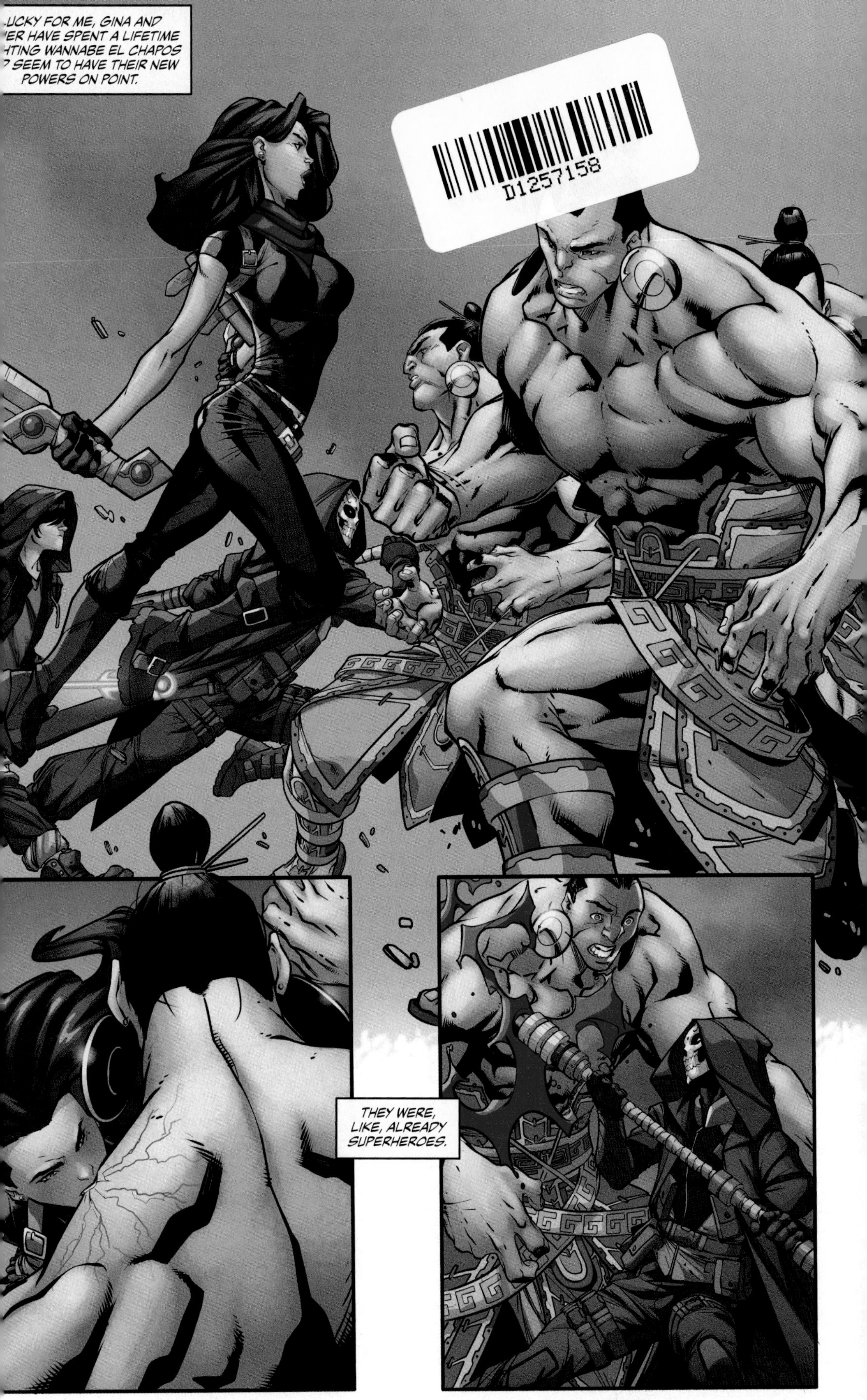

LUCKY FOR ME, GINA AND
VER HAVE SPENT A LIFETIME
HTING WANNABE EL CHAPOS
D SEEM TO HAVE THEIR NEW
POWERS ON POINT.
THEY WERE, LIKE, ALREADY SUPERHEROES.

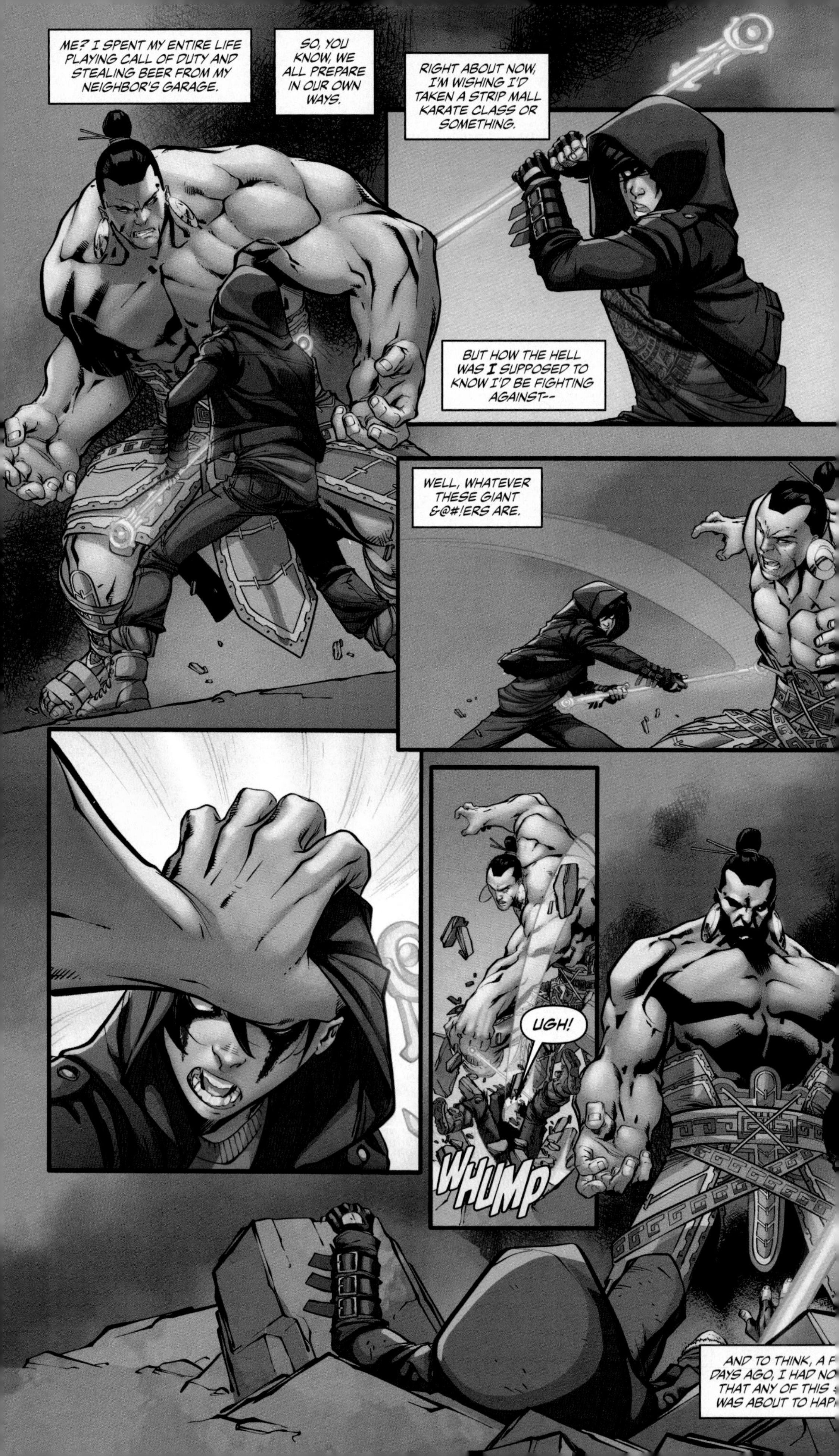
ME? I SPENT MY ENTIRE LIFE PLAYING CALL OF DUTY AND STEALING BEER FROM MY NEIGHBOR'S GARAGE.
SO, YOU KNOW, WE ALL PREPARE IN OUR OWN WAYS.
RIGHT ABOUT NOW, I'M WISHING I'D TAKEN A STRIP MALL KARATE CLASS OR SOMETHING.
BUT HOW THE HELL WAS I SUPPOSED TO KNOW I'D BE FIGHTING AGAINST--
WELL, WHATEVER THESE GIANT &@#!ERS ARE.
UGH!
WHUMP

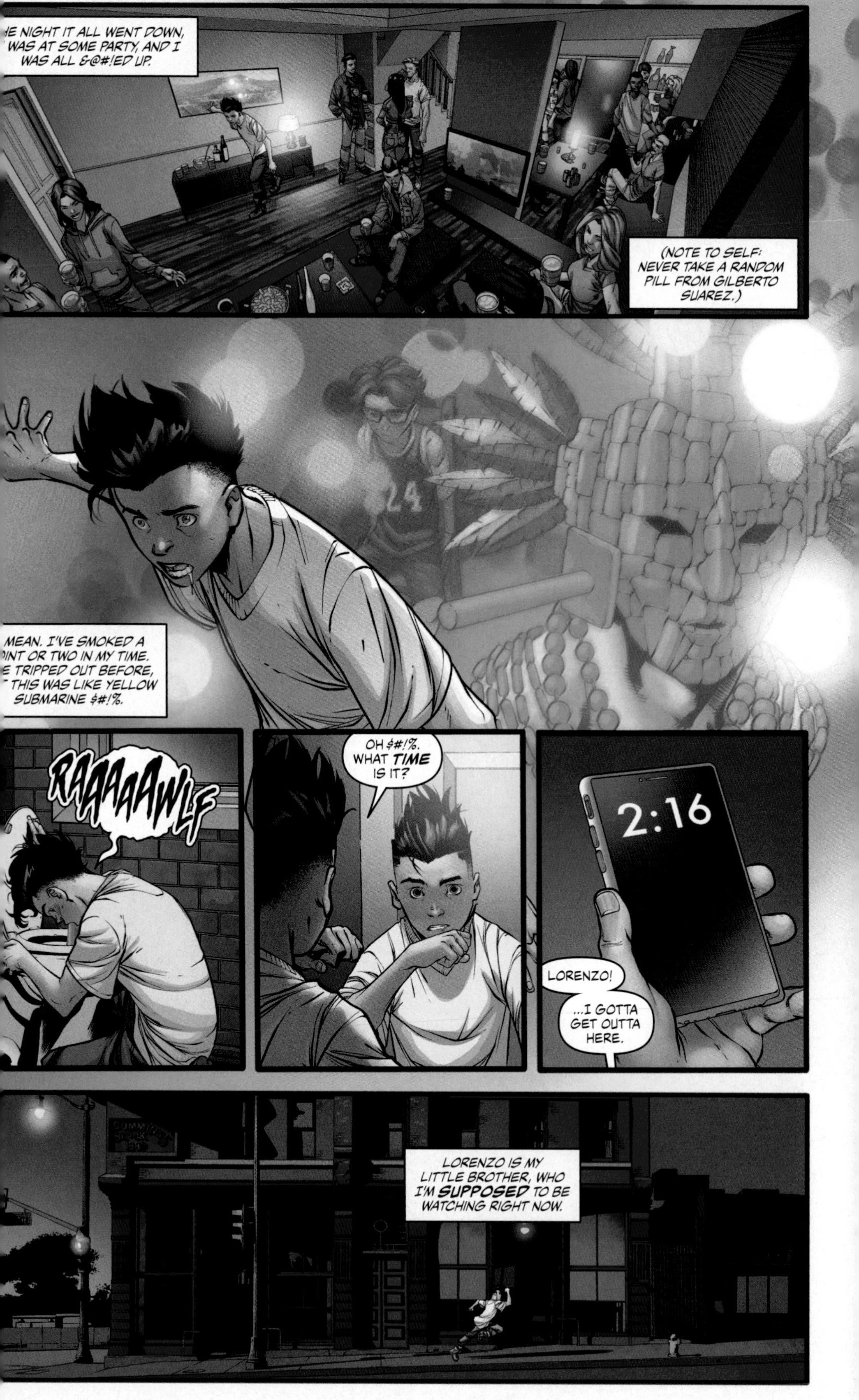

HE NIGHT IT ALL WENT DOWN, WAS AT SOME PARTY, AND I WAS ALL &@#!ED UP.
(NOTE TO SELF: NEVER TAKE A RANDOM PILL FROM GILBERTO SUAREZ.)
MEAN. I'VE SMOKED A OINT OR TWO IN MY TIME. E TRIPPED OUT BEFORE, THIS WAS LIKE YELLOW SUBMARINE $#!%.
RAAAAAAWLF
OH $#!%. WHAT TIME IS IT?
2:16
LORENZO!
...I GOTTA GET OUTTA HERE.
LORENZO IS MY LITTLE BROTHER, WHO I'M SUPPOSED TO BE WATCHING RIGHT NOW.

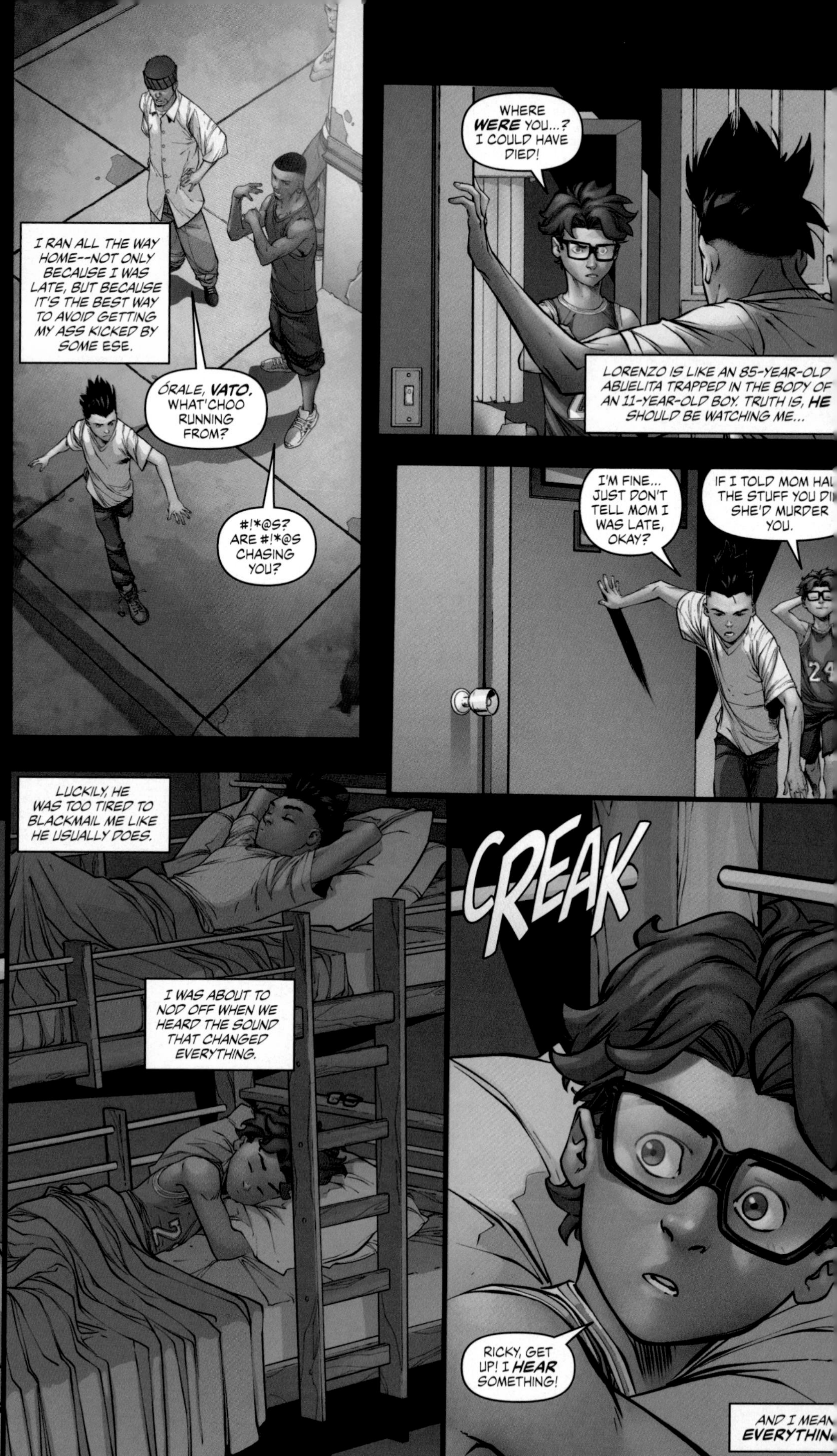
I RAN ALL THE WAY HOME--NOT ONLY BECAUSE I WAS LATE, BUT BECAUSE IT'S THE BEST WAY TO AVOID GETTING MY ASS KICKED BY SOME ESE.
ÓRALE, VATO. WHAT'CHOO RUNNING FROM?
#!*@S? ARE #!*@S CHASING YOU?
WHERE WERE YOU...? I COULD HAVE DIED!
LORENZO IS LIKE AN 85-YEAR-OLD ABUELITA TRAPPED IN THE BODY OF AN 11-YEAR-OLD BOY. TRUTH IS, HE SHOULD BE WATCHING ME...
I'M FINE... JUST DON'T TELL MOM I WAS LATE, OKAY?
IF I TOLD MOM HAL THE STUFF YOU DI SHE'D MURDER YOU.
LUCKILY, HE WAS TOO TIRED TO BLACKMAIL ME LIKE HE USUALLY DOES.
I WAS ABOUT TO NOD OFF WHEN WE HEARD THE SOUND THAT CHANGED EVERYTHING.
CREAK
RICKY, GET UP! I HEAR SOMETHING!
AND I MEAN EVERYTHIN

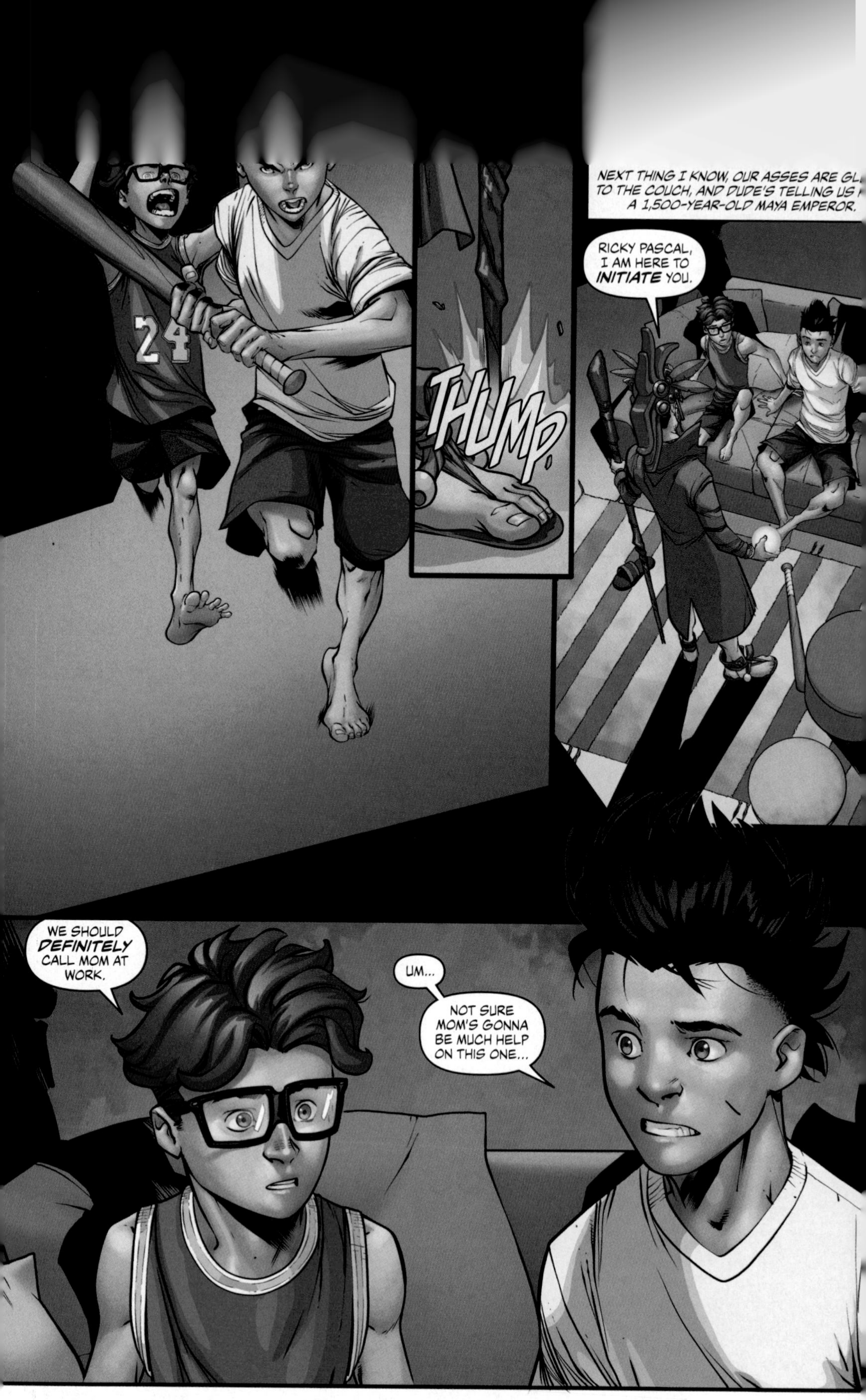
THUMP
NEXT THING I KNOW, OUR ASSES ARE GL
TO THE COUCH, AND DUDE'S TELLING US
A 1,500-YEAR-OLD MAYA EMPEROR.
RICKY PASCAL, I AM HERE TO *INITIATE* YOU.
WE SHOULD *DEFINITELY* CALL MOM AT WORK.
UM...
NOT SURE MOM'S GONNA BE MUCH HELP ON THIS ONE...

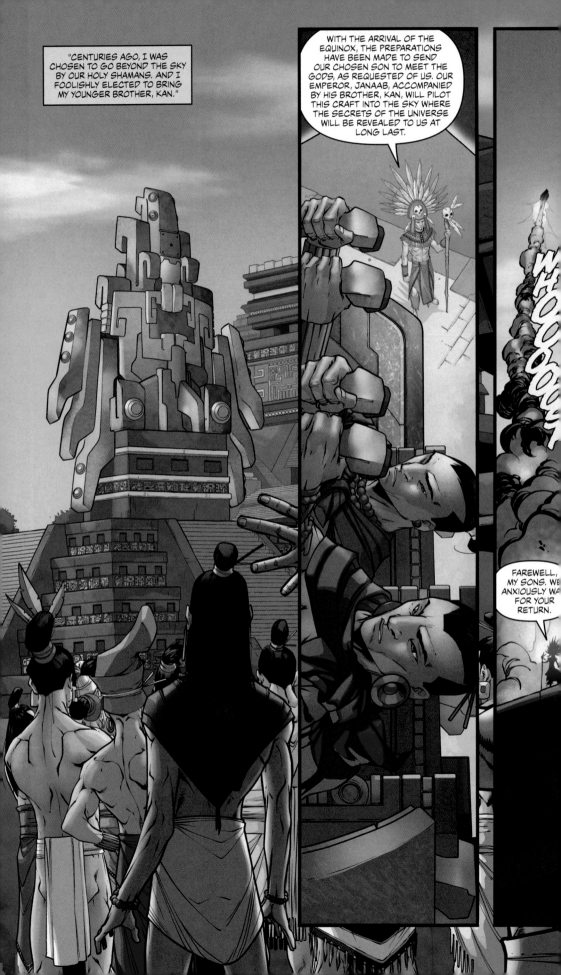

"CENTURIES AGO, I WAS CHOSEN TO GO BEYOND THE SKY BY OUR HOLY SHAMANS. AND I FOOLISHLY ELECTED TO BRING MY YOUNGER BROTHER, KAN."

WITH THE ARRIVAL OF THE EQUINOX, THE PREPARATIONS HAVE BEEN MADE TO SEND OUR CHOSEN SON TO MEET THE GODS, AS REQUESTED OF US. OUR EMPEROR, JANAAB, ACCOMPANIED BY HIS BROTHER, KAN, WILL PILOT THIS CRAFT INTO THE SKY WHERE THE SECRETS OF THE UNIVERSE WILL BE REVEALED TO US AT LONG LAST.

WHO-O-O-OOSH

FAREWELL, MY SONS. WE ANXIOUSLY WA FOR YOUR RETURN.

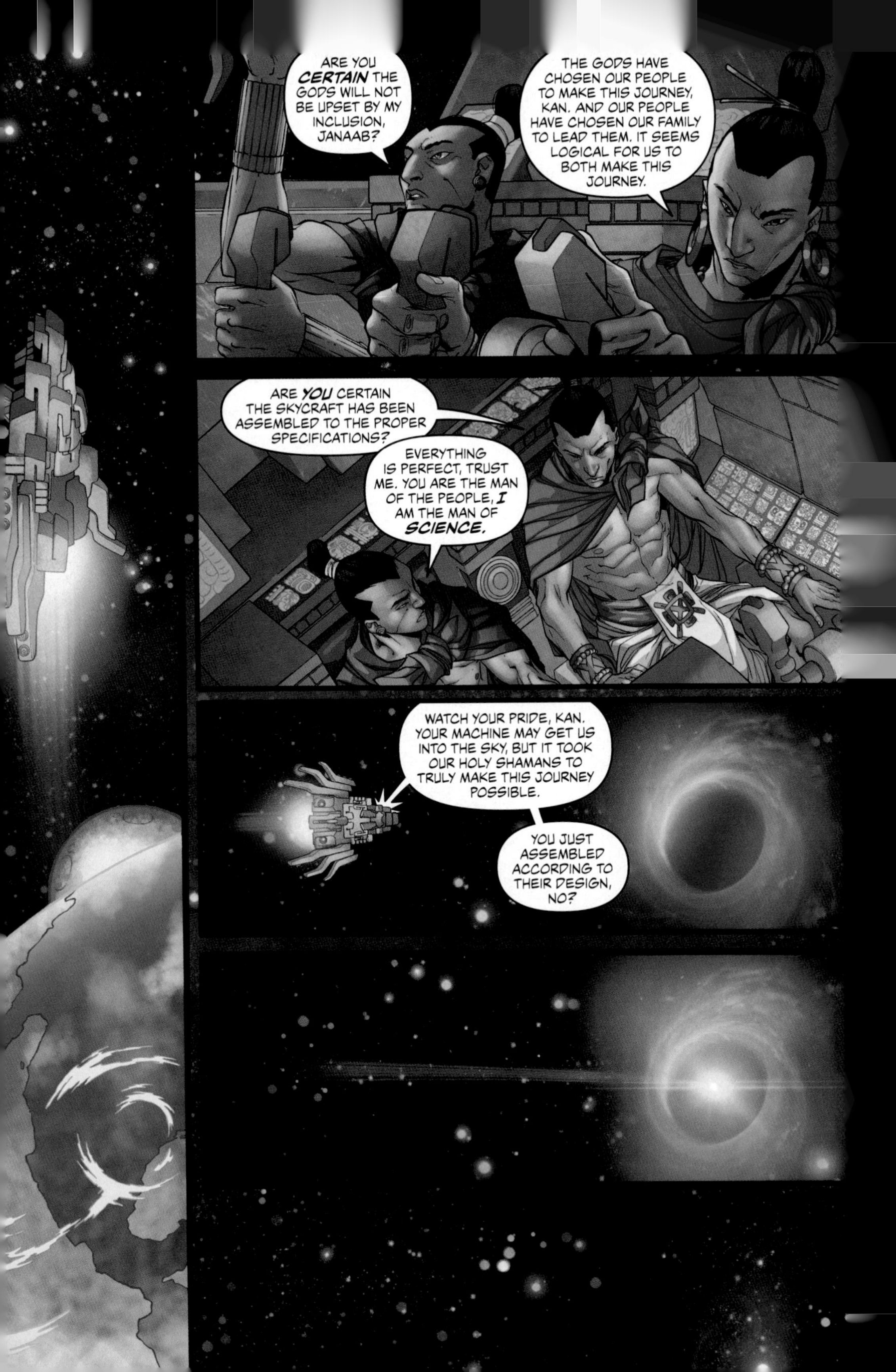
ARE YOU CERTAIN THE GODS WILL NOT BE UPSET BY MY INCLUSION, JANAAB?
THE GODS HAVE CHOSEN OUR PEOPLE TO MAKE THIS JOURNEY, KAN. AND OUR PEOPLE HAVE CHOSEN OUR FAMILY TO LEAD THEM. IT SEEMS LOGICAL FOR US TO BOTH MAKE THIS JOURNEY.
ARE YOU CERTAIN THE SKYCRAFT HAS BEEN ASSEMBLED TO THE PROPER SPECIFICATIONS?
EVERYTHING IS PERFECT, TRUST ME. YOU ARE THE MAN OF THE PEOPLE, I AM THE MAN OF SCIENCE.
WATCH YOUR PRIDE, KAN. YOUR MACHINE MAY GET US INTO THE SKY, BUT IT TOOK OUR HOLY SHAMANS TO TRULY MAKE THIS JOURNEY POSSIBLE.
YOU JUST ASSEMBLED ACCORDING TO THEIR DESIGN, NO?

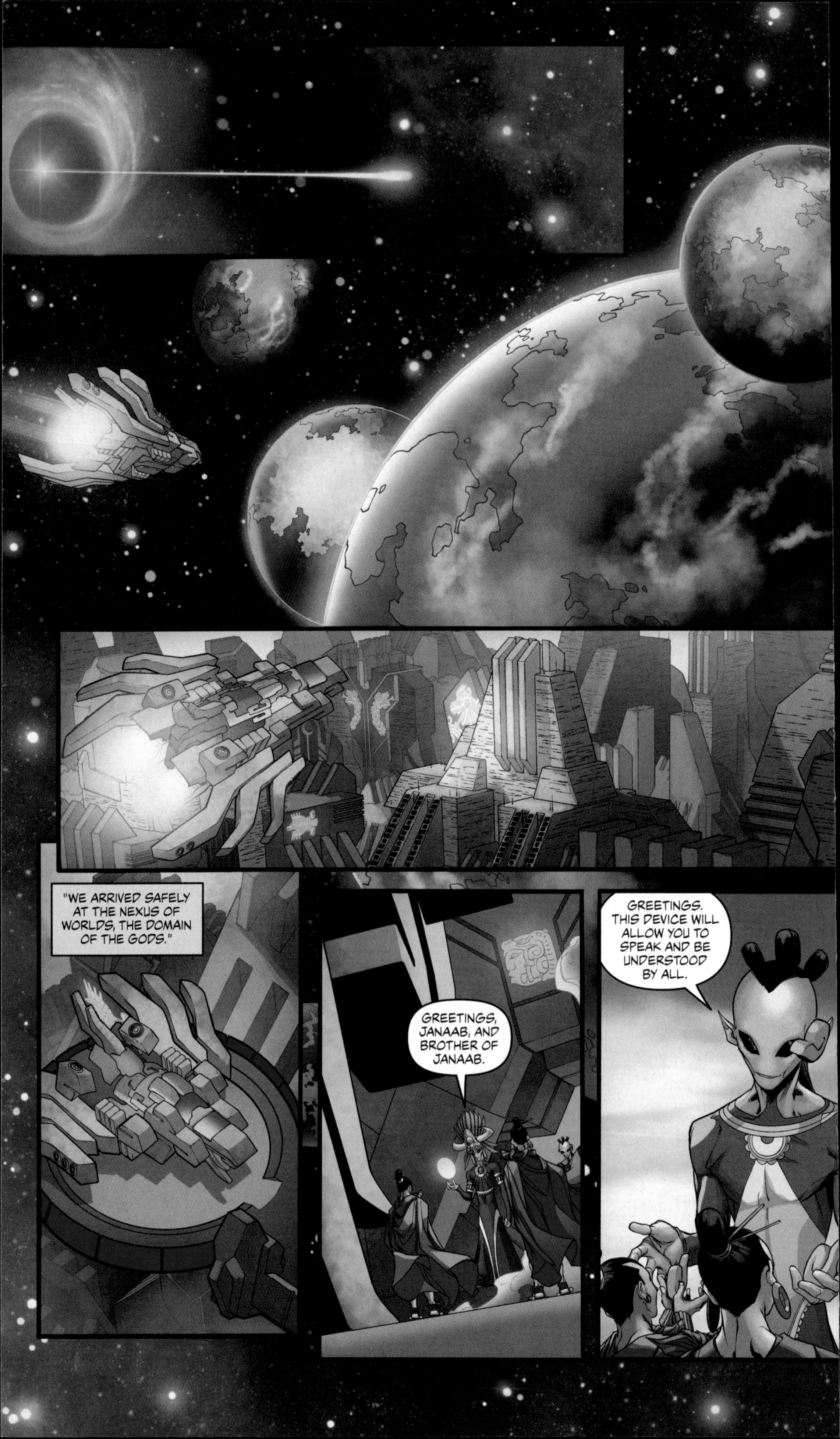
"WE ARRIVED SAFELY AT THE NEXUS OF WORLDS, THE DOMAIN OF THE GODS."
GREETINGS, JANAAB, AND BROTHER OF JANAAB.
GREETINGS. THIS DEVICE WILL ALLOW YOU TO SPEAK AND BE UNDERSTOOD BY ALL.

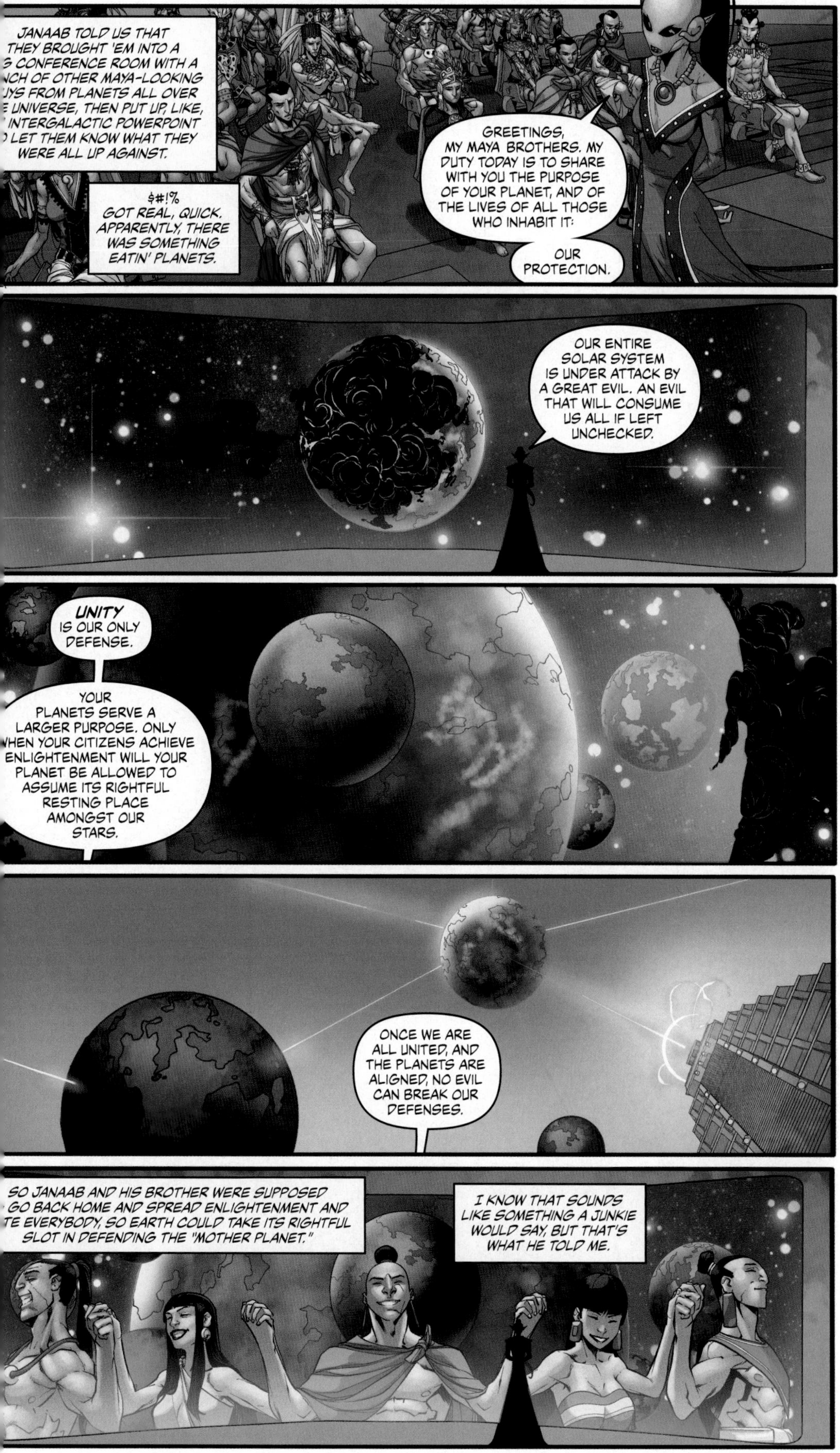

JANAAB TOLD US THAT THEY BROUGHT 'EM INTO A S CONFERENCE ROOM WITH A NCH OF OTHER MAYA-LOOKING UYS FROM PLANETS ALL OVER E UNIVERSE, THEN PUT UP, LIKE, INTERGALACTIC POWERPOINT D LET THEM KNOW WHAT THEY WERE ALL UP AGAINST.
$#!% GOT REAL, QUICK. APPARENTLY, THERE WAS SOMETHING EATIN' PLANETS.
GREETINGS, MY MAYA BROTHERS. MY DUTY TODAY IS TO SHARE WITH YOU THE PURPOSE OF YOUR PLANET, AND OF THE LIVES OF ALL THOSE WHO INHABIT IT:
OUR PROTECTION.
OUR ENTIRE SOLAR SYSTEM IS UNDER ATTACK BY A GREAT EVIL. AN EVIL THAT WILL CONSUME US ALL IF LEFT UNCHECKED.
UNITY IS OUR ONLY DEFENSE.
YOUR PLANETS SERVE A LARGER PURPOSE. ONLY WHEN YOUR CITIZENS ACHIEVE ENLIGHTENMENT WILL YOUR PLANET BE ALLOWED TO ASSUME ITS RIGHTFUL RESTING PLACE AMONGST OUR STARS.
ONCE WE ARE ALL UNITED, AND THE PLANETS ARE ALIGNED, NO EVIL CAN BREAK OUR DEFENSES.
SO JANAAB AND HIS BROTHER WERE SUPPOSED GO BACK HOME AND SPREAD ENLIGHTENMENT AND TE EVERYBODY, SO EARTH COULD TAKE ITS RIGHTFUL SLOT IN DEFENDING THE "MOTHER PLANET."
I KNOW THAT SOUNDS LIKE SOMETHING A JUNKIE WOULD SAY, BUT THAT'S WHAT HE TOLD ME.

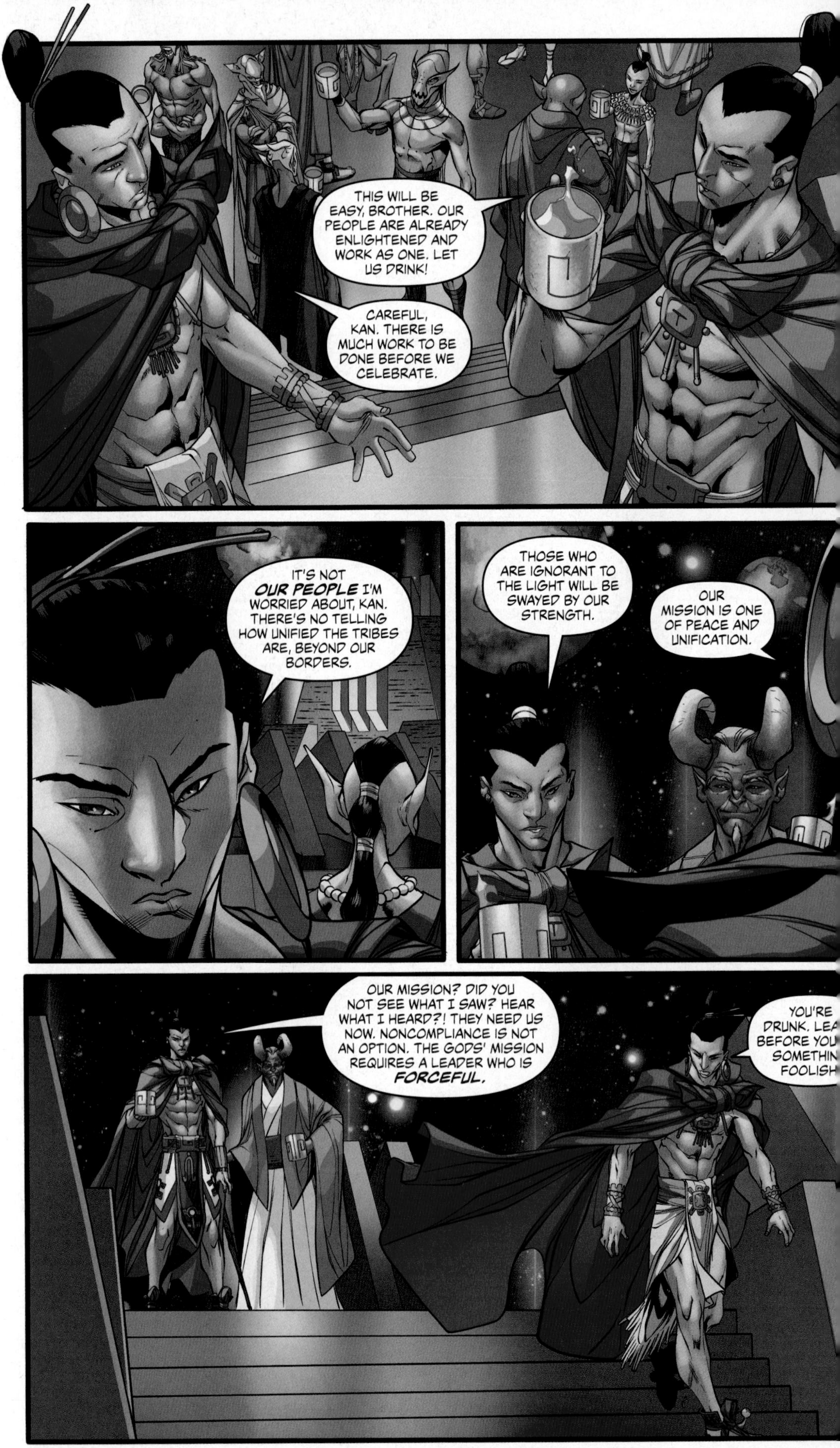
THIS WILL BE EASY, BROTHER. OUR PEOPLE ARE ALREADY ENLIGHTENED AND WORK AS ONE. LET US DRINK!
CAREFUL, KAN. THERE IS MUCH WORK TO BE DONE BEFORE WE CELEBRATE.
IT'S NOT ***OUR PEOPLE*** I'M WORRIED ABOUT, KAN. THERE'S NO TELLING HOW UNIFIED THE TRIBES ARE, BEYOND OUR BORDERS.
THOSE WHO ARE IGNORANT TO THE LIGHT WILL BE SWAYED BY OUR STRENGTH.
OUR MISSION IS ONE OF PEACE AND UNIFICATION.
OUR MISSION? DID YOU NOT SEE WHAT I SAW? HEAR WHAT I HEARD?! THEY NEED US NOW. NONCOMPLIANCE IS NOT AN OPTION. THE GODS' MISSION REQUIRES A LEADER WHO IS ***FORCEFUL.***
YOU'RE DRUNK. LEA BEFORE YOU SOMETHIN FOOLISH

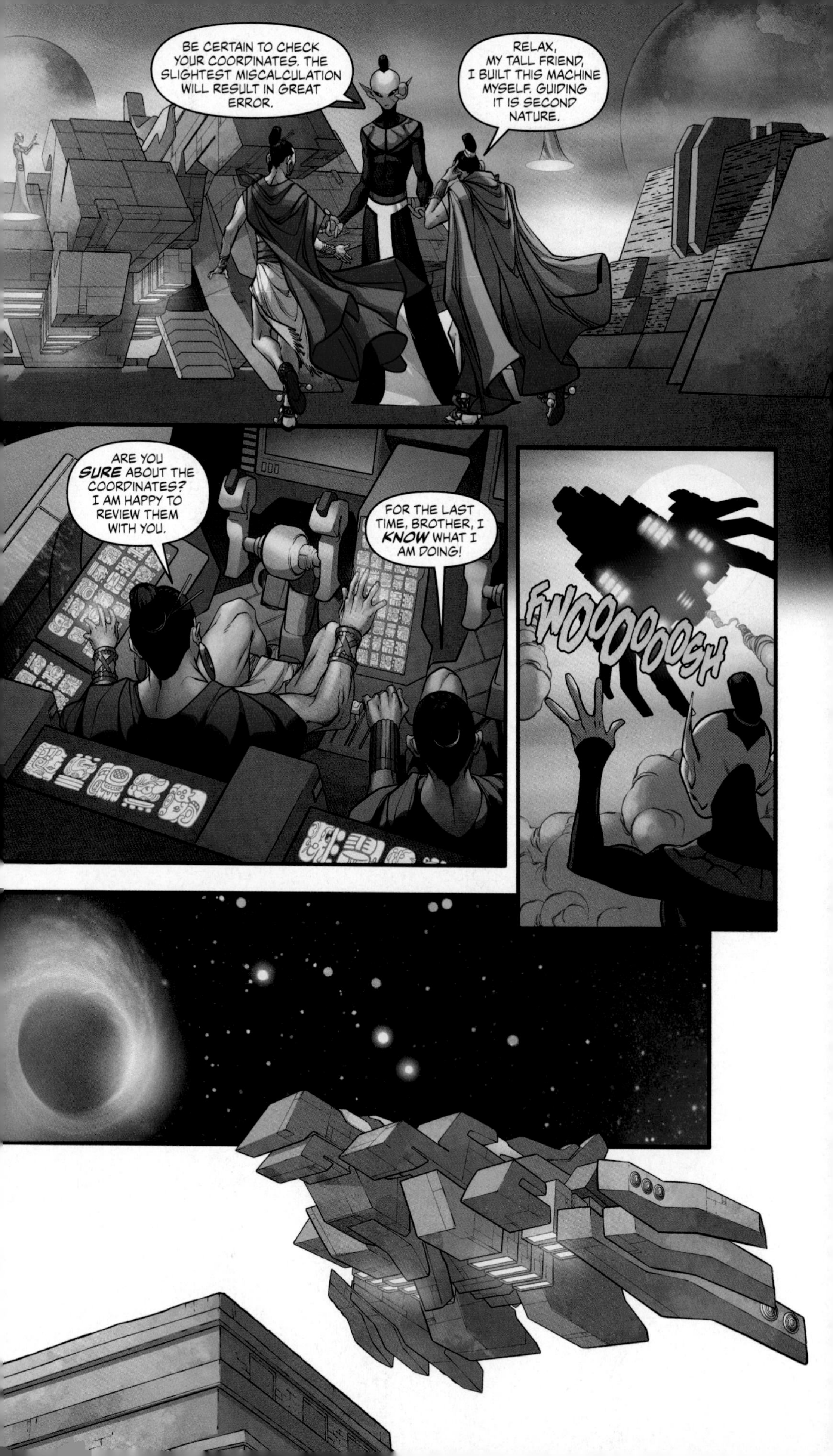
BE CERTAIN TO CHECK YOUR COORDINATES. THE SLIGHTEST MISCALCULATION WILL RESULT IN GREAT ERROR.
RELAX, MY TALL FRIEND, I BUILT THIS MACHINE MYSELF. GUIDING IT IS SECOND NATURE.
ARE YOU SURE ABOUT THE COORDINATES? I AM HAPPY TO REVIEW THEM WITH YOU.
FOR THE LAST TIME, BROTHER, I KNOW WHAT I AM DOING!
FWOOOOOOOSH

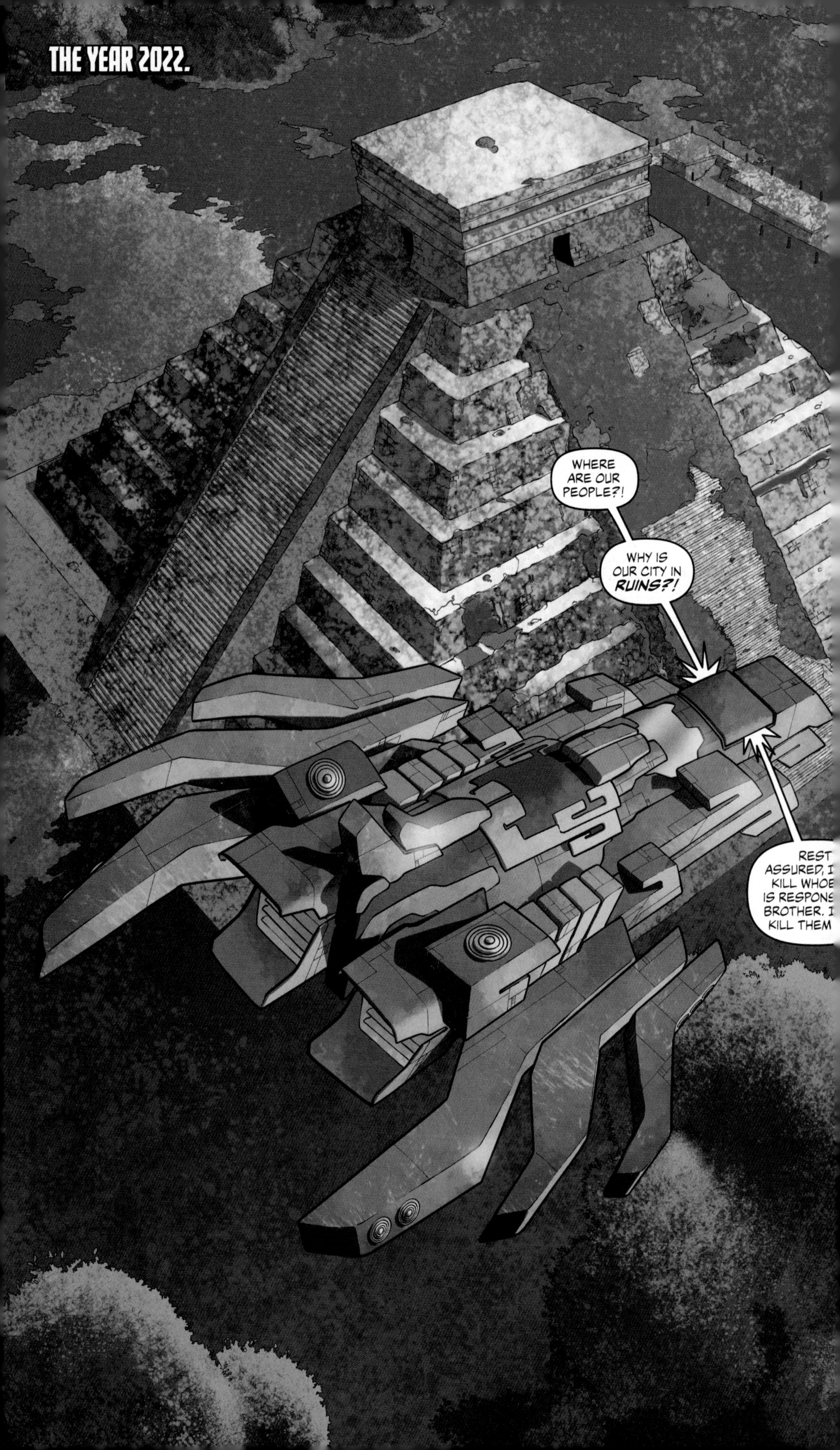
THE YEAR 2022.
WHERE ARE OUR PEOPLE?!
WHY IS OUR CITY IN *RUINS?!*
REST ASSURED, I KILL WHOE IS RESPONS BROTHER. I KILL THEM

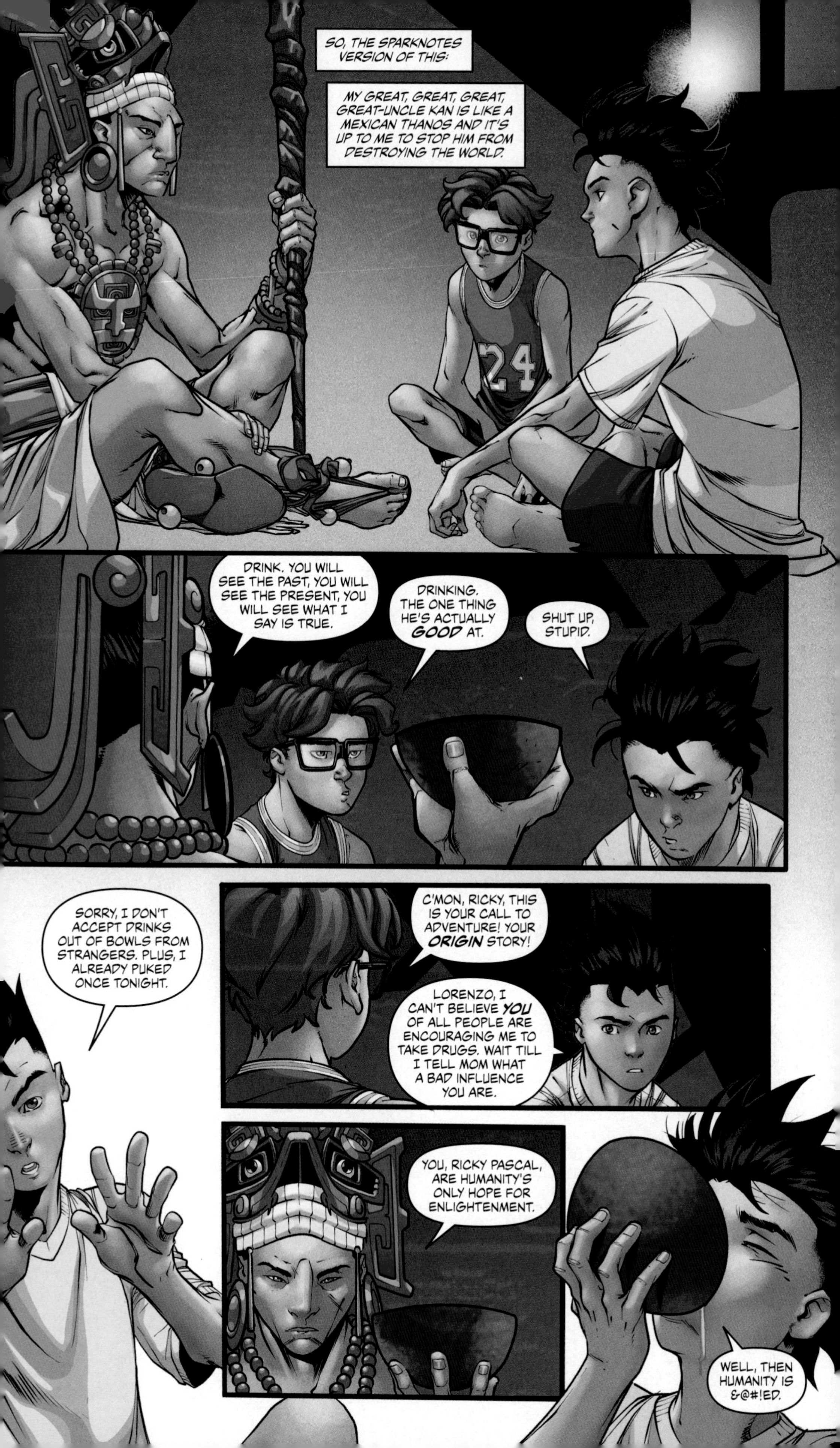
SO, THE SPARKNOTES VERSION OF THIS:
MY GREAT, GREAT, GREAT, GREAT-UNCLE KAN IS LIKE A MEXICAN THANOS AND IT'S UP TO ME TO STOP HIM FROM DESTROYING THE WORLD.
24
DRINK. YOU WILL SEE THE PAST, YOU WILL SEE THE PRESENT, YOU WILL SEE WHAT I SAY IS TRUE.
DRINKING. THE ONE THING HE'S ACTUALLY *GOOD* AT.
SHUT UP, STUPID.
SORRY, I DON'T ACCEPT DRINKS OUT OF BOWLS FROM STRANGERS. PLUS, I ALREADY PUKED ONCE TONIGHT.
C'MON, RICKY, THIS IS YOUR CALL TO ADVENTURE! YOUR *ORIGIN* STORY!
LORENZO, I CAN'T BELIEVE *YOU* OF ALL PEOPLE ARE ENCOURAGING ME TO TAKE DRUGS. WAIT TILL I TELL MOM WHAT A BAD INFLUENCE YOU ARE.
YOU, RICKY PASCAL, ARE HUMANITY'S ONLY HOPE FOR ENLIGHTENMENT.
WELL, THEN HUMANITY IS &@#!ED.

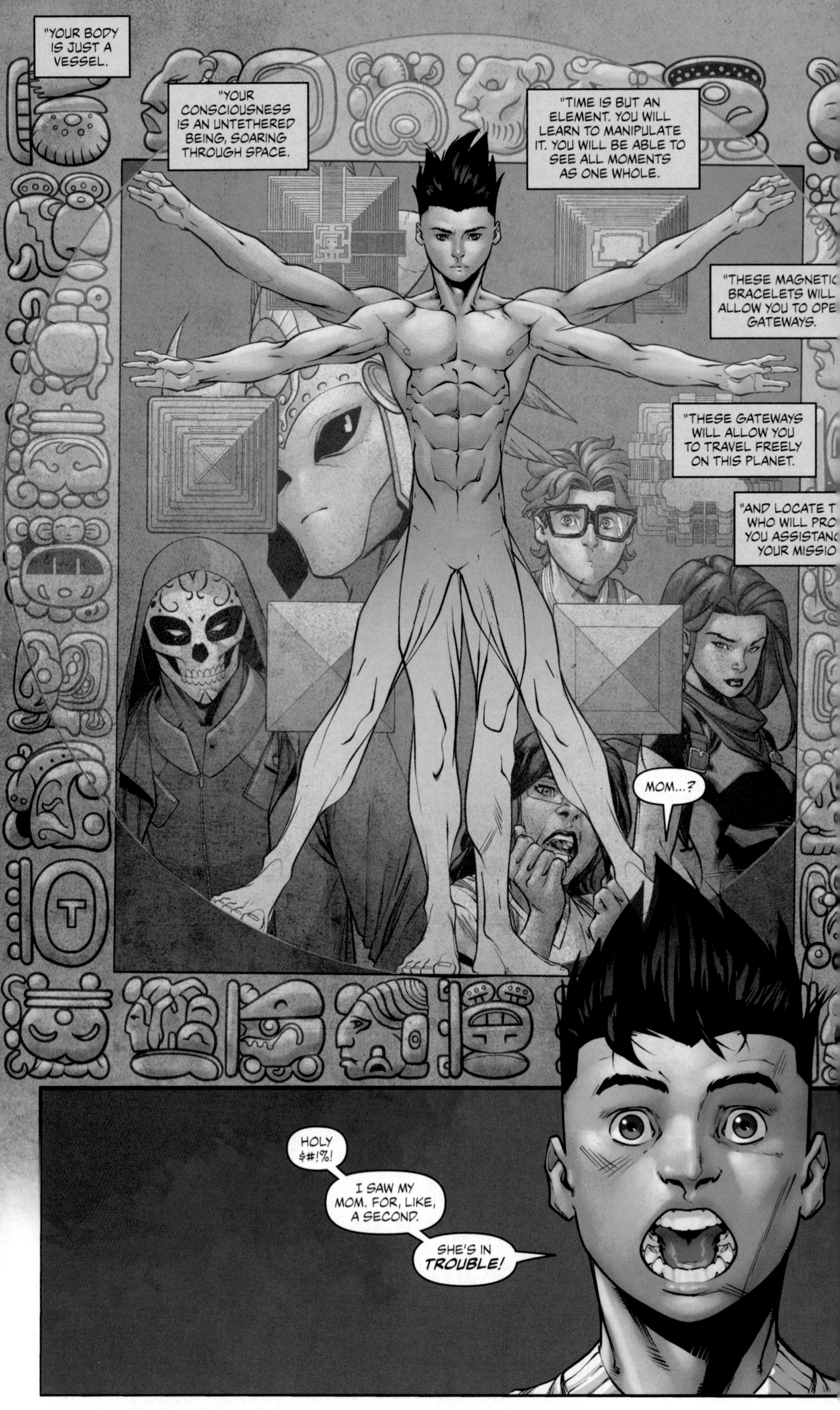
"YOUR BODY IS JUST A VESSEL.
"YOUR CONSCIOUSNESS IS AN UNTETHERED BEING, SOARING THROUGH SPACE.
"TIME IS BUT AN ELEMENT. YOU WILL LEARN TO MANIPULATE IT. YOU WILL BE ABLE TO SEE ALL MOMENTS AS ONE WHOLE.
"THESE MAGNETIC BRACELETS WILL ALLOW YOU TO OPE GATEWAYS.
"THESE GATEWAYS WILL ALLOW YOU TO TRAVEL FREELY ON THIS PLANET.
"AND LOCATE T WHO WILL PRO YOU ASSISTANC YOUR MISSIO
MOM...?
HOLY $#!%!
I SAW MY MOM. FOR, LIKE, A SECOND.
SHE'S IN TROUBLE!

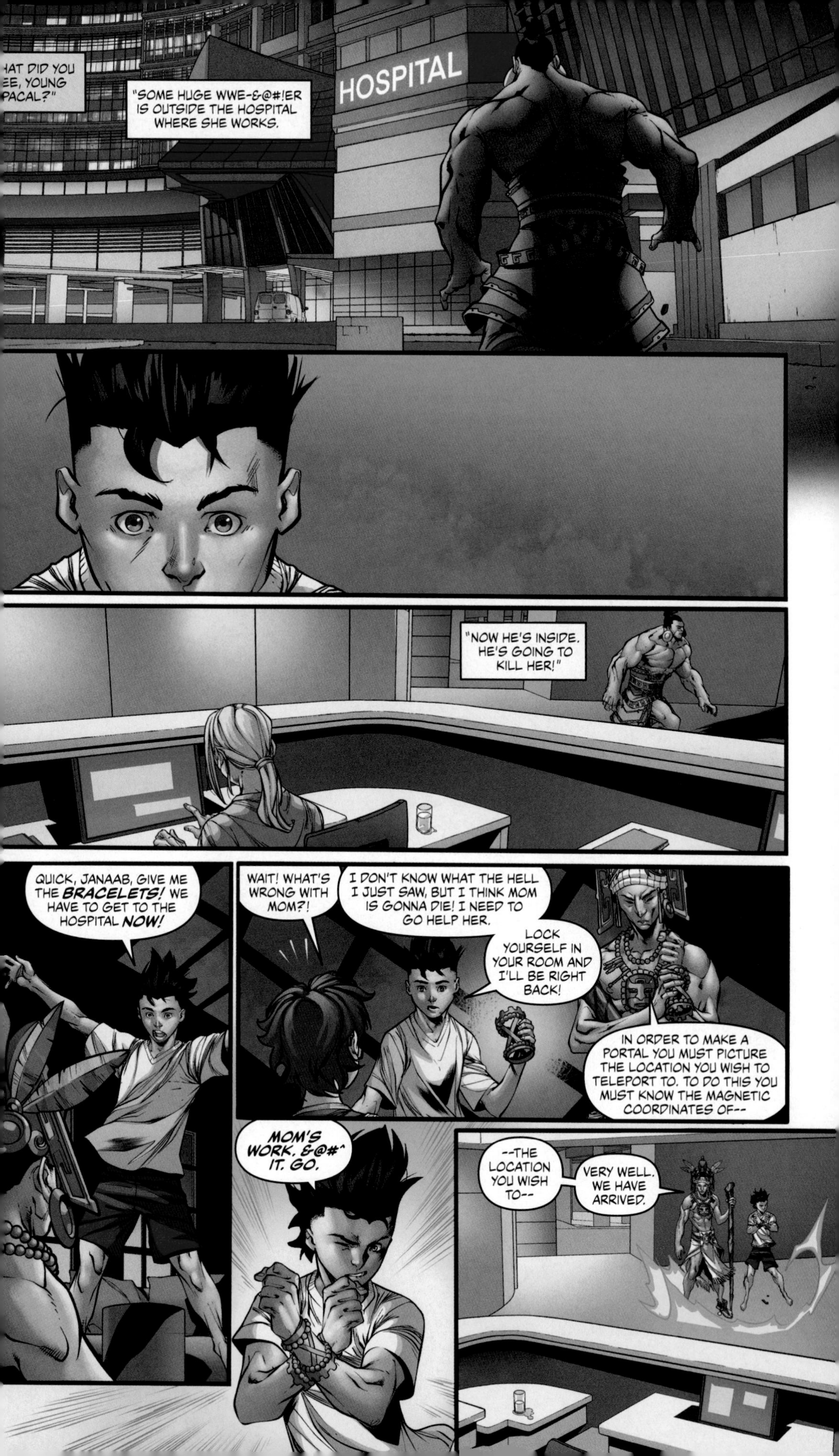

HAT DID YOU
EE, YOUNG
PACAL?"
"SOME HUGE WWE-&@#!ER IS OUTSIDE THE HOSPITAL WHERE SHE WORKS.
HOSPITAL
"NOW HE'S INSIDE. HE'S GOING TO KILL HER!"
QUICK, JANAAB, GIVE ME THE BRACELETS! WE HAVE TO GET TO THE HOSPITAL NOW!
WAIT! WHAT'S WRONG WITH MOM?!
I DON'T KNOW WHAT THE HELL I JUST SAW, BUT I THINK MOM IS GONNA DIE! I NEED TO GO HELP HER.
LOCK YOURSELF IN YOUR ROOM AND I'LL BE RIGHT BACK!
IN ORDER TO MAKE A PORTAL YOU MUST PICTURE THE LOCATION YOU WISH TO TELEPORT TO. TO DO THIS YOU MUST KNOW THE MAGNETIC COORDINATES OF--
MOM'S WORK. &@#^ IT. GO.
--THE LOCATION YOU WISH TO--
VERY WELL. WE HAVE ARRIVED.

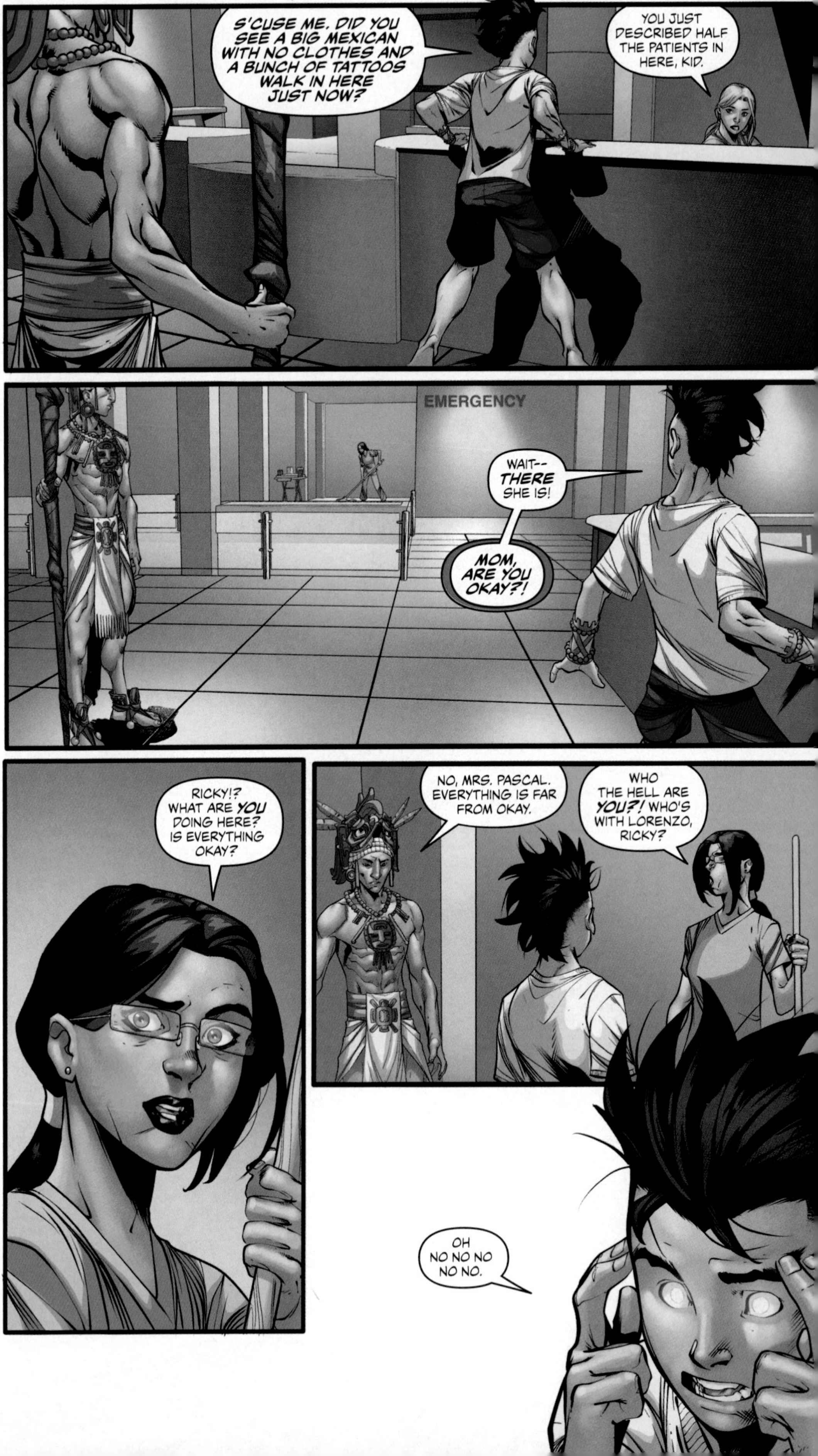
S'CUSE ME. DID YOU SEE A BIG MEXICAN WITH NO CLOTHES AND A BUNCH OF TATTOOS WALK IN HERE JUST NOW?
YOU JUST DESCRIBED HALF THE PATIENTS IN HERE, KID.
EMERGENCY
WAIT-- THERE SHE IS!
MOM, ARE YOU OKAY?!
RICKY!? WHAT ARE YOU DOING HERE? IS EVERYTHING OKAY?
NO, MRS. PASCAL. EVERYTHING IS FAR FROM OKAY.
WHO THE HELL ARE YOU?! WHO'S WITH LORENZO, RICKY?
OH NO NO NO NO NO.

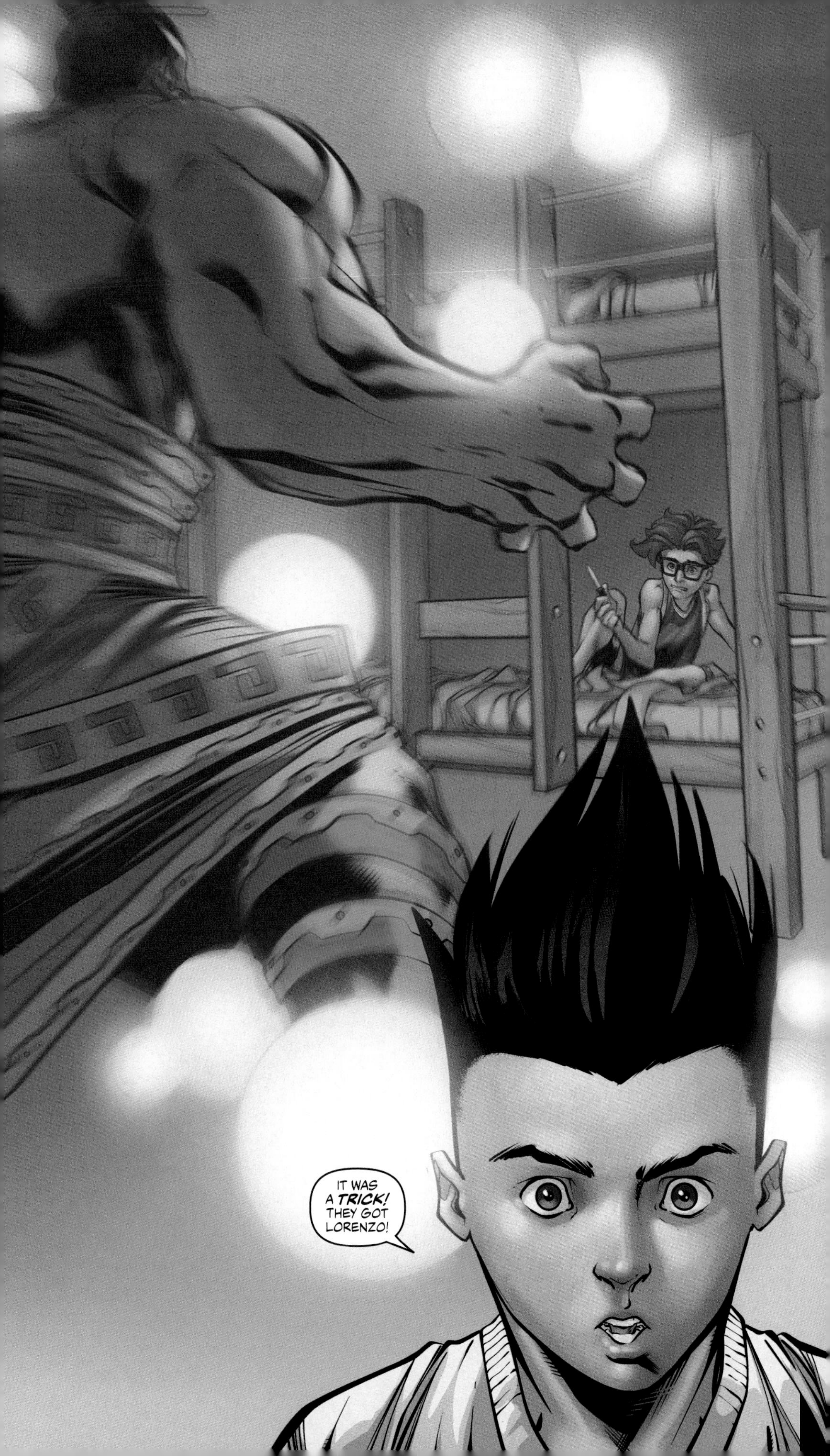
IT WAS A **TRICK!** THEY GOT LORENZO!

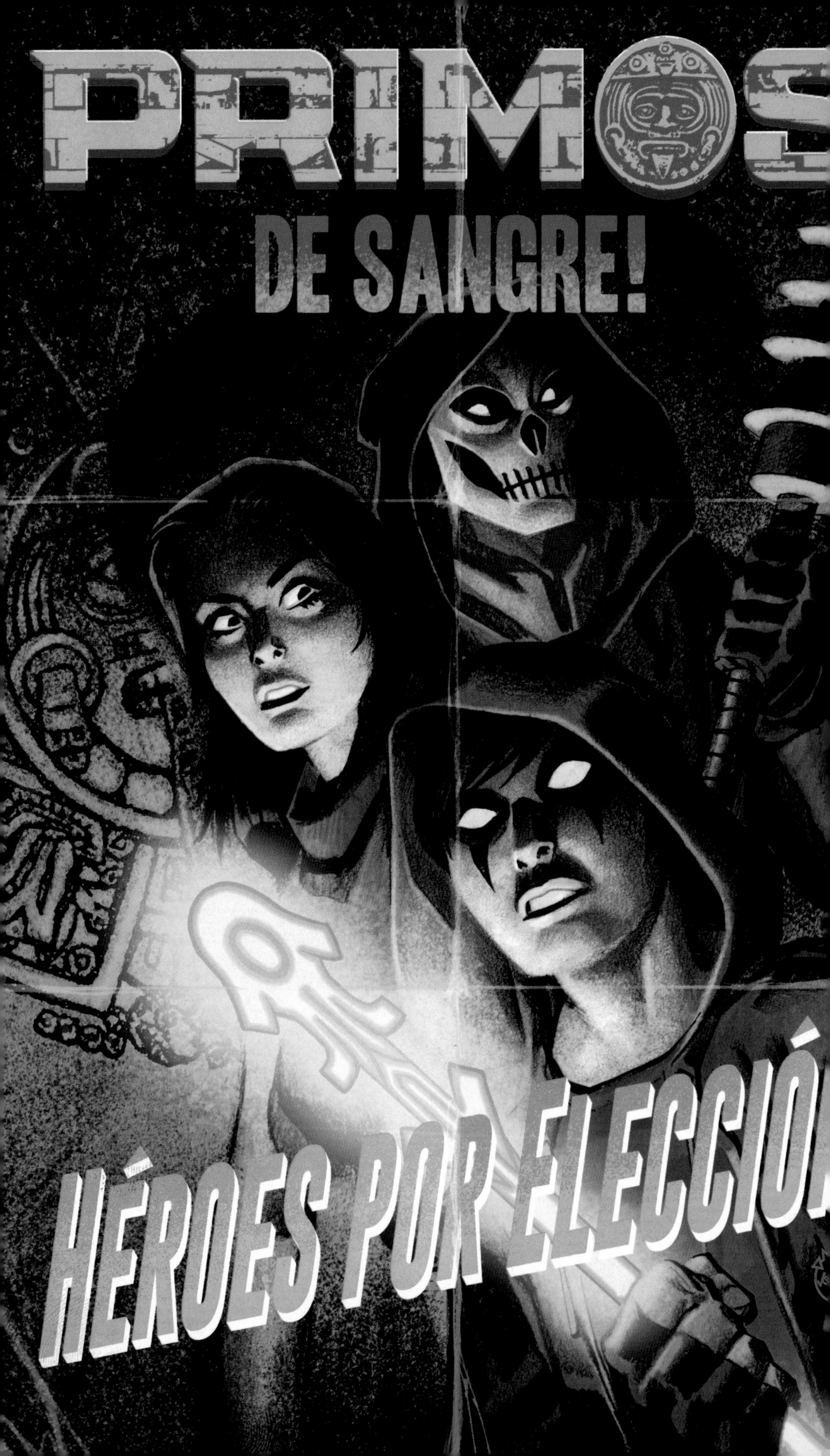
PRIMOS
DE SANGRE!
HÉROES POR ELECCIÓN

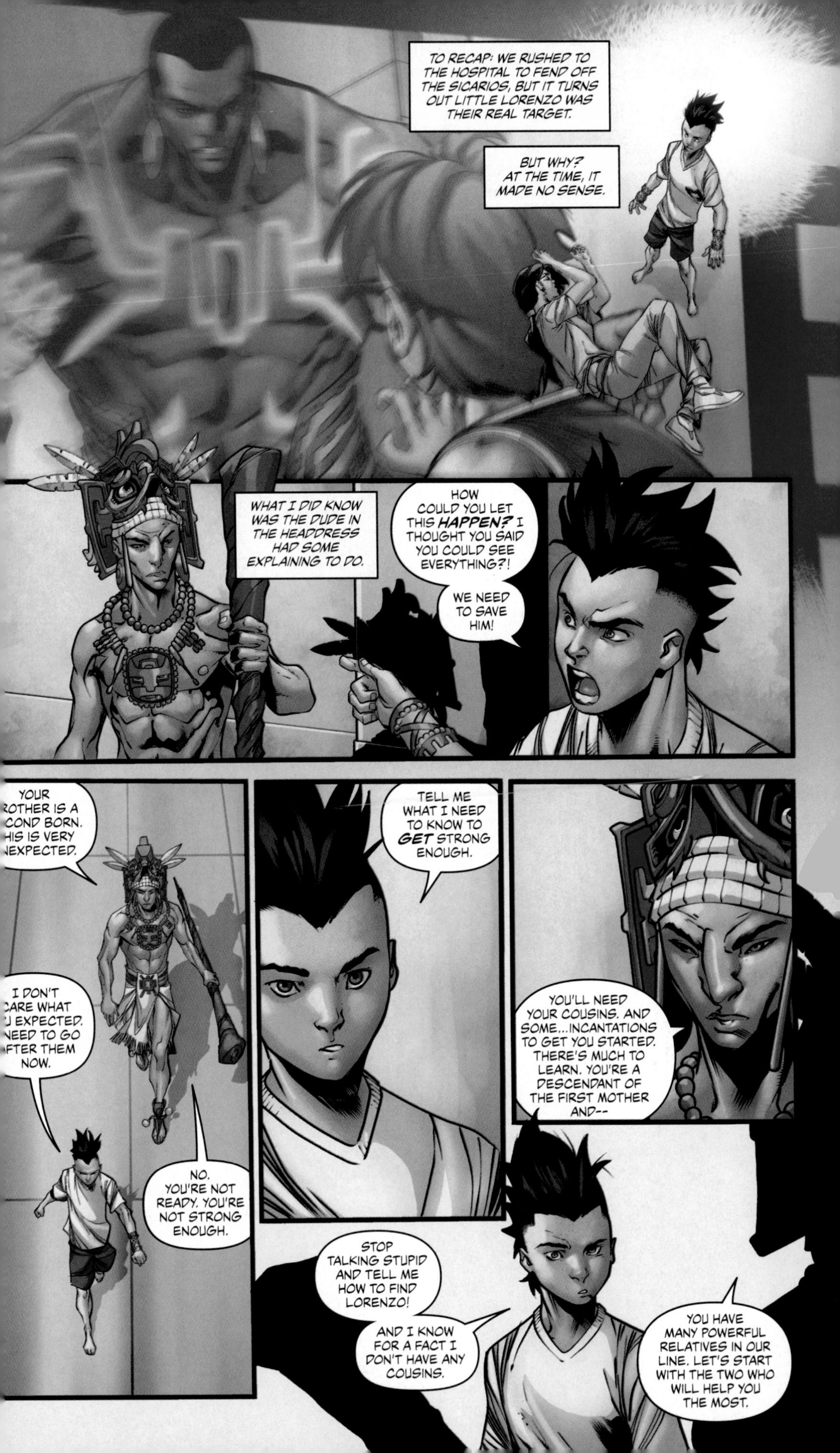
TO RECAP: WE RUSHED TO THE HOSPITAL TO FEND OFF THE SICARIOS, BUT IT TURNS OUT LITTLE LORENZO WAS THEIR REAL TARGET.
BUT WHY? AT THE TIME, IT MADE NO SENSE.
WHAT I DID KNOW WAS THE DUDE IN THE HEADDRESS HAD SOME EXPLAINING TO DO.
HOW COULD YOU LET THIS HAPPEN? I THOUGHT YOU SAID YOU COULD SEE EVERYTHING?!
WE NEED TO SAVE HIM!
YOUR ROTHER IS A COND BORN. HIS IS VERY NEXPECTED.
I DON'T CARE WHAT U EXPECTED. NEED TO GO FTER THEM NOW.
NO. YOU'RE NOT READY. YOU'RE NOT STRONG ENOUGH.
TELL ME WHAT I NEED TO KNOW TO GET STRONG ENOUGH.
YOU'LL NEED YOUR COUSINS. AND SOME...INCANTATIONS TO GET YOU STARTED. THERE'S MUCH TO LEARN. YOU'RE A DESCENDANT OF THE FIRST MOTHER AND--
STOP TALKING STUPID AND TELL ME HOW TO FIND LORENZO!
AND I KNOW FOR A FACT I DON'T HAVE ANY COUSINS.
YOU HAVE MANY POWERFUL RELATIVES IN OUR LINE. LET'S START WITH THE TWO WHO WILL HELP YOU THE MOST.

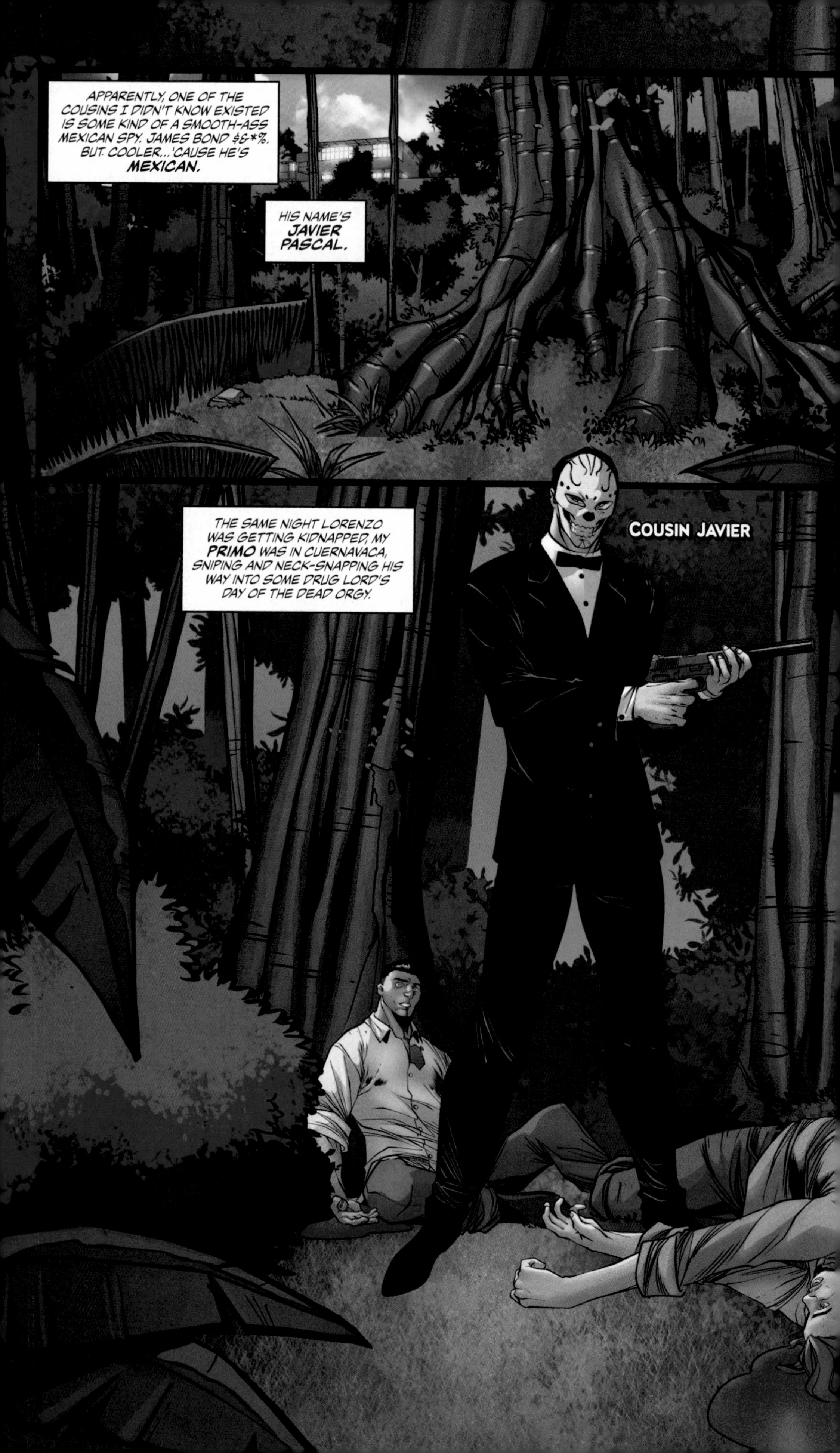
APPARENTLY, ONE OF THE COUSINS I DIDN'T KNOW EXISTED IS SOME KIND OF A SMOOTH-ASS MEXICAN SPY. JAMES BOND $&*%. BUT COOLER...'CAUSE HE'S **MEXICAN.**
HIS NAME'S **JAVIER PASCAL.**
THE SAME NIGHT LORENZO WAS GETTING KIDNAPPED, MY **PRIMO** WAS IN CUERNAVACA, SNIPING AND NECK-SNAPPING HIS WAY INTO SOME DRUG LORD'S DAY OF THE DEAD ORGY.
COUSIN JAVIER

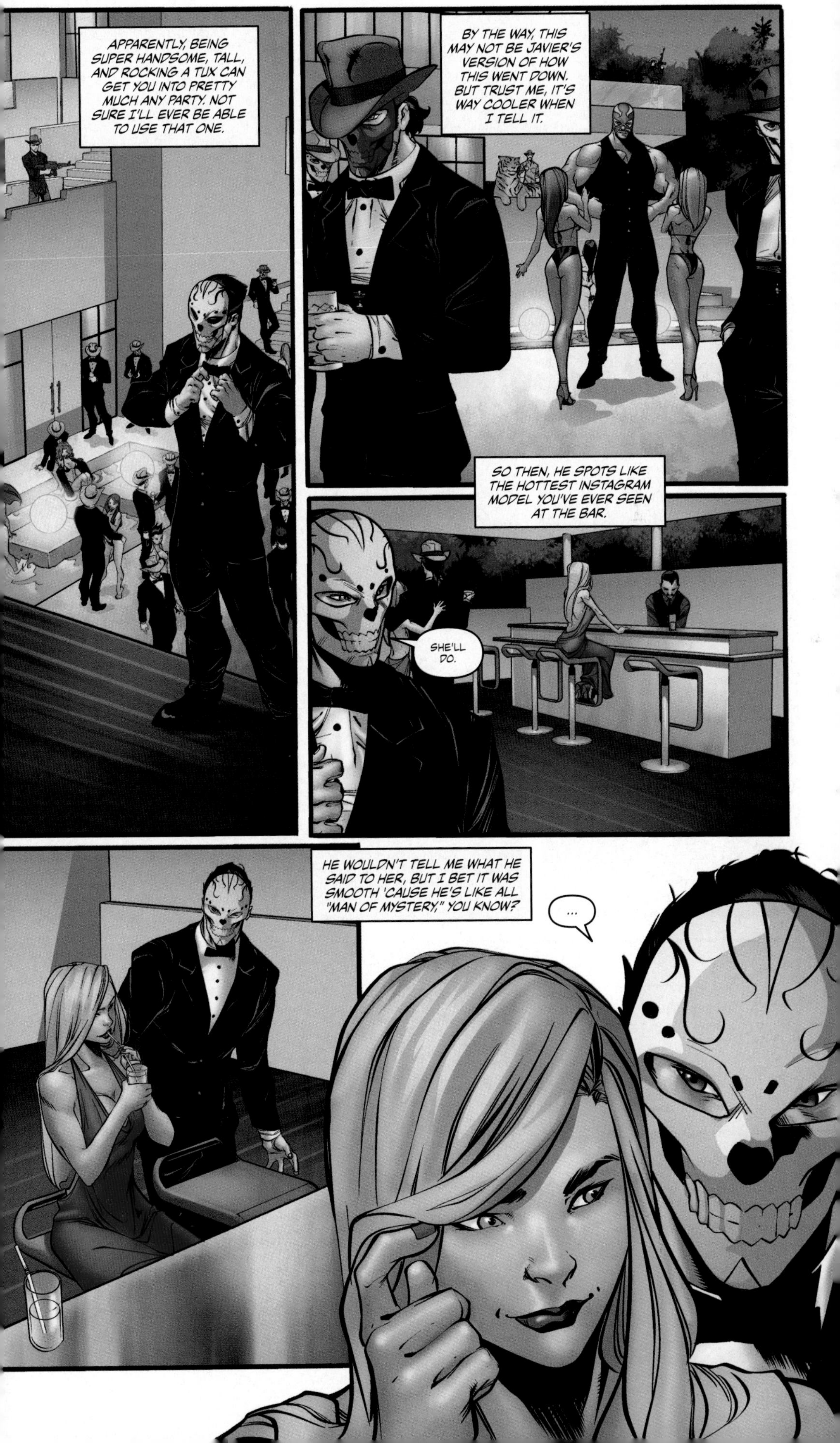

APPARENTLY, BEING SUPER HANDSOME, TALL, AND ROCKING A TUX CAN GET YOU INTO PRETTY MUCH ANY PARTY. NOT SURE I'LL EVER BE ABLE TO USE THAT ONE.
BY THE WAY, THIS MAY NOT BE JAVIER'S VERSION OF HOW THIS WENT DOWN. BUT TRUST ME, IT'S WAY COOLER WHEN I TELL IT.
SO THEN, HE SPOTS LIKE THE HOTTEST INSTAGRAM MODEL YOU'VE EVER SEEN AT THE BAR.
SHE'LL DO.
HE WOULDN'T TELL ME WHAT HE SAID TO HER, BUT I BET IT WAS SMOOTH 'CAUSE HE'S LIKE ALL "MAN OF MYSTERY," YOU KNOW?
...

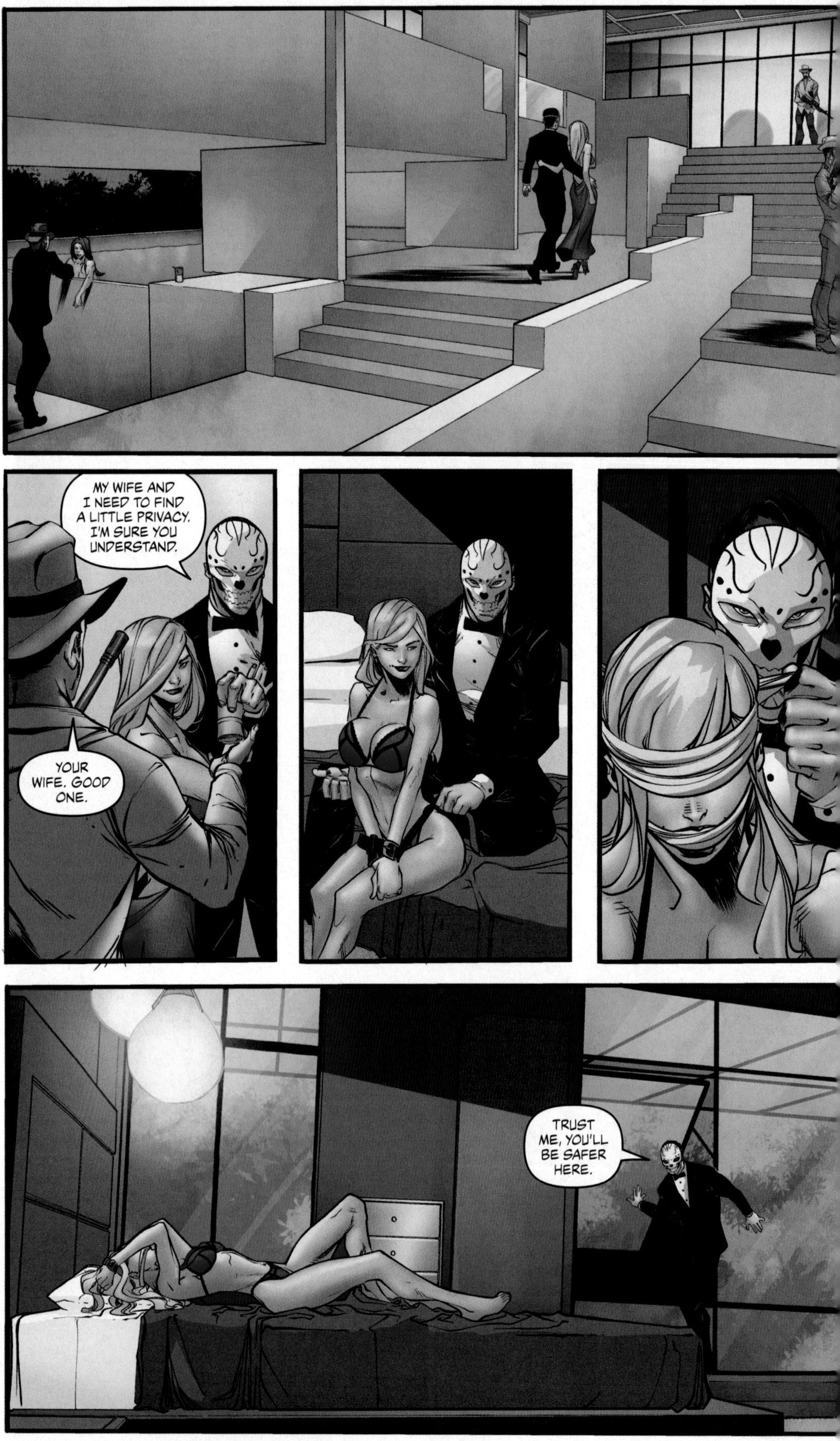
MY WIFE AND I NEED TO FIND A LITTLE PRIVACY. I'M SURE YOU UNDERSTAND.
YOUR WIFE. GOOD ONE.
TRUST ME, YOU'LL BE SAFER HERE.

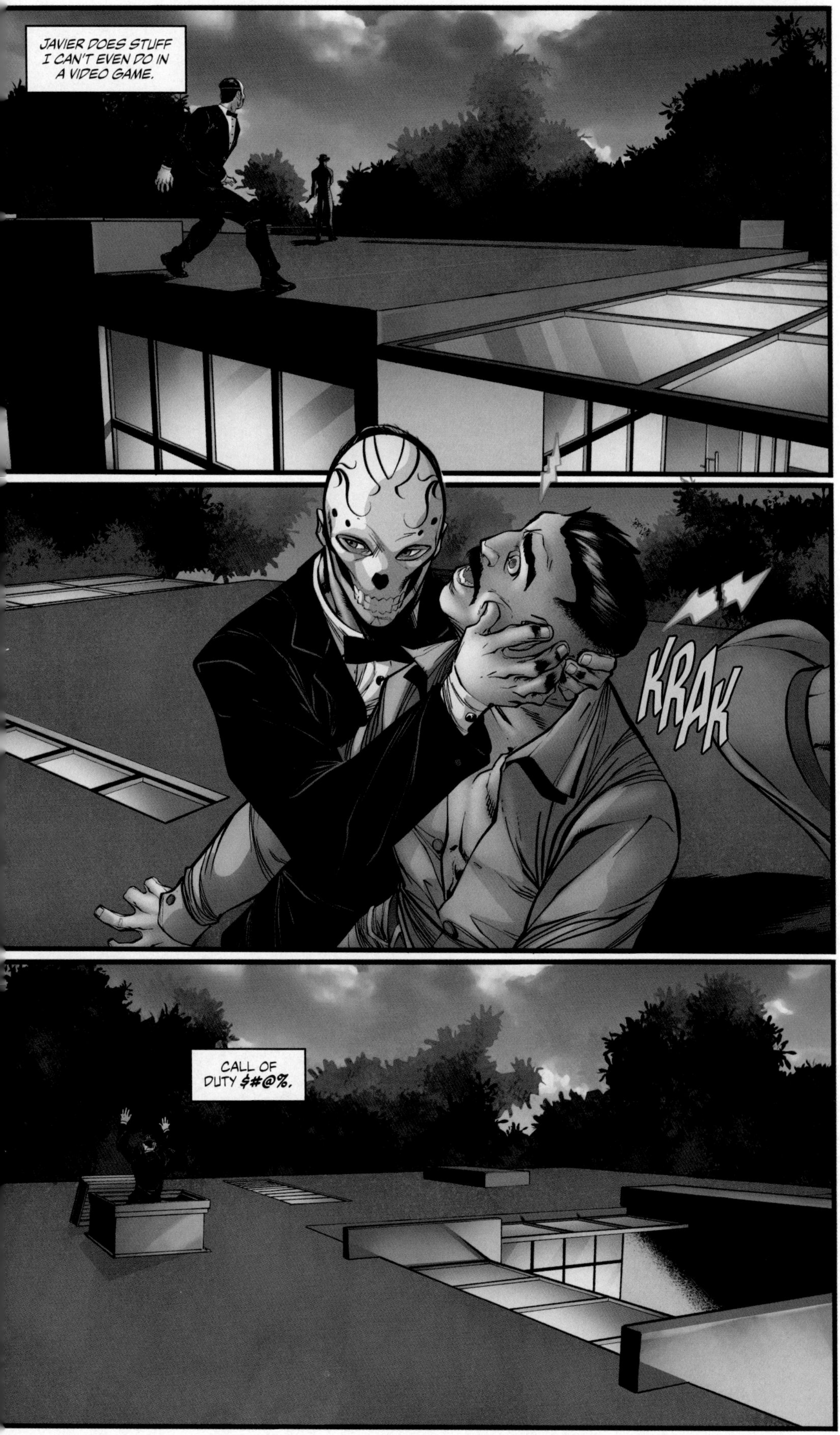
JAVIER DOES STUFF I CAN'T EVEN DO IN A VIDEO GAME.
KRAK
CALL OF DUTY $#@%.

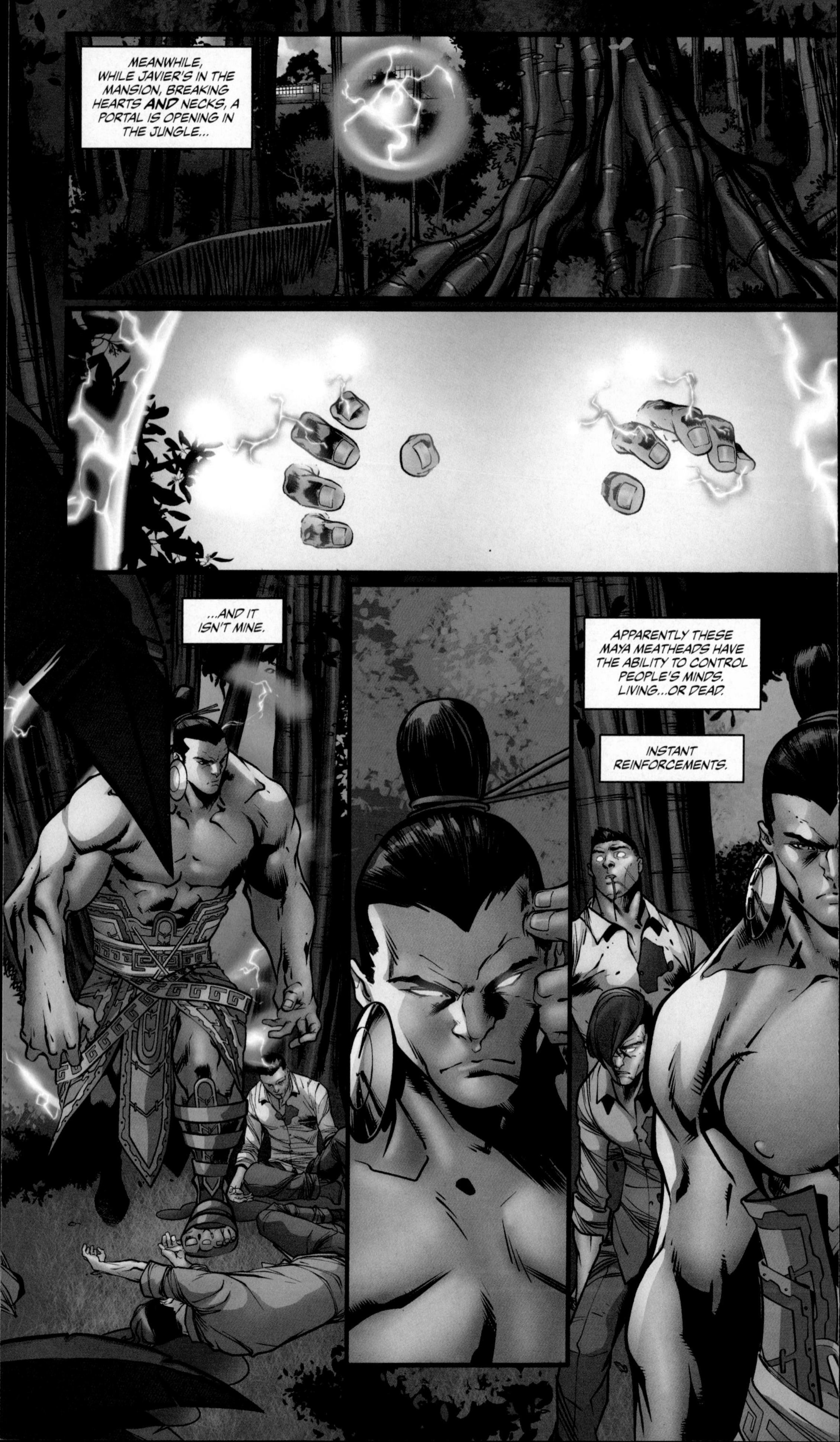
MEANWHILE, WHILE JAVIER'S IN THE MANSION, BREAKING HEARTS AND NECKS, A PORTAL IS OPENING IN THE JUNGLE...
...AND IT ISN'T MINE.
APPARENTLY THESE MAYA MEATHEADS HAVE THE ABILITY TO CONTROL PEOPLE'S MINDS. LIVING...OR DEAD.
INSTANT REINFORCEMENTS.

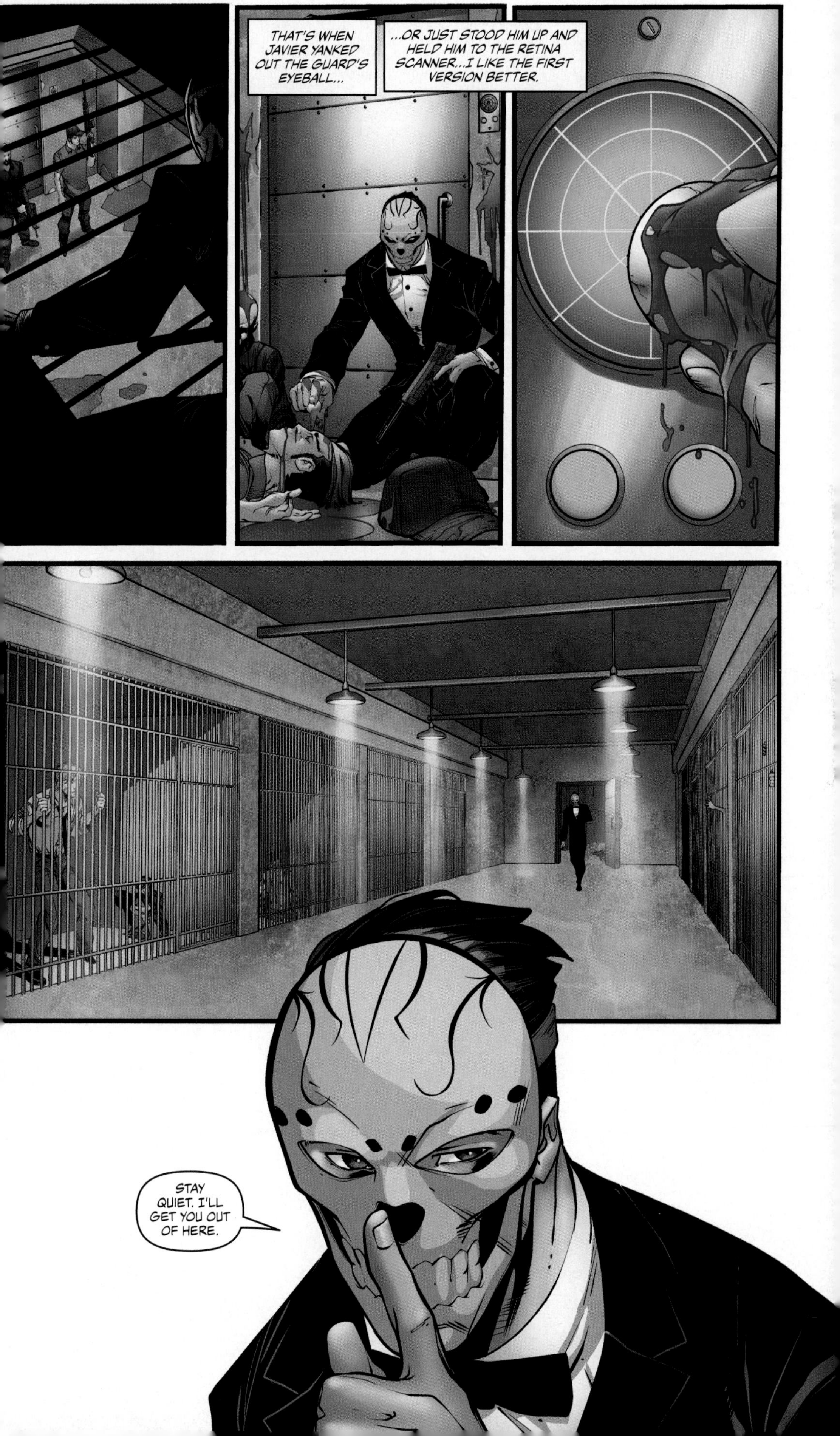
THAT'S WHEN JAVIER YANKED OUT THE GUARD'S EYEBALL...
...OR JUST STOOD HIM UP AND HELD HIM TO THE RETINA SCANNER...I LIKE THE FIRST VERSION BETTER.
STAY QUIET. I'LL GET YOU OUT OF HERE.

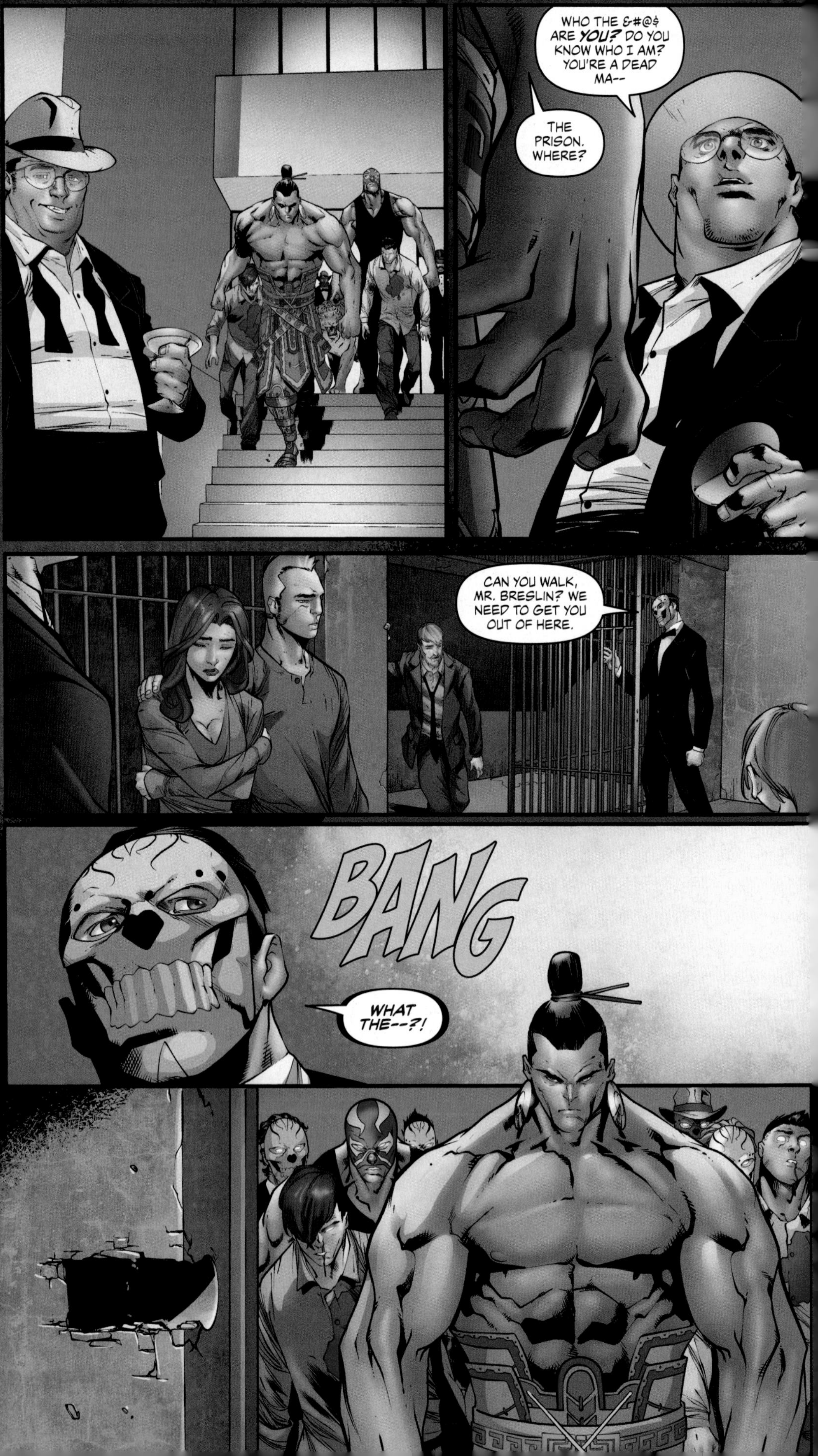
WHO THE &#@$ ARE YOU? DO YOU KNOW WHO I AM? YOU'RE A DEAD MA--
THE PRISON. WHERE?
CAN YOU WALK, MR. BRESLIN? WE NEED TO GET YOU OUT OF HERE.
BANG
WHAT THE--?!

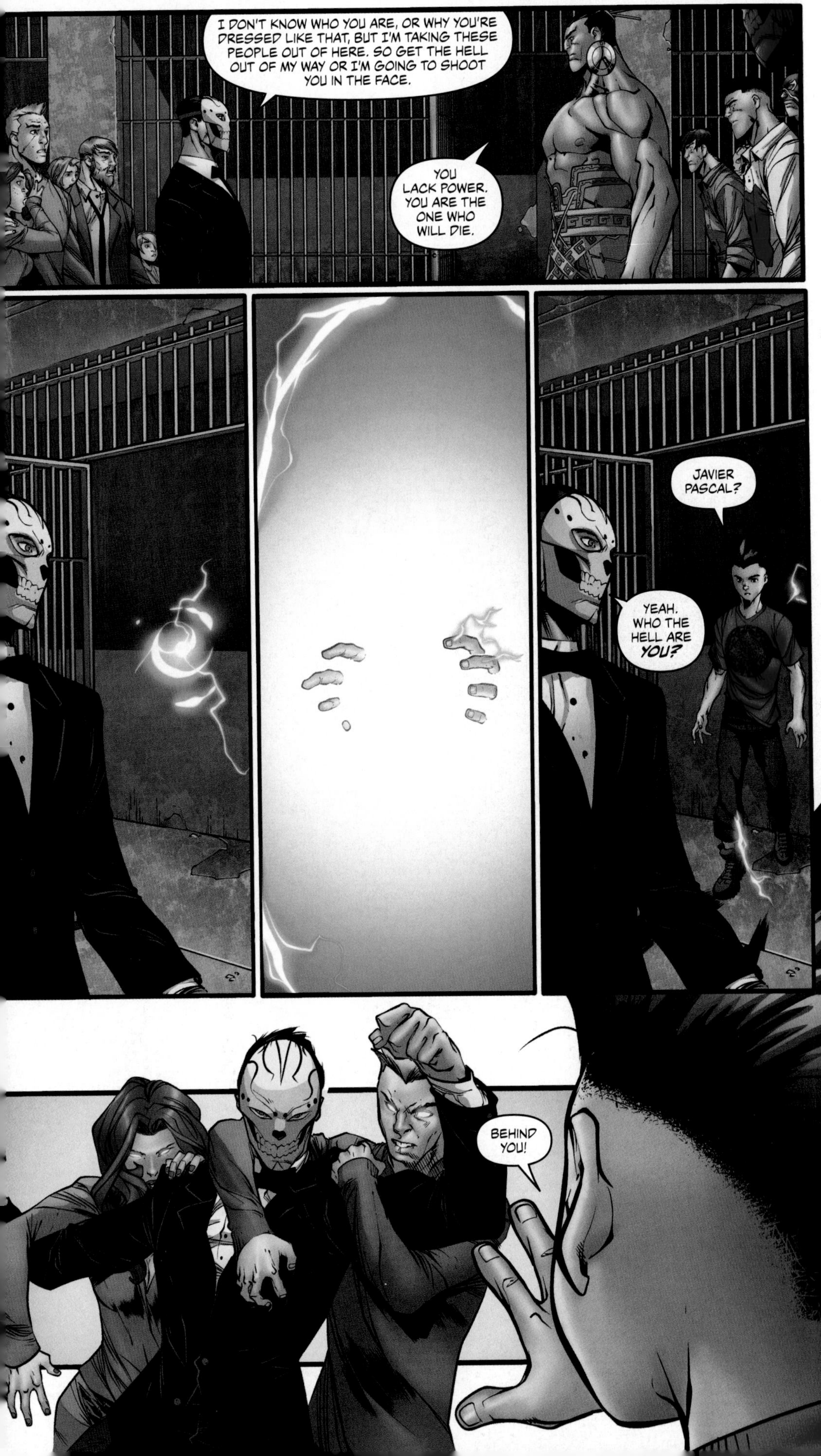
I DON'T KNOW WHO YOU ARE, OR WHY YOU'RE DRESSED LIKE THAT, BUT I'M TAKING THESE PEOPLE OUT OF HERE. SO GET THE HELL OUT OF MY WAY OR I'M GOING TO SHOOT YOU IN THE FACE.
YOU LACK POWER. YOU ARE THE ONE WHO WILL DIE.
JAVIER PASCAL?
YEAH. WHO THE HELL ARE ***YOU?***
BEHIND YOU!

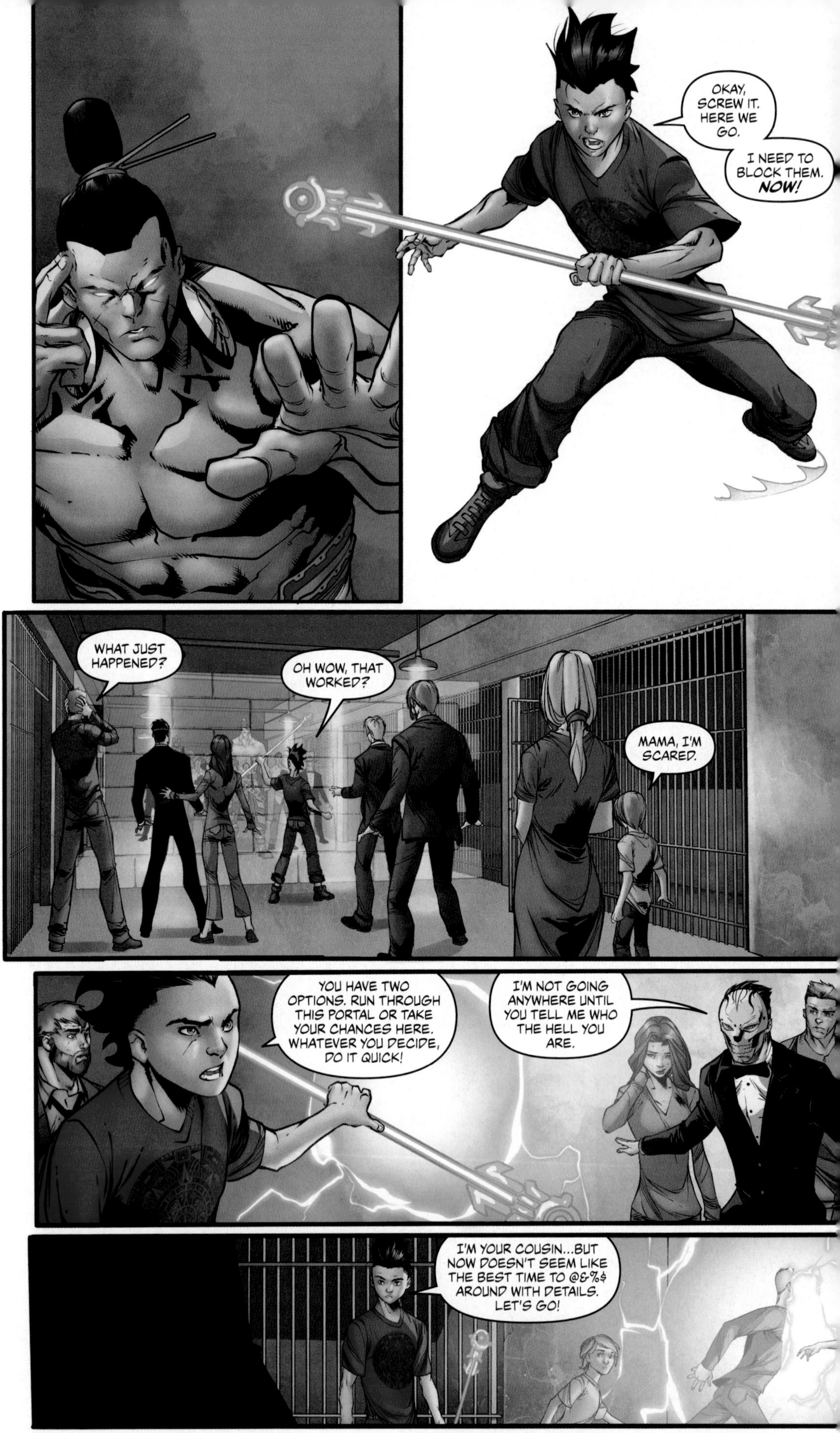

OKAY, SCREW IT. HERE WE GO.
I NEED TO BLOCK THEM. NOW!
WHAT JUST HAPPENED?
OH WOW, THAT WORKED?
MAMA, I'M SCARED.
YOU HAVE TWO OPTIONS. RUN THROUGH THIS PORTAL OR TAKE YOUR CHANCES HERE. WHATEVER YOU DECIDE, DO IT QUICK!
I'M NOT GOING ANYWHERE UNTIL YOU TELL ME WHO THE HELL YOU ARE.
I'M YOUR COUSIN...BUT NOW DOESN'T SEEM LIKE THE BEST TIME TO @&%$ AROUND WITH DETAILS. LET'S GO!

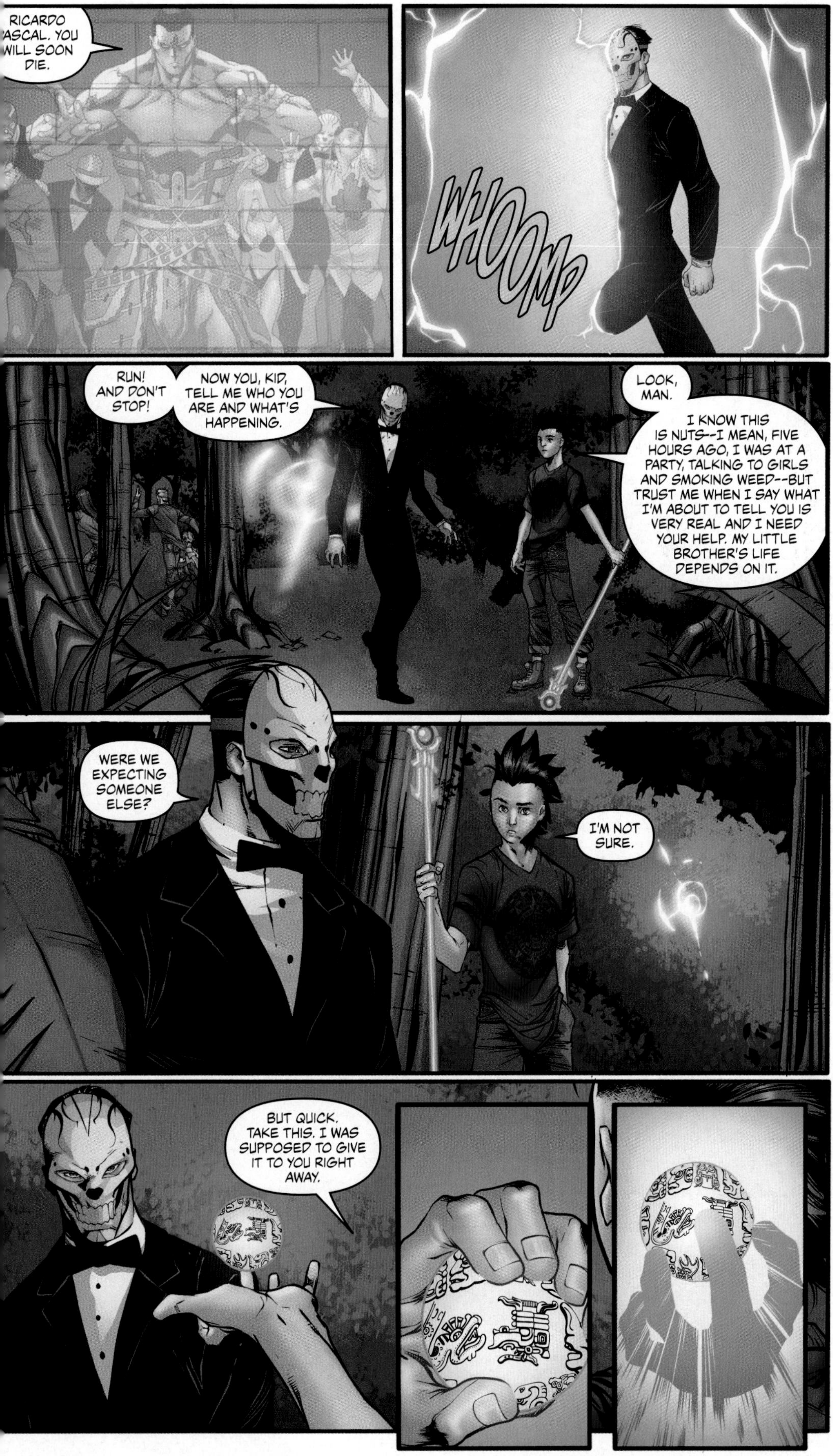
RICARDO PASCAL. YOU WILL SOON DIE.
WHOOMP
RUN! AND DON'T STOP!
NOW YOU, KID, TELL ME WHO YOU ARE AND WHAT'S HAPPENING.
LOOK, MAN.
I KNOW THIS IS NUTS--I MEAN, FIVE HOURS AGO, I WAS AT A PARTY, TALKING TO GIRLS AND SMOKING WEED--BUT TRUST ME WHEN I SAY WHAT I'M ABOUT TO TELL YOU IS VERY REAL AND I NEED YOUR HELP. MY LITTLE BROTHER'S LIFE DEPENDS ON IT.
WERE WE EXPECTING SOMEONE ELSE?
I'M NOT SURE.
BUT QUICK. TAKE THIS. I WAS SUPPOSED TO GIVE IT TO YOU RIGHT AWAY.

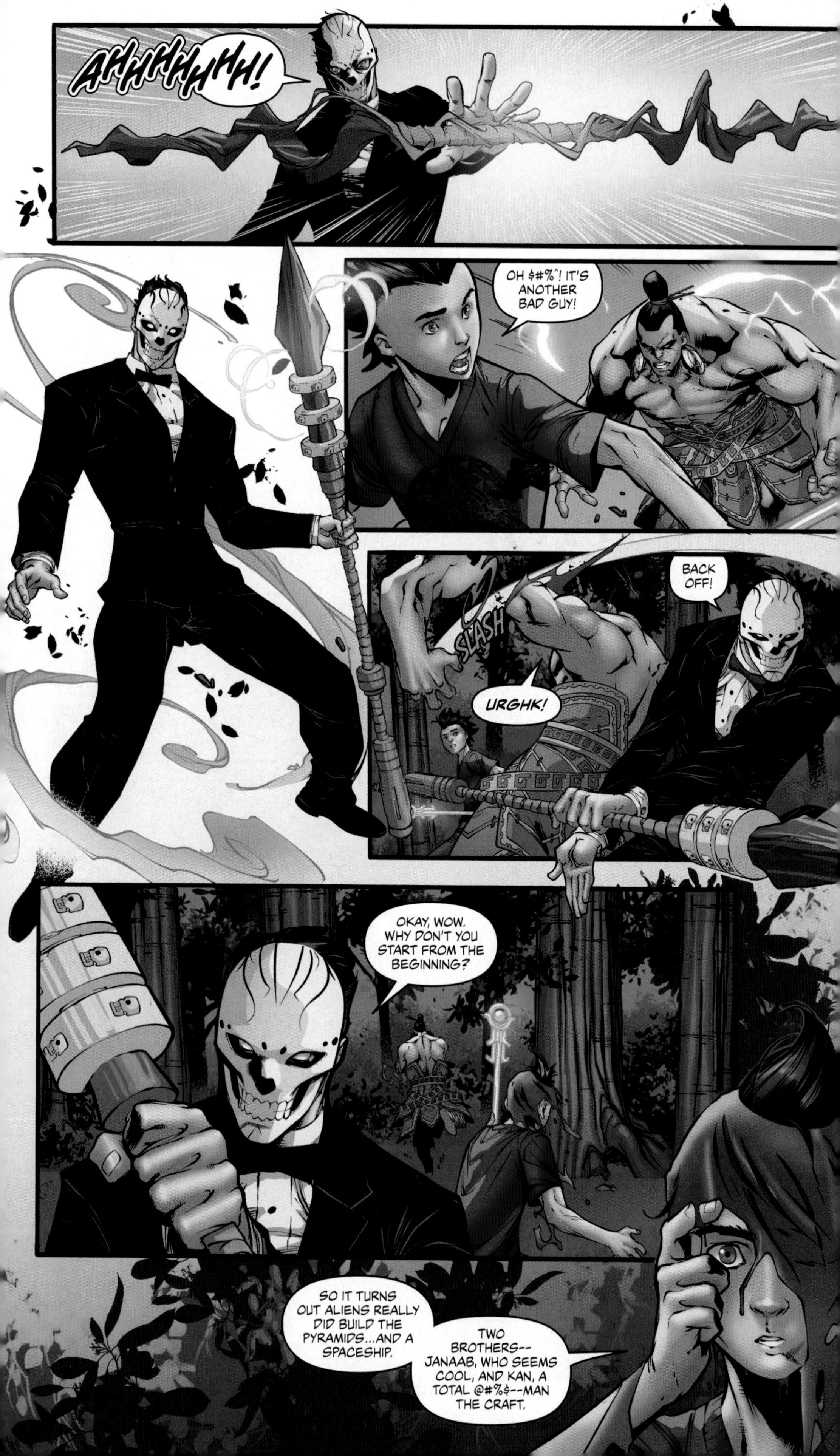
AHHHHHHHH!
OH $#%^! IT'S ANOTHER BAD GUY!
BACK OFF!
SLASH
URGHK!
OKAY, WOW. WHY DON'T YOU START FROM THE BEGINNING?
SO IT TURNS OUT ALIENS REALLY DID BUILD THE PYRAMIDS...AND A SPACESHIP.
TWO BROTHERS-- JANAAB, WHO SEEMS COOL, AND KAN, A TOTAL @#%$--MAN THE CRAFT.

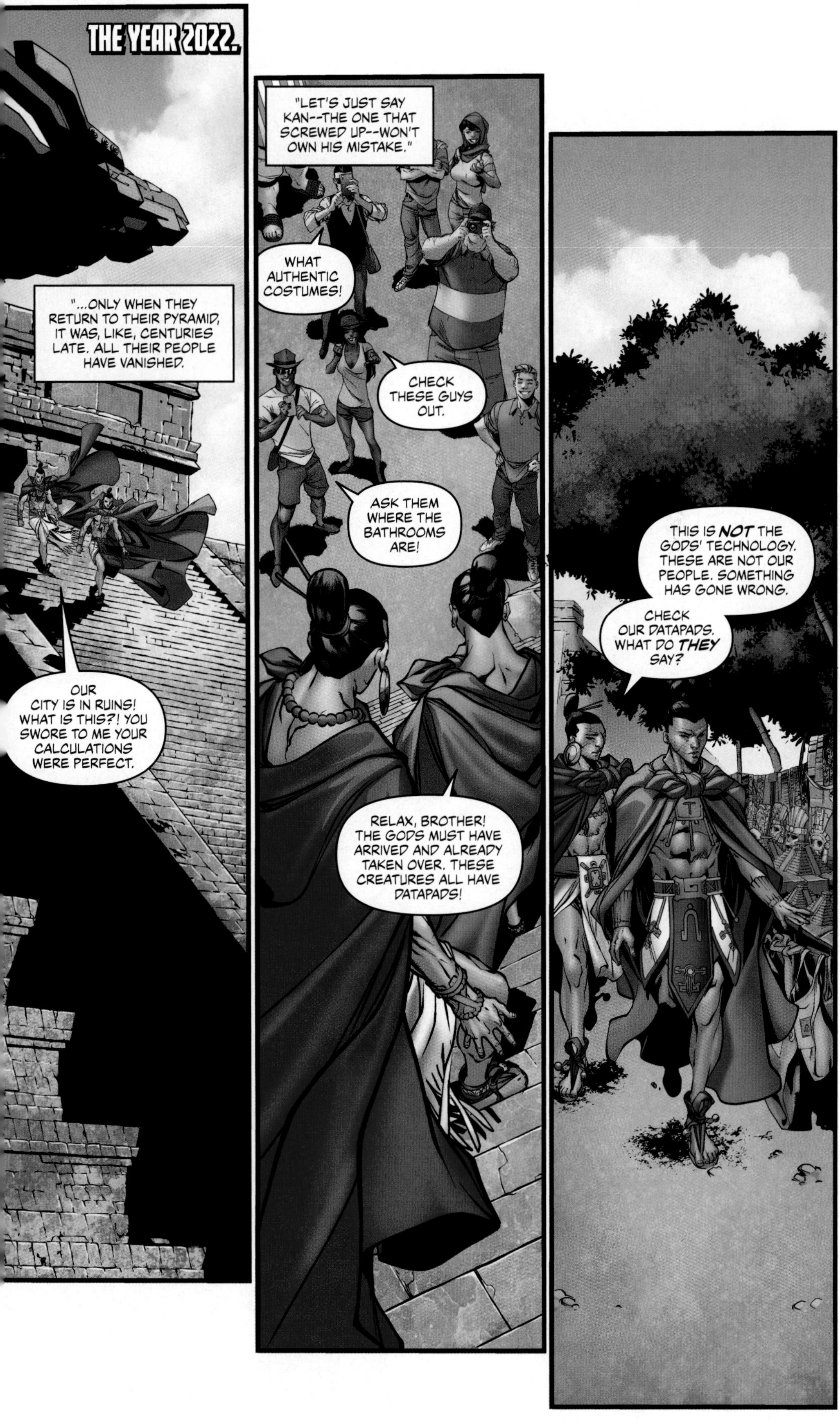
THE YEAR 2022.
"...ONLY WHEN THEY RETURN TO THEIR PYRAMID, IT WAS, LIKE, CENTURIES LATE. ALL THEIR PEOPLE HAVE VANISHED.
OUR CITY IS IN RUINS! WHAT IS THIS?! YOU SWORE TO ME YOUR CALCULATIONS WERE PERFECT.
"LET'S JUST SAY KAN--THE ONE THAT SCREWED UP--WON'T OWN HIS MISTAKE."
WHAT AUTHENTIC COSTUMES!
CHECK THESE GUYS OUT.
ASK THEM WHERE THE BATHROOMS ARE!
RELAX, BROTHER! THE GODS MUST HAVE ARRIVED AND ALREADY TAKEN OVER. THESE CREATURES ALL HAVE DATAPADS!
THIS IS NOT THE GODS' TECHNOLOGY. THESE ARE NOT OUR PEOPLE. SOMETHING HAS GONE WRONG.
CHECK OUR DATAPADS. WHAT DO THEY SAY?

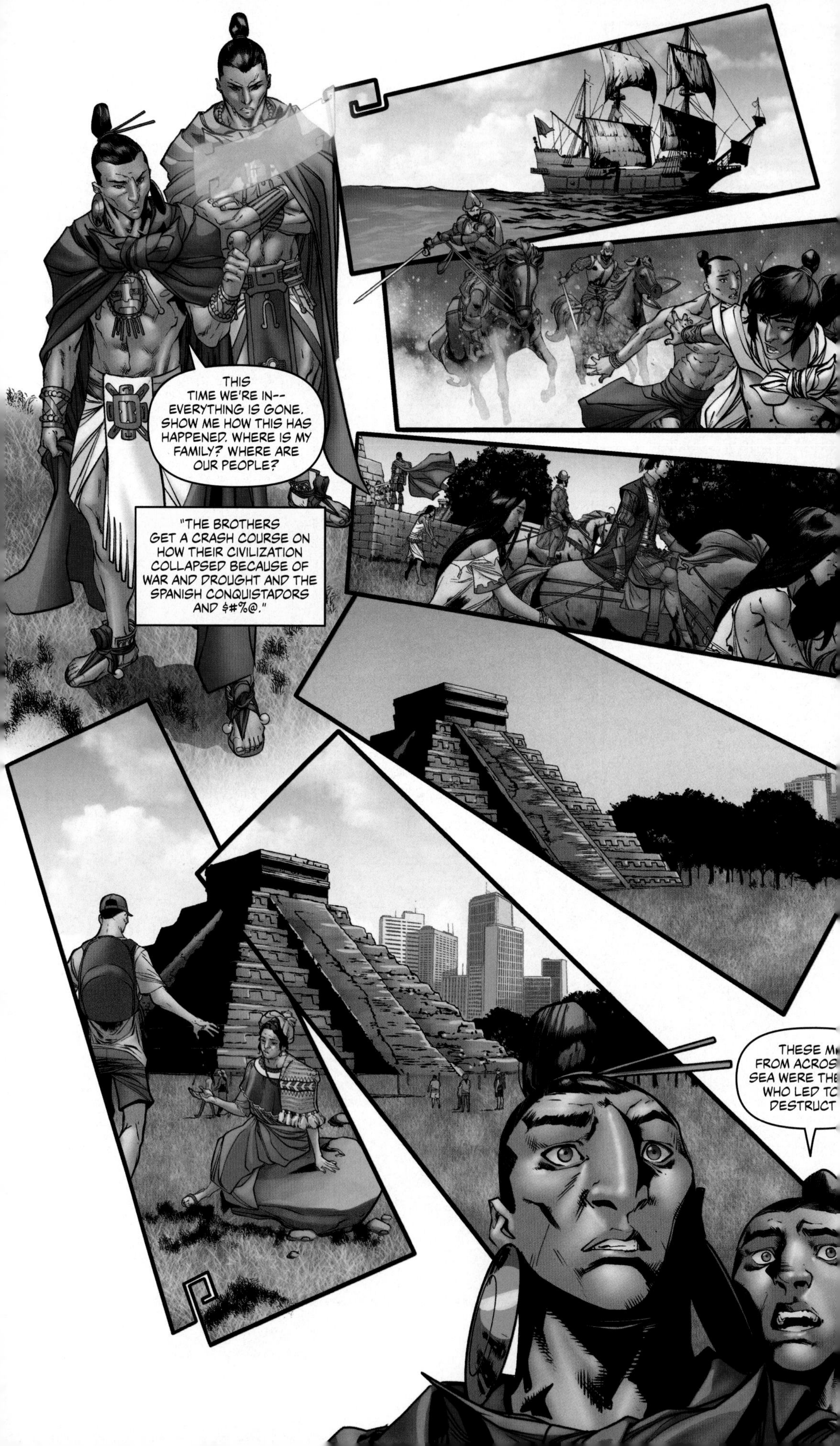
THIS TIME WE'RE IN-- EVERYTHING IS GONE. SHOW ME HOW THIS HAS HAPPENED. WHERE IS MY FAMILY? WHERE ARE OUR PEOPLE?
"THE BROTHERS GET A CRASH COURSE ON HOW THEIR CIVILIZATION COLLAPSED BECAUSE OF WAR AND DROUGHT AND THE SPANISH CONQUISTADORS AND $#%@."
THESE M FROM ACROS SEA WERE THE WHO LED T DESTRUCT

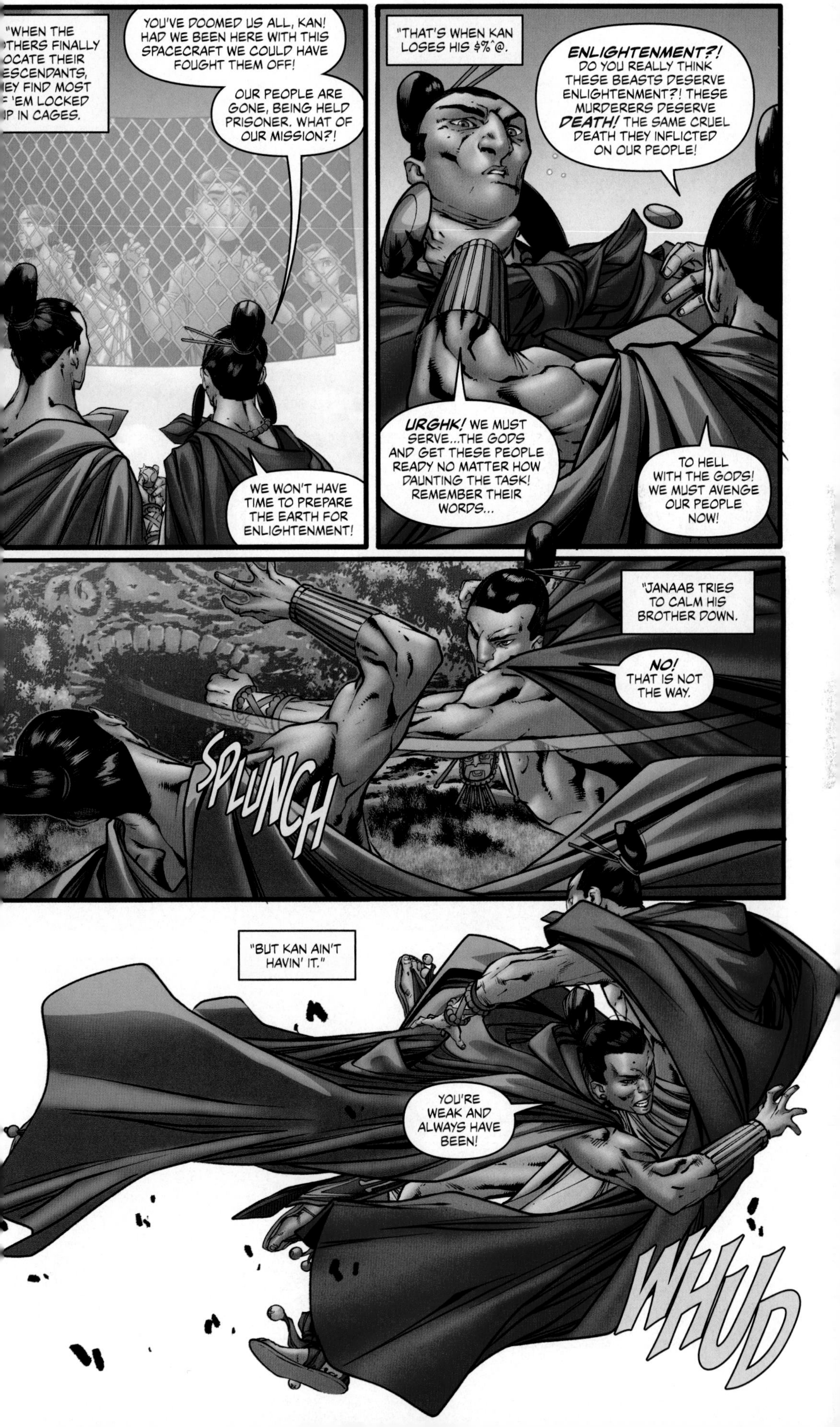
"WHEN THE OTHERS FINALLY LOCATE THEIR DESCENDANTS, THEY FIND MOST OF 'EM LOCKED UP IN CAGES.
YOU'VE DOOMED US ALL, KAN! HAD WE BEEN HERE WITH THIS SPACECRAFT WE COULD HAVE FOUGHT THEM OFF!
OUR PEOPLE ARE GONE, BEING HELD PRISONER. WHAT OF OUR MISSION?!
WE WON'T HAVE TIME TO PREPARE THE EARTH FOR ENLIGHTENMENT!
"THAT'S WHEN KAN LOSES HIS $%@.
ENLIGHTENMENT?! DO YOU REALLY THINK THESE BEASTS DESERVE ENLIGHTENMENT?! THESE MURDERERS DESERVE DEATH! THE SAME CRUEL DEATH THEY INFLICTED ON OUR PEOPLE!
URGHK! WE MUST SERVE...THE GODS AND GET THESE PEOPLE READY NO MATTER HOW DAUNTING THE TASK! REMEMBER THEIR WORDS...
TO HELL WITH THE GODS! WE MUST AVENGE OUR PEOPLE NOW!
"JANAAB TRIES TO CALM HIS BROTHER DOWN.
NO! THAT IS NOT THE WAY.
SPLUNCH
"BUT KAN AIN'T HAVIN' IT."
YOU'RE WEAK AND ALWAYS HAVE BEEN!
WHUD

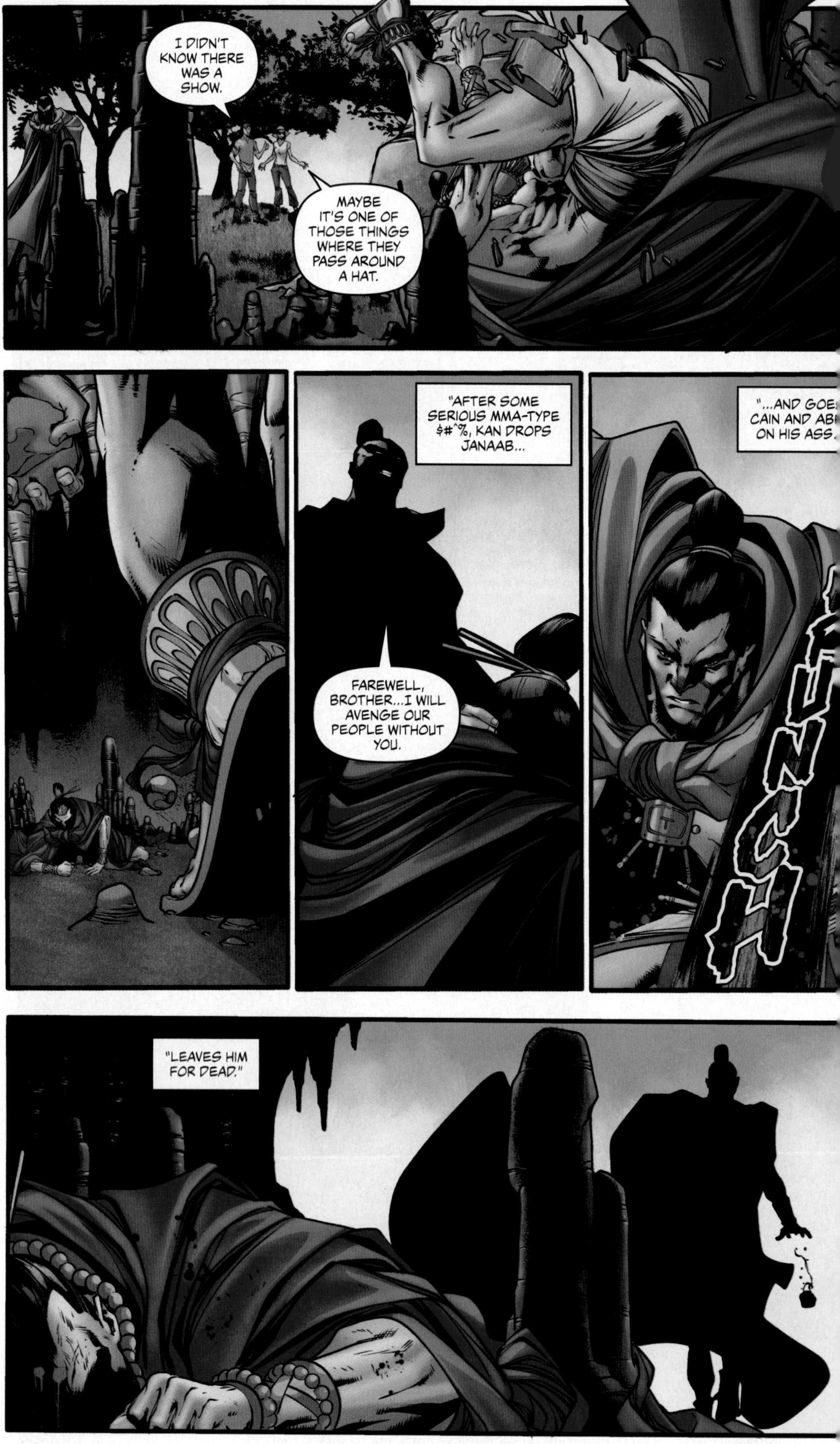
I DIDN'T KNOW THERE WAS A SHOW.
MAYBE IT'S ONE OF THOSE THINGS WHERE THEY PASS AROUND A HAT.
"AFTER SOME SERIOUS MMA-TYPE $#^%, KAN DROPS JANAAB...
FAREWELL, BROTHER...I WILL AVENGE OUR PEOPLE WITHOUT YOU.
"...AND GOE
CAIN AND AB
ON HIS ASS.
"LEAVES HIM FOR DEAD."

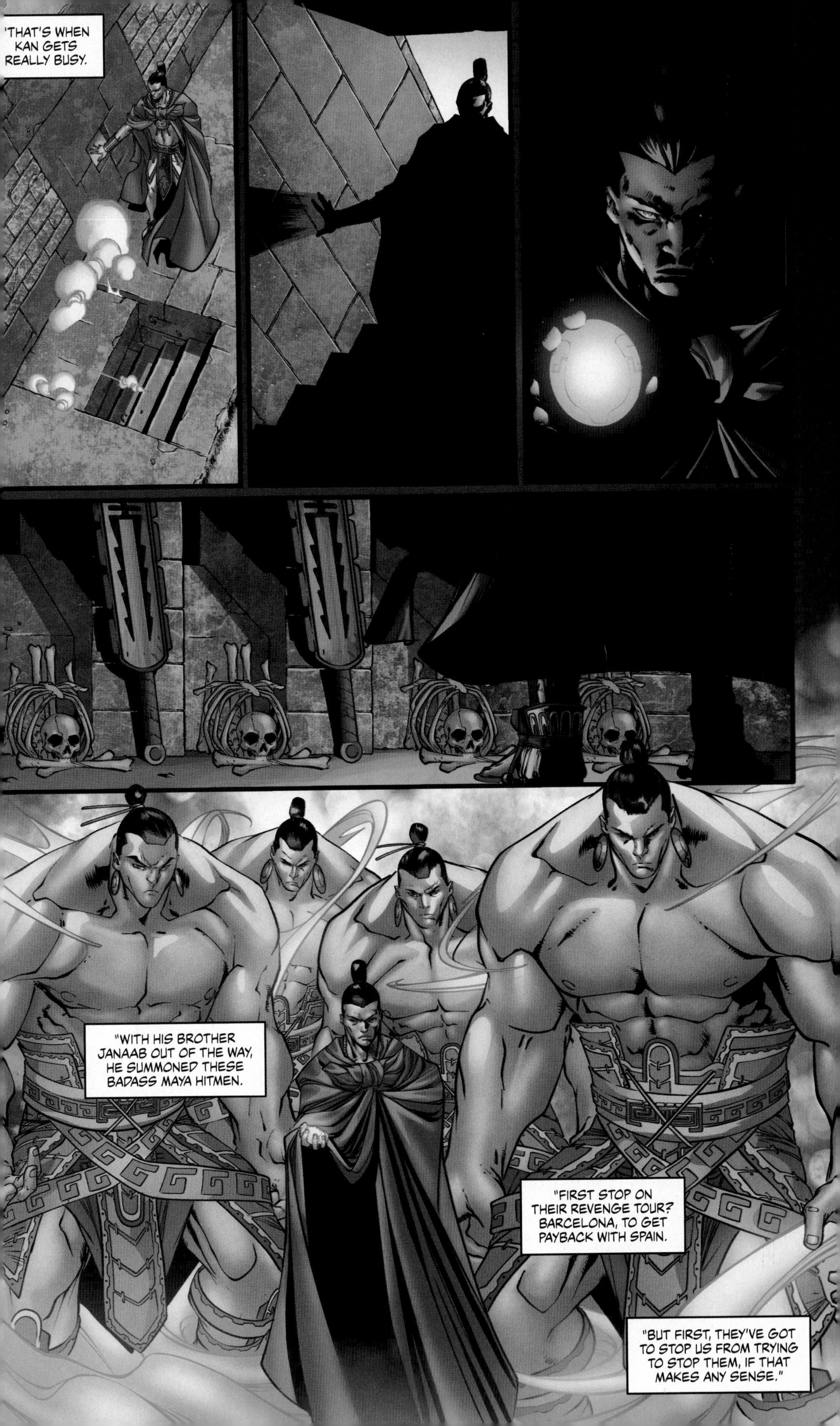
'THAT'S WHEN KAN GETS REALLY BUSY.
"WITH HIS BROTHER JANAAB OUT OF THE WAY, HE SUMMONED THESE BADASS MAYA HITMEN.
"FIRST STOP ON THEIR REVENGE TOUR? BARCELONA, TO GET PAYBACK WITH SPAIN.
"BUT FIRST, THEY'VE GOT TO STOP US FROM TRYING TO STOP THEM, IF THAT MAKES ANY SENSE."

...SO THAT'S EVERYTHING I KNOW. JANAAB TOLD ME THAT ONCE WE'RE ALL TOGETHER, WE CAN SAVE MY BROTHER.

WAIT. ISN'T JANAAB *DEAD?*

NO, I SAID "LEFT FOR DEAD." AS IN WEAK AF AND NOT ABLE TO HELP US SAVE THE EARTH FROM KAN'S CRAZY ASS.

WHO DO YOU THINK TOLD ME THIS WHOLE STORY?

OKAY. I'LL COME WITH YOU.

I'M CONVINCED.

WHAT PUT YOU OVER THE TOP? WAS IT THE MAGICAL BALL THAT TURNED INTO A SPEAR I GAVE YOU OR THE PORTAL?

ALL OF THE ABOVE, SMARTASS. ALSO, I'VE HAD DREAMS ABOUT MAYA WARRIORS AS FAR BACK AS I CAN REMEMBER.

I'VE HAD CRAZY DREAMS, TOO. I JUST THOUGHT I WAS DROPPED ON THE HEAD AS A BABY OR SOMETHING.

OKAY, WE SHOULD GO. WE NEED TO FIND OUR OTHER COUSIN.

EVER BEEN TO EL PASO?

IF WE'RE GOIN TO EL PASO, WE GOING TO NEED GO TO MEXICO AND PICK UP FEW THINGS.

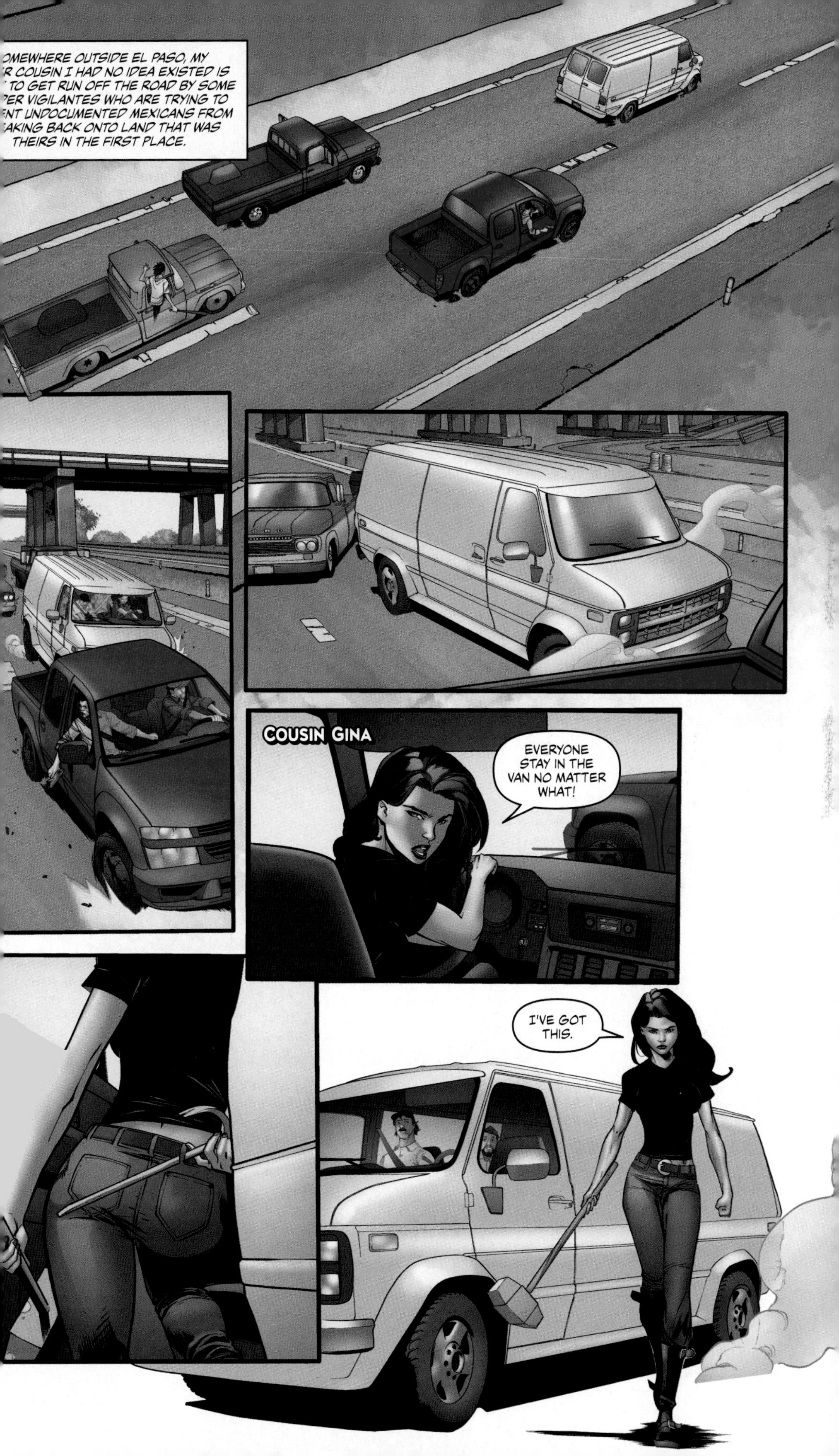
OMEWHERE OUTSIDE EL PASO, MY
R COUSIN I HAD NO IDEA EXISTED IS
TO GET RUN OFF THE ROAD BY SOME
PER VIGILANTES WHO ARE TRYING TO
NT UNDOCUMENTED MEXICANS FROM
AKING BACK ONTO LAND THAT WAS
THEIRS IN THE FIRST PLACE.
COUSIN GINA
EVERYONE STAY IN THE VAN NO MATTER WHAT!
I'VE GOT THIS.

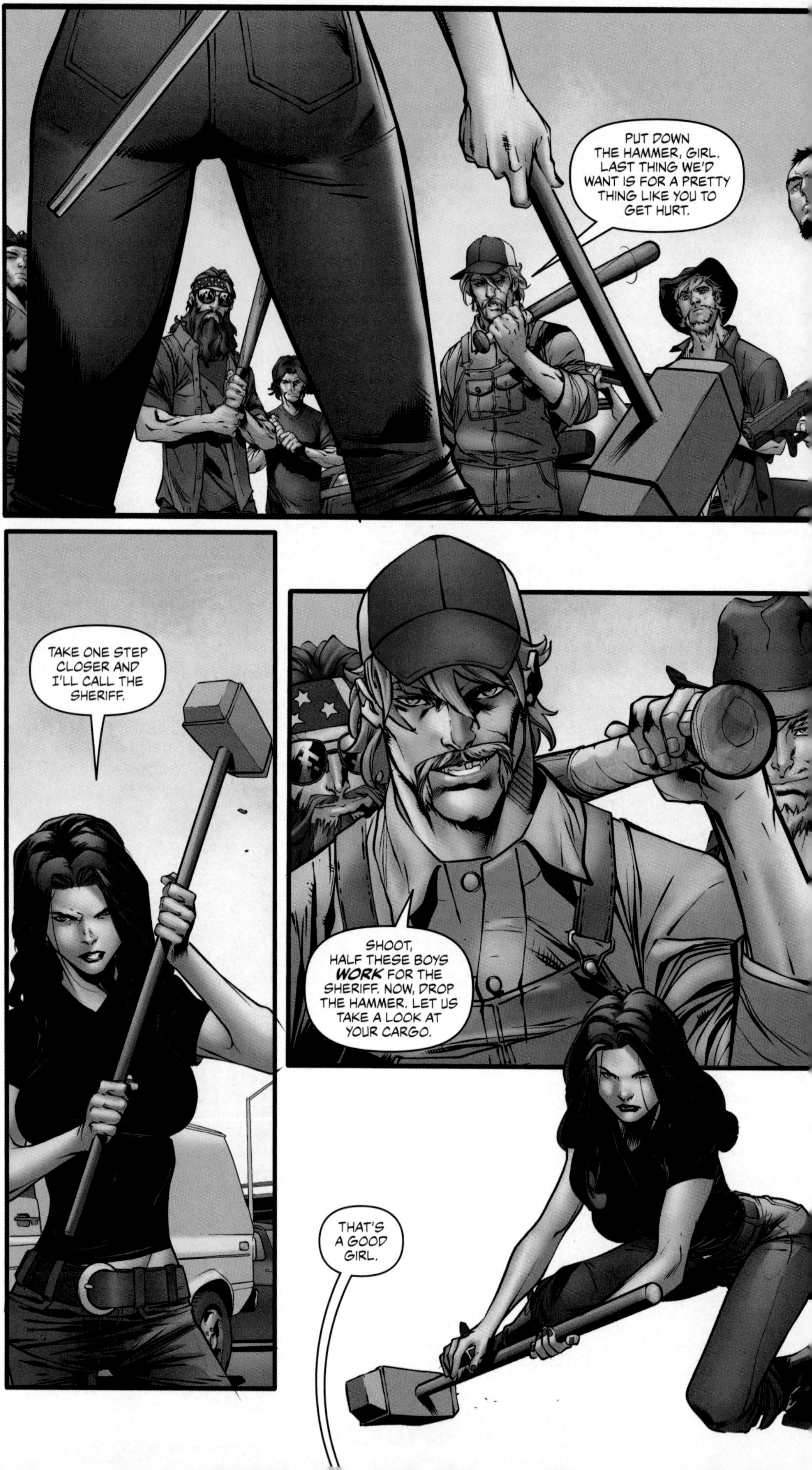
PUT DOWN THE HAMMER, GIRL. LAST THING WE'D WANT IS FOR A PRETTY THING LIKE YOU TO GET HURT.
TAKE ONE STEP CLOSER AND I'LL CALL THE SHERIFF.
SHOOT, HALF THESE BOYS WORK FOR THE SHERIFF. NOW, DROP THE HAMMER. LET US TAKE A LOOK AT YOUR CARGO.
THAT'S A GOOD GIRL.

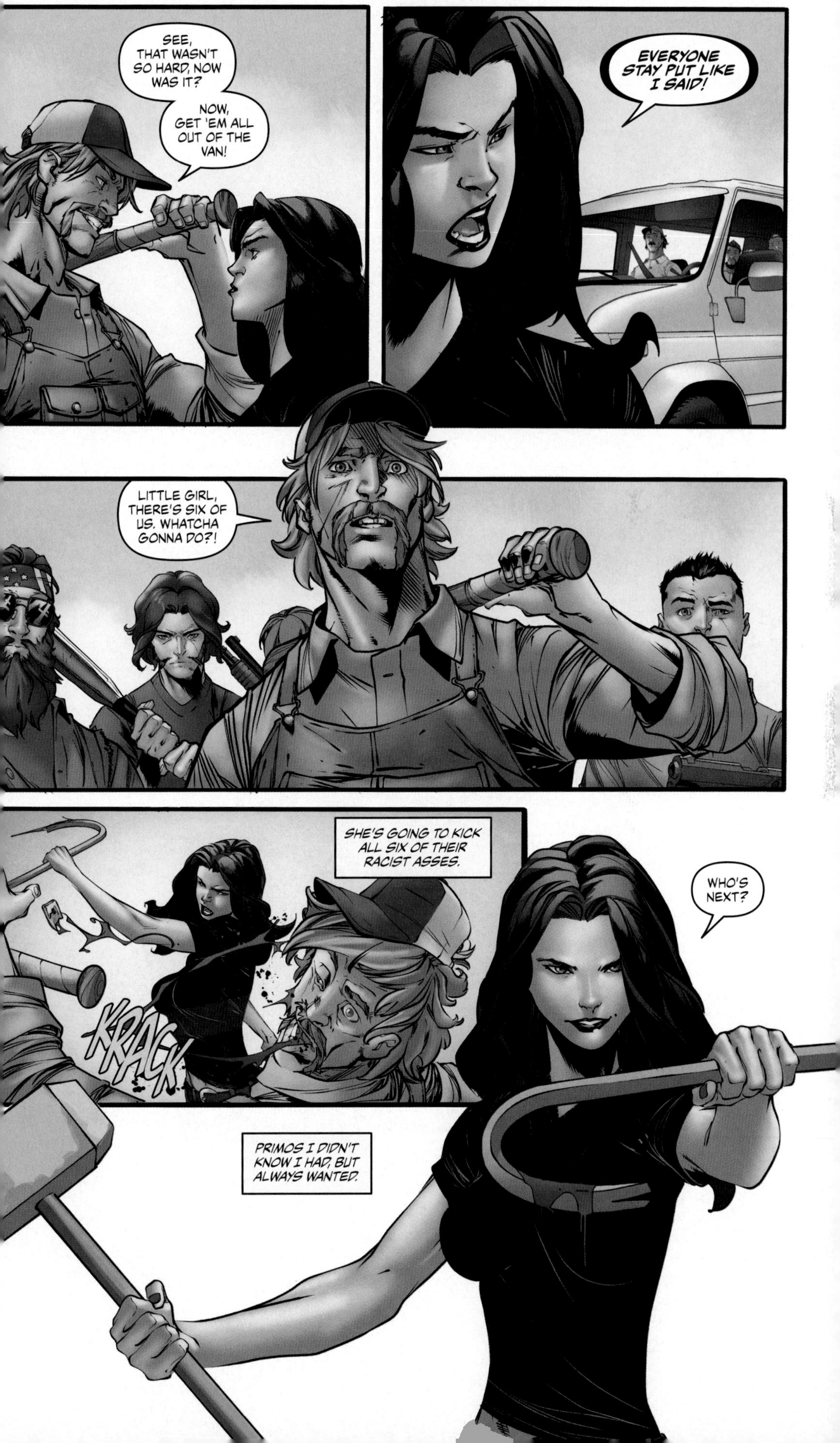
SEE, THAT WASN'T SO HARD, NOW WAS IT?
NOW, GET 'EM ALL OUT OF THE VAN!
EVERYONE STAY PUT LIKE I SAID!
LITTLE GIRL, THERE'S SIX OF US. WHATCHA GONNA DO?!
SHE'S GOING TO KICK ALL SIX OF THEIR RACIST ASSES.
KRACK
WHO'S NEXT?
PRIMOS I DIDN'T KNOW I HAD, BUT ALWAYS WANTED.

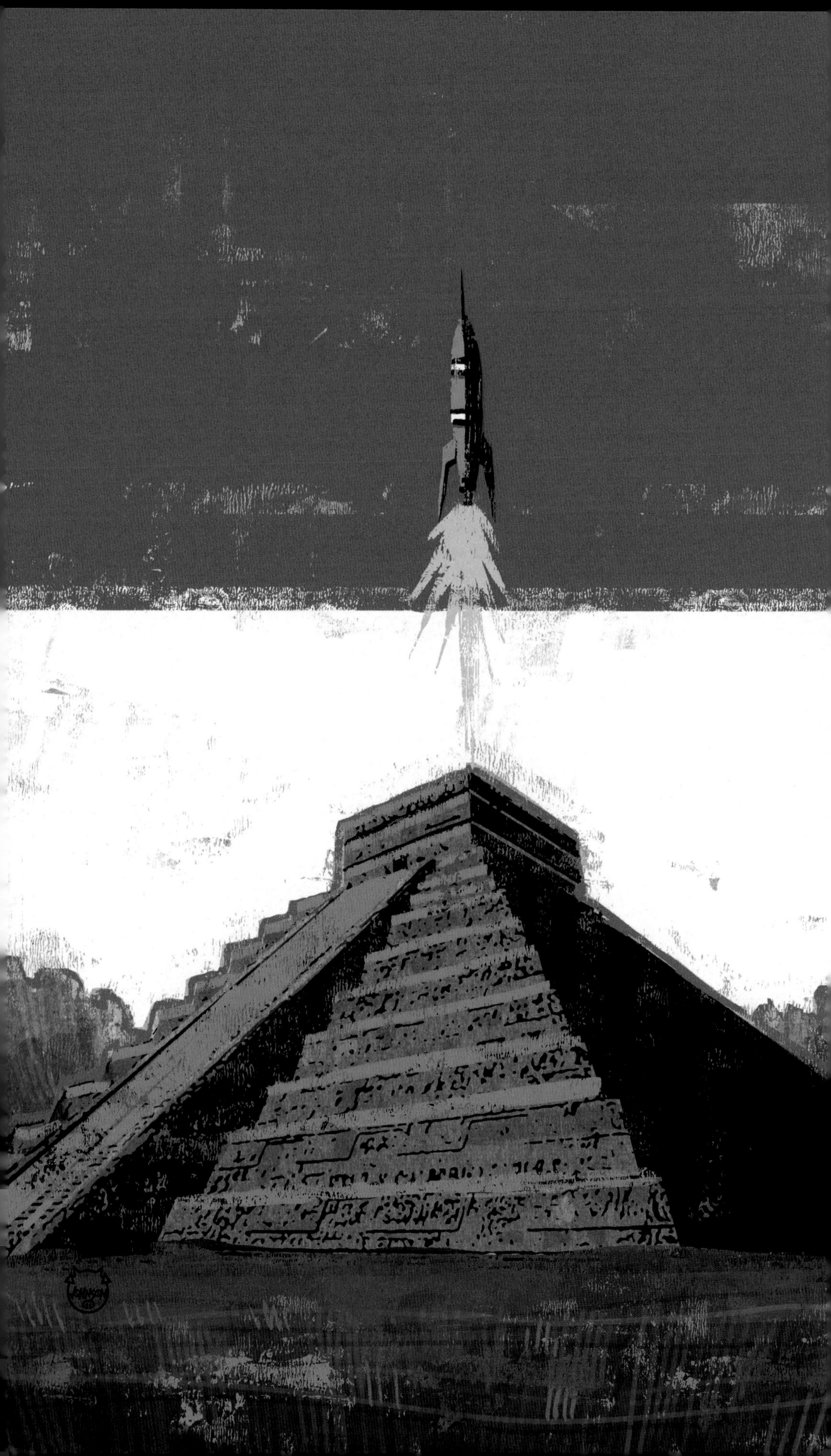

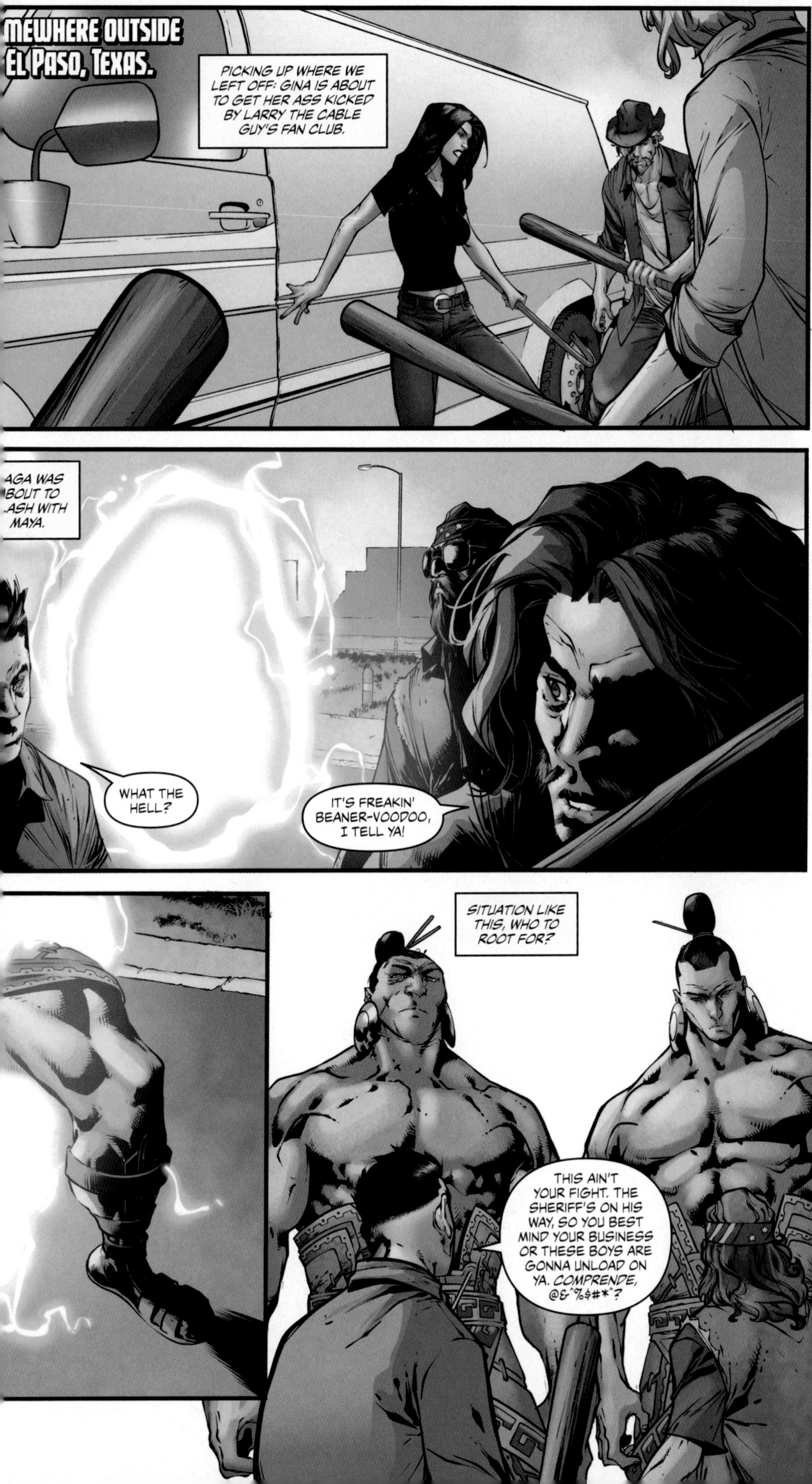
MEWHERE OUTSIDE
EL PASO, TEXAS.
PICKING UP WHERE WE LEFT OFF: GINA IS ABOUT TO GET HER ASS KICKED BY LARRY THE CABLE GUY'S FAN CLUB.
AGA WAS BOUT TO ASH WITH MAYA.
WHAT THE HELL?
IT'S FREAKIN' BEANER-VOODOO, I TELL YA!
SITUATION LIKE THIS, WHO TO ROOT FOR?
THIS AIN'T YOUR FIGHT. THE SHERIFF'S ON HIS WAY, SO YOU BEST MIND YOUR BUSINESS OR THESE BOYS ARE GONNA UNLOAD ON YA. *COMPRENDE*, @&^%$#*^?

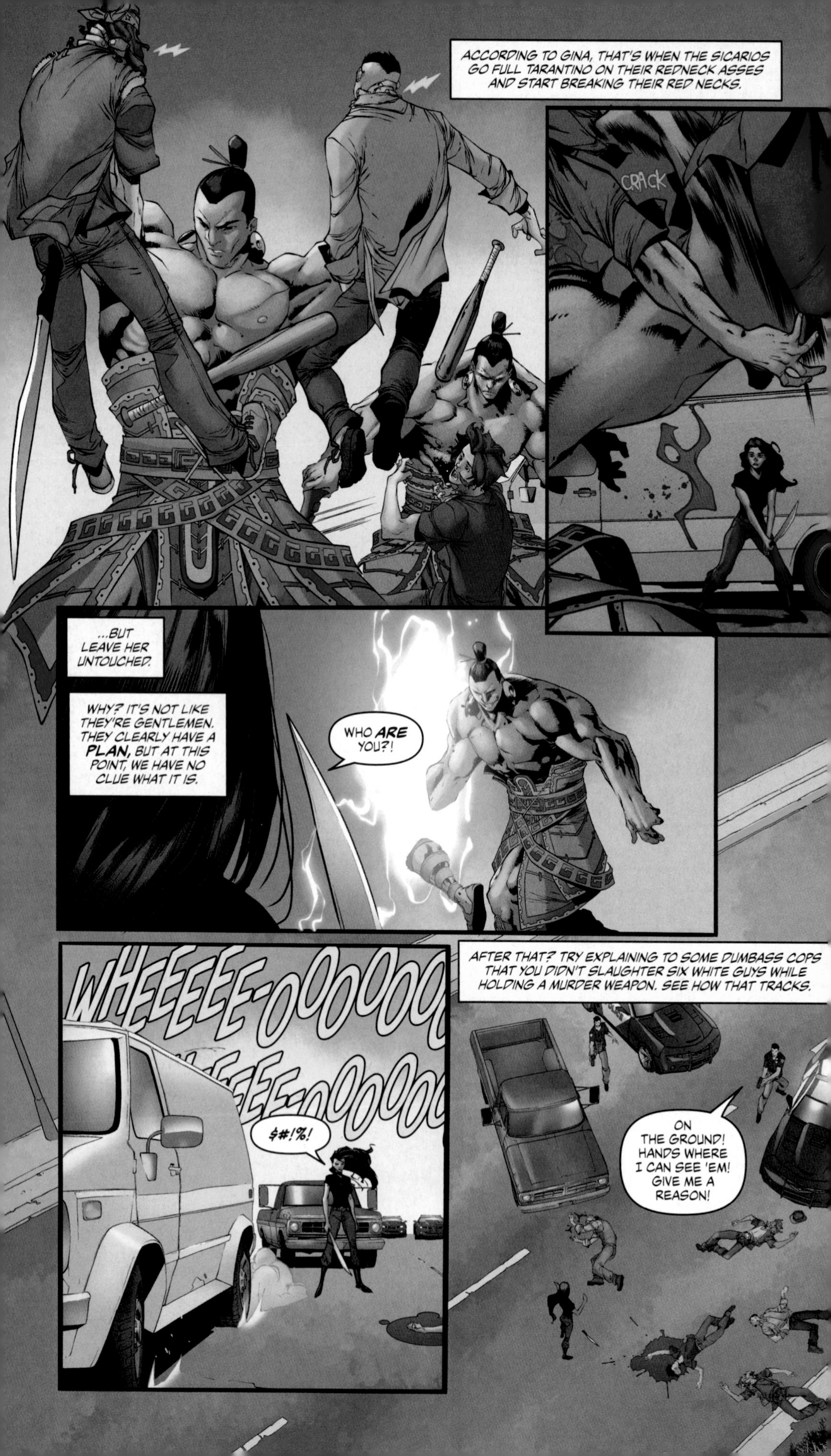

ACCORDING TO GINA, THAT'S WHEN THE SICARIOS GO FULL TARANTINO ON THEIR REDNECK ASSES AND START BREAKING THEIR RED NECKS.
CRACK
...BUT LEAVE HER UNTOUCHED.
WHY? IT'S NOT LIKE THEY'RE GENTLEMEN. THEY CLEARLY HAVE A PLAN, BUT AT THIS POINT, WE HAVE NO CLUE WHAT IT IS.
WHO ARE YOU?!
WHEEEEE-OOOOOO
$#!%!
AFTER THAT? TRY EXPLAINING TO SOME DUMBASS COPS THAT YOU DIDN'T SLAUGHTER SIX WHITE GUYS WHILE HOLDING A MURDER WEAPON. SEE HOW THAT TRACKS.
ON THE GROUND! HANDS WHERE I CAN SEE 'EM! GIVE ME A REASON!

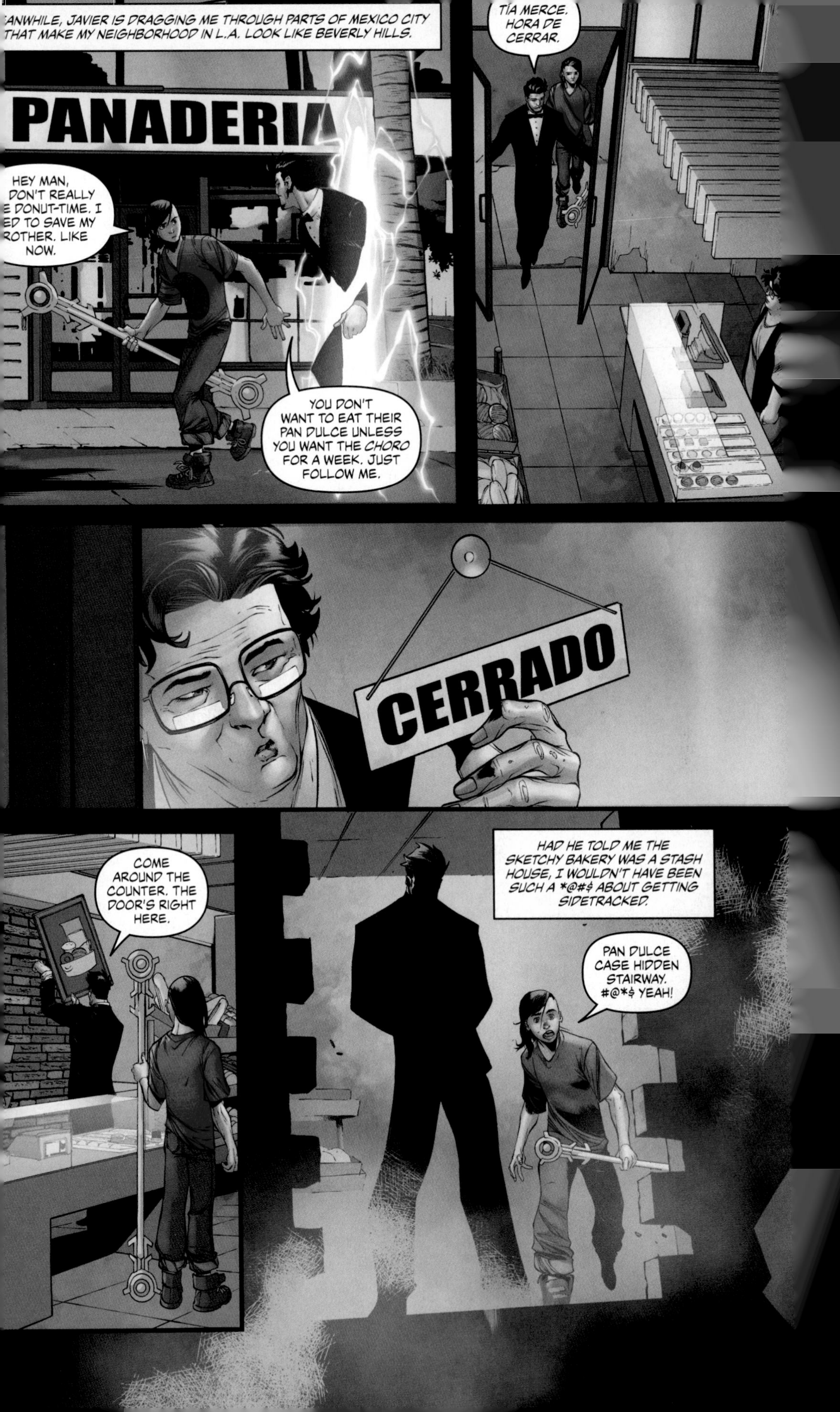

ANWHILE, JAVIER IS DRAGGING ME THROUGH PARTS OF MEXICO CITY THAT MAKE MY NEIGHBORHOOD IN L.A. LOOK LIKE BEVERLY HILLS.
PANADERIA
HEY MAN, DON'T REALLY E DONUT-TIME. I ED TO SAVE MY ROTHER. LIKE NOW.
YOU DON'T WANT TO EAT THEIR PAN DULCE UNLESS YOU WANT THE CHORO FOR A WEEK. JUST FOLLOW ME.
TÍA MERCE. HORA DE CERRAR.
CERRADO
COME AROUND THE COUNTER. THE DOOR'S RIGHT HERE.
HAD HE TOLD ME THE SKETCHY BAKERY WAS A STASH HOUSE, I WOULDN'T HAVE BEEN SUCH A *@#$ ABOUT GETTING SIDETRACKED.
PAN DULCE CASE HIDDEN STAIRWAY. #@*$ YEAH!

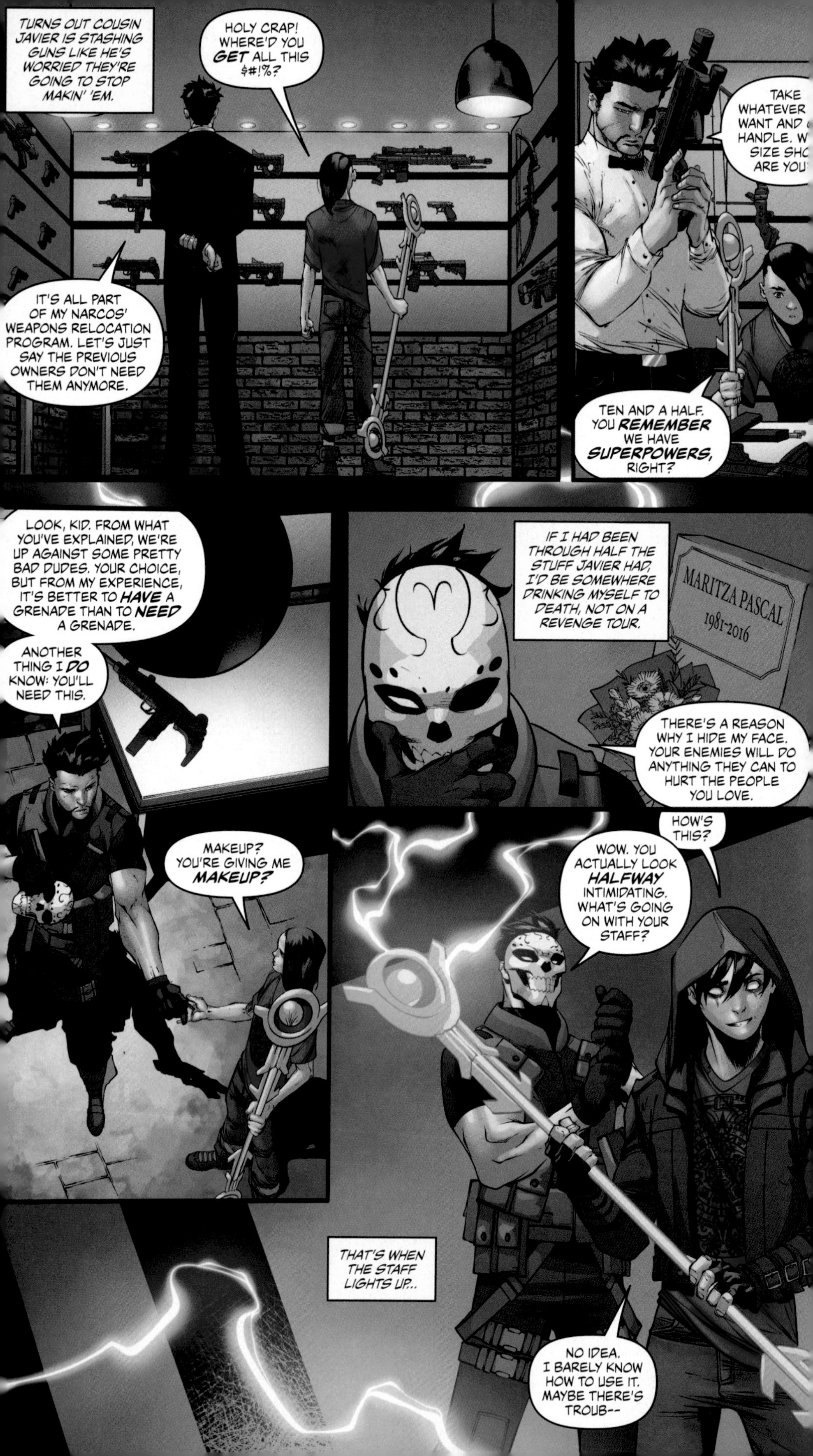
TURNS OUT COUSIN JAVIER IS STASHING GUNS LIKE HE'S WORRIED THEY'RE GOING TO STOP MAKIN' 'EM.
HOLY CRAP! WHERE'D YOU GET ALL THIS $#!%?
IT'S ALL PART OF MY NARCOS' WEAPONS RELOCATION PROGRAM. LET'S JUST SAY THE PREVIOUS OWNERS DON'T NEED THEM ANYMORE.
TEN AND A HALF. YOU REMEMBER WE HAVE SUPERPOWERS, RIGHT?
LOOK, KID. FROM WHAT YOU'VE EXPLAINED, WE'RE UP AGAINST SOME PRETTY BAD DUDES. YOUR CHOICE, BUT FROM MY EXPERIENCE, IT'S BETTER TO HAVE A GRENADE THAN TO NEED A GRENADE.
ANOTHER THING I DO KNOW: YOU'LL NEED THIS.
MAKEUP? YOU'RE GIVING ME MAKEUP?
IF I HAD BEEN THROUGH HALF THE STUFF JAVIER HAD, I'D BE SOMEWHERE DRINKING MYSELF TO DEATH, NOT ON A REVENGE TOUR.
MARITZA PASCAL
1981-2016
THERE'S A REASON WHY I HIDE MY FACE. YOUR ENEMIES WILL DO ANYTHING THEY CAN TO HURT THE PEOPLE YOU LOVE.
HOW'S THIS?
WOW. YOU ACTUALLY LOOK HALFWAY INTIMIDATING. WHAT'S GOING ON WITH YOUR STAFF?
THAT'S WHEN THE STAFF LIGHTS UP...
NO IDEA. I BARELY KNOW HOW TO USE IT. MAYBE THERE'S TROUB--

...AND JUMPS OUR ASSES UNDER THE PYRAMID.

--BLE. OR MAYBE IT'S TELEPORTING US TO A BIG-ASS CAVE.

LOOK ALIVE. THERE'S A LIGHT COMING FROM DOWN THERE.

IT'S EASY TO FORGET YOU HAVE SUPERPOWERS WHEN YOU'RE SCARED $#!%LESS.

WATCH OUR SIX. ONE OF THOSE THINGS SHOWS UP, SHOOT IT IN THE FACE.

I'M REALLY MORE OF A RUN-AS-FAST-AS-YOU-CAN-AWAY-FROM-DANGER KIND OF GUY, BUT I'LL HOLD ON TO IT IF IT MAKES YOU FEEL BETTER.

BETTER WATCH WHAT WE TOUCH. PRETTY SURE IF WE MOVE THE WRONG THING, A LARGE BOULDER WILL START ROLLING AT US.

CHECK IT OUT. THE NOT-SO-ANCIENT HISTORY OF THIS MORNING.

...ULD WE ...NOCK?

NOT WHEN IT LOOKS LIKE YOU'RE HOLDING THE KEY.

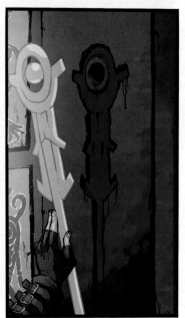

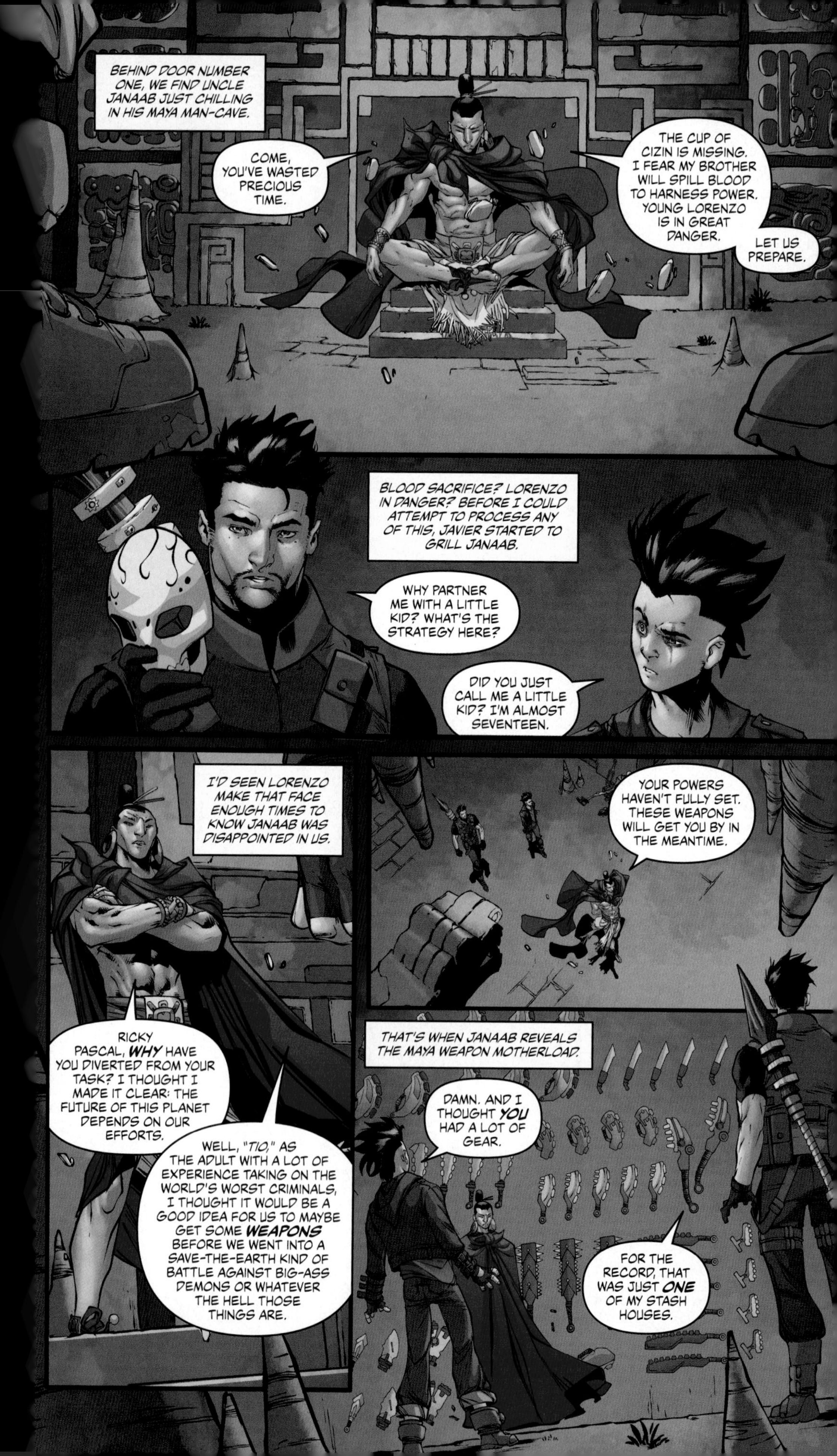
BEHIND DOOR NUMBER ONE, WE FIND UNCLE JANAAB JUST CHILLING IN HIS MAYA MAN-CAVE.
COME, YOU'VE WASTED PRECIOUS TIME.
THE CUP OF CIZIN IS MISSING. I FEAR MY BROTHER WILL SPILL BLOOD TO HARNESS POWER. YOUNG LORENZO IS IN GREAT DANGER.
LET US PREPARE.
BLOOD SACRIFICE? LORENZO IN DANGER? BEFORE I COULD ATTEMPT TO PROCESS ANY OF THIS, JAVIER STARTED TO GRILL JANAAB.
WHY PARTNER ME WITH A LITTLE KID? WHAT'S THE STRATEGY HERE?
DID YOU JUST CALL ME A LITTLE KID? I'M ALMOST SEVENTEEN.
I'D SEEN LORENZO MAKE THAT FACE ENOUGH TIMES TO KNOW JANAAB WAS DISAPPOINTED IN US.
RICKY PASCAL, WHY HAVE YOU DIVERTED FROM YOUR TASK? I THOUGHT I MADE IT CLEAR: THE FUTURE OF THIS PLANET DEPENDS ON OUR EFFORTS.
WELL, "TIO," AS THE ADULT WITH A LOT OF EXPERIENCE TAKING ON THE WORLD'S WORST CRIMINALS, I THOUGHT IT WOULD BE A GOOD IDEA FOR US TO MAYBE GET SOME WEAPONS BEFORE WE WENT INTO A SAVE-THE-EARTH KIND OF BATTLE AGAINST BIG-ASS DEMONS OR WHATEVER THE HELL THOSE THINGS ARE.
YOUR POWERS HAVEN'T FULLY SET. THESE WEAPONS WILL GET YOU BY IN THE MEANTIME.
THAT'S WHEN JANAAB REVEALS THE MAYA WEAPON MOTHERLOAD.
DAMN. AND I THOUGHT YOU HAD A LOT OF GEAR.
FOR THE RECORD, THAT WAS JUST ONE OF MY STASH HOUSES.

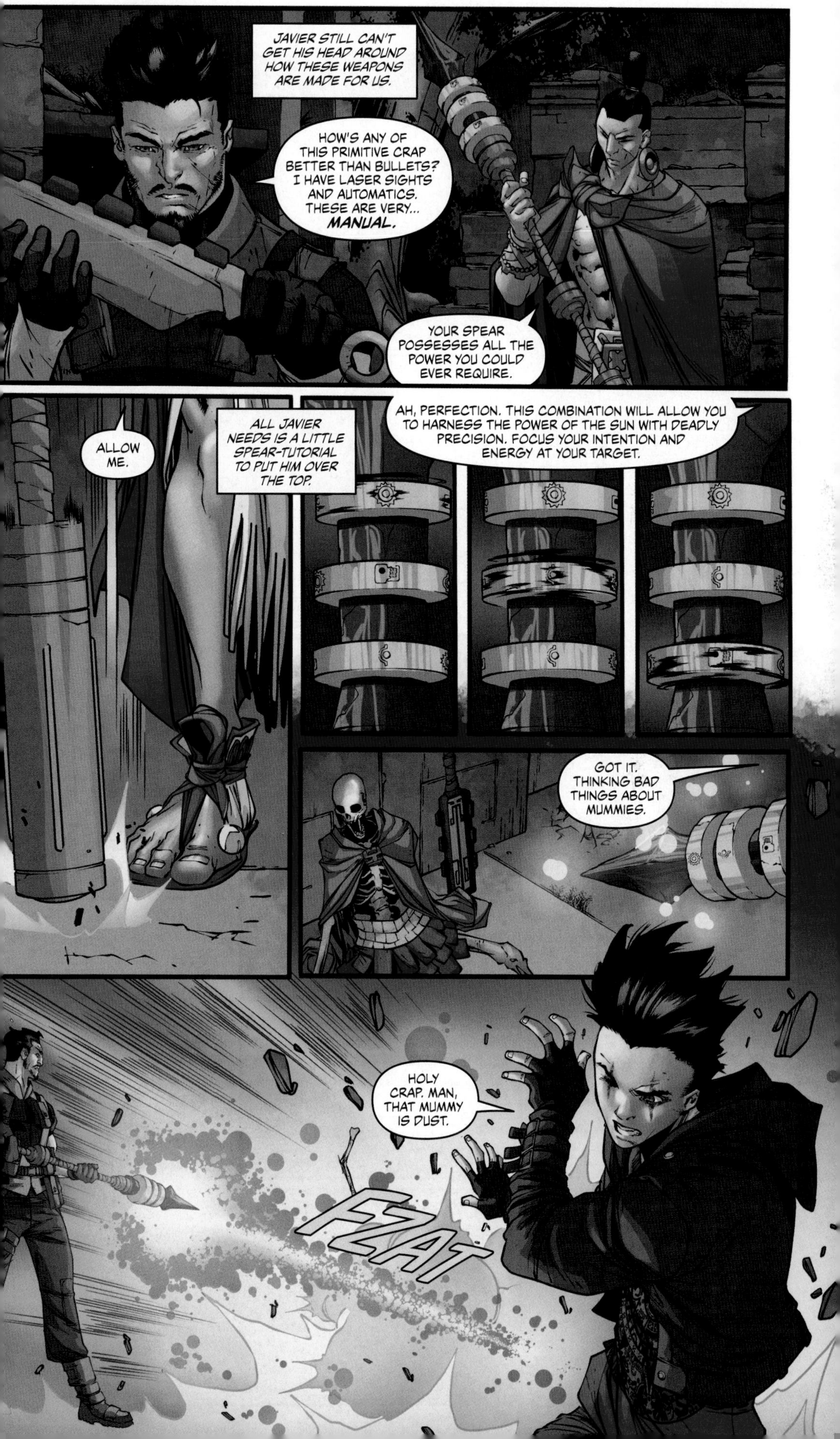
JAVIER STILL CAN'T GET HIS HEAD AROUND HOW THESE WEAPONS ARE MADE FOR US.
HOW'S ANY OF THIS PRIMITIVE CRAP BETTER THAN BULLETS? I HAVE LASER SIGHTS AND AUTOMATICS. THESE ARE VERY... MANUAL.
YOUR SPEAR POSSESSES ALL THE POWER YOU COULD EVER REQUIRE.
ALLOW ME.
ALL JAVIER NEEDS IS A LITTLE SPEAR-TUTORIAL TO PUT HIM OVER THE TOP.
AH, PERFECTION. THIS COMBINATION WILL ALLOW YOU TO HARNESS THE POWER OF THE SUN WITH DEADLY PRECISION. FOCUS YOUR INTENTION AND ENERGY AT YOUR TARGET.
GOT IT. THINKING BAD THINGS ABOUT MUMMIES.
HOLY CRAP. MAN, THAT MUMMY IS DUST.
FZZAT

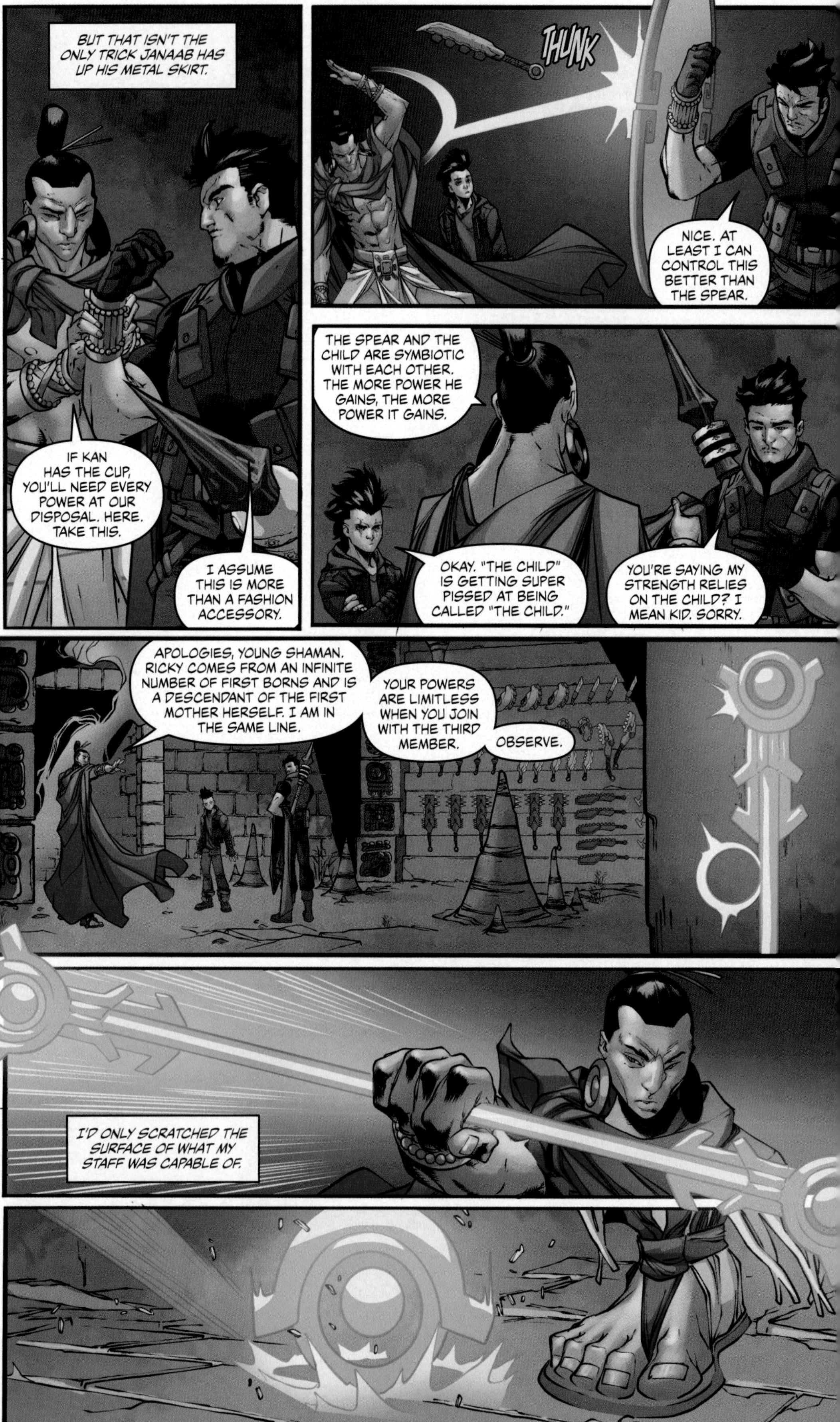

BUT THAT ISN'T THE ONLY TRICK JANAAB HAS UP HIS METAL SKIRT.
IF KAN HAS THE CUP, YOU'LL NEED EVERY POWER AT OUR DISPOSAL. HERE. TAKE THIS.
I ASSUME THIS IS MORE THAN A FASHION ACCESSORY.
THUNK
NICE. AT LEAST I CAN CONTROL THIS BETTER THAN THE SPEAR.
THE SPEAR AND THE CHILD ARE SYMBIOTIC WITH EACH OTHER. THE MORE POWER HE GAINS, THE MORE POWER IT GAINS.
YOU'RE SAYING MY STRENGTH RELIES ON THE CHILD? I MEAN KID. SORRY.
OKAY. "THE CHILD" IS GETTING SUPER PISSED AT BEING CALLED "THE CHILD."
APOLOGIES, YOUNG SHAMAN. RICKY COMES FROM AN INFINITE NUMBER OF FIRST BORNS AND IS A DESCENDANT OF THE FIRST MOTHER HERSELF. I AM IN THE SAME LINE.
YOUR POWERS ARE LIMITLESS WHEN YOU JOIN WITH THE THIRD MEMBER.
OBSERVE.
I'D ONLY SCRATCHED THE SURFACE OF WHAT MY STAFF WAS CAPABLE OF.

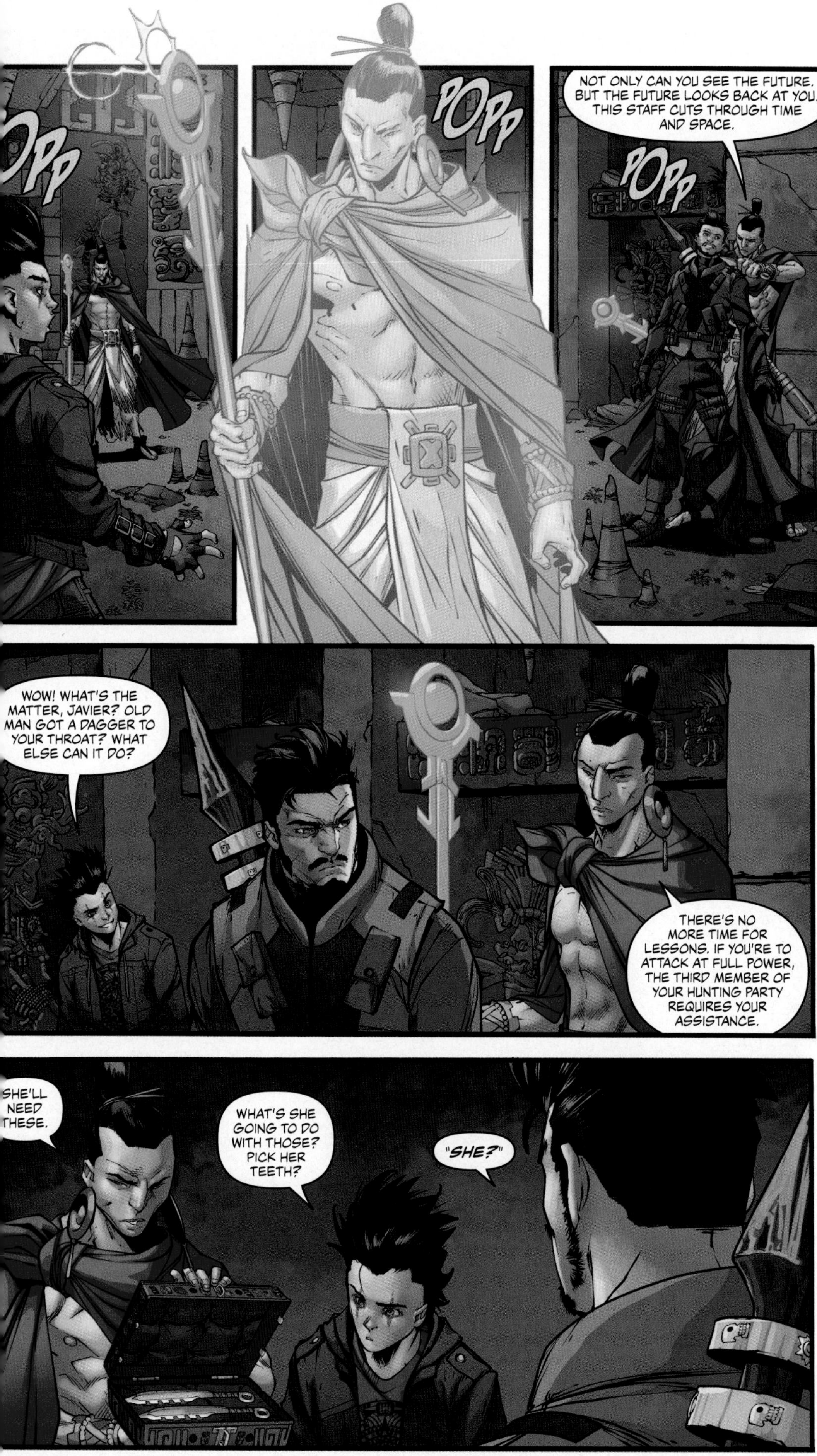
POPP
POPP
NOT ONLY CAN YOU SEE THE FUTURE. BUT THE FUTURE LOOKS BACK AT YOU. THIS STAFF CUTS THROUGH TIME AND SPACE.
POPP
WOW! WHAT'S THE MATTER, JAVIER? OLD MAN GOT A DAGGER TO YOUR THROAT? WHAT ELSE CAN IT DO?
THERE'S NO MORE TIME FOR LESSONS. IF YOU'RE TO ATTACK AT FULL POWER, THE THIRD MEMBER OF YOUR HUNTING PARTY REQUIRES YOUR ASSISTANCE.
SHE'LL NEED THESE.
WHAT'S SHE GOING TO DO WITH THOSE? PICK HER TEETH?
"SHE?"

EL PASO COUNTY SHERIFF'S OFFICE HEADQUARTERS

TELL ME WHY I SHOULDN'T KILL YOU RIGHT NOW?!

LAWS? YOUR *OATH*? *DUE PROCESS*? WHERE DO YOU WANT ME TO STOP?

WHEEEE-OOO WHEEEE-OO WHEEEE-OOO

WATCH HE IF SHE MOV SHOOT HER A SHE TRIED T FOR YOUR G

WHOOMP

COULDN'T HAVE TELEPORTED US DIRECTLY INTO THE ROOM?

BUT THEN YOU WOULDN GET TO SHO ANYTHING.

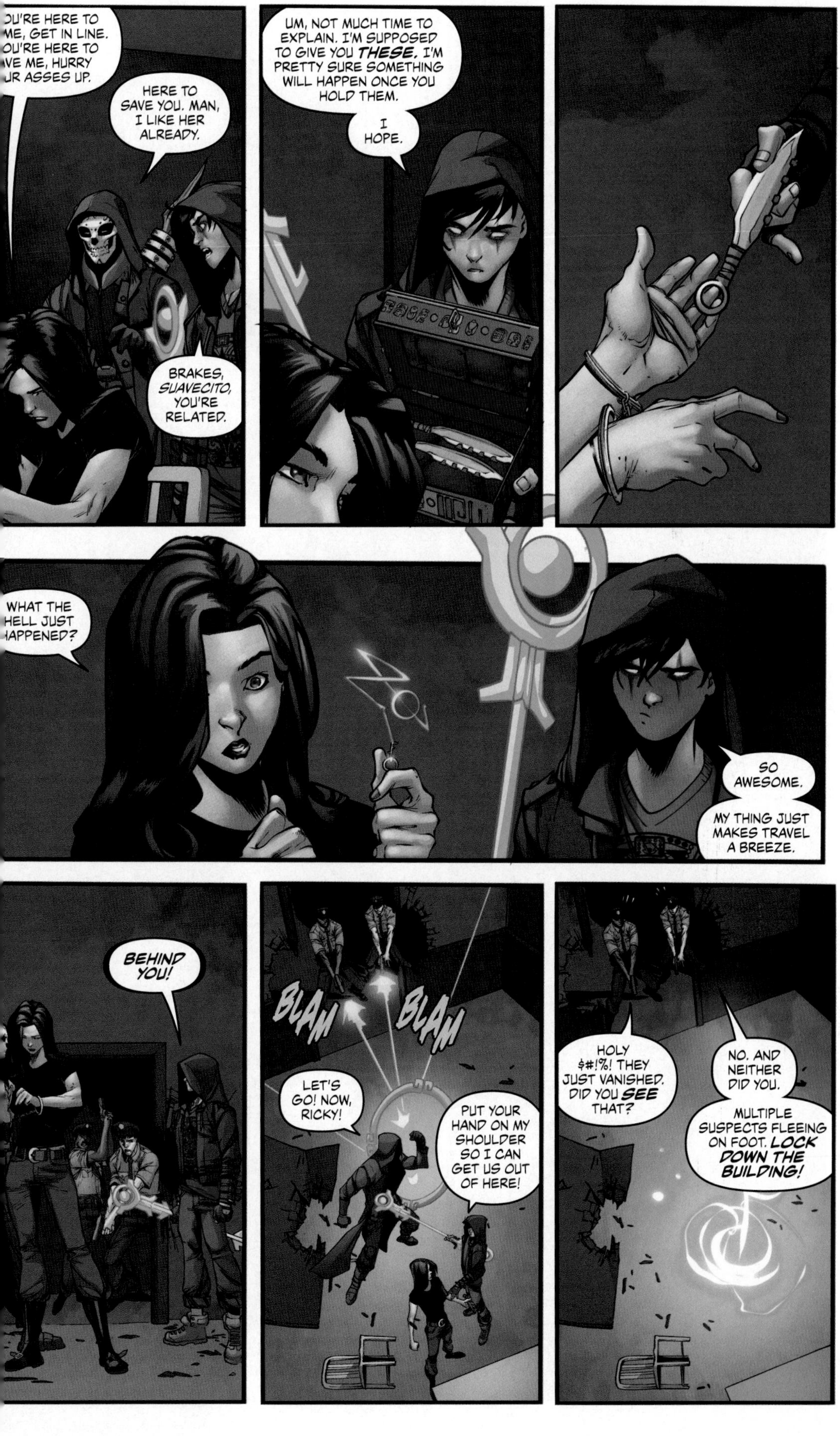
OU'RE HERE TO ME, GET IN LINE. OU'RE HERE TO VE ME, HURRY UR ASSES UP.
HERE TO SAVE YOU. MAN, I LIKE HER ALREADY.
BRAKES, SUAVECITO, YOU'RE RELATED.
UM, NOT MUCH TIME TO EXPLAIN. I'M SUPPOSED TO GIVE YOU THESE. I'M PRETTY SURE SOMETHING WILL HAPPEN ONCE YOU HOLD THEM.
I HOPE.
WHAT THE HELL JUST APPENED?
SO AWESOME.
MY THING JUST MAKES TRAVEL A BREEZE.
BEHIND YOU!
BLAM
BLAM
LET'S GO! NOW, RICKY!
PUT YOUR HAND ON MY SHOULDER SO I CAN GET US OUT OF HERE!
HOLY $#!%! THEY JUST VANISHED. DID YOU SEE THAT?
NO. AND NEITHER DID YOU.
MULTIPLE SUSPECTS FLEEING ON FOOT. LOCK DOWN THE BUILDING!

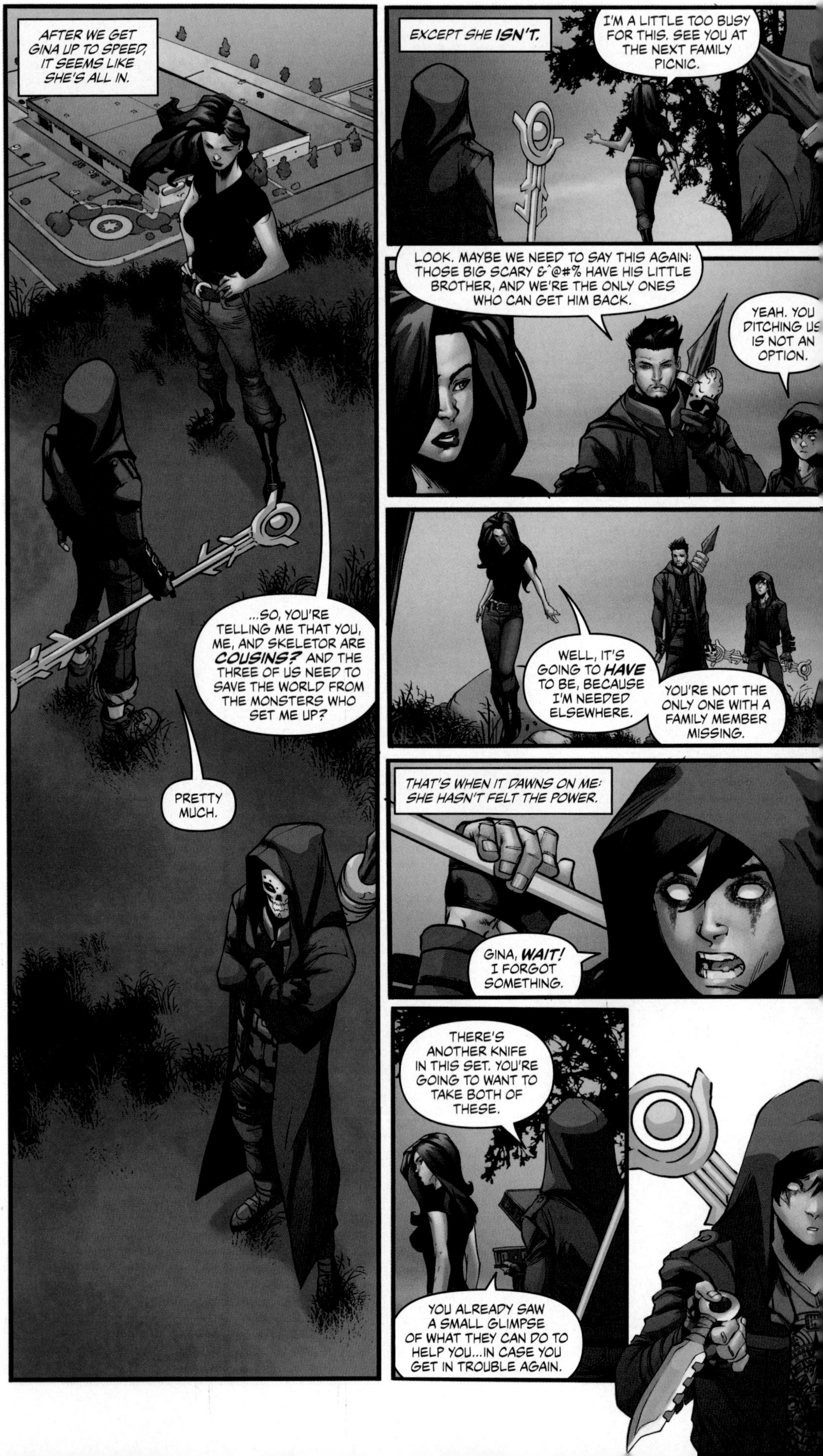
AFTER WE GET GINA UP TO SPEED, IT SEEMS LIKE SHE'S ALL IN.
...SO, YOU'RE TELLING ME THAT YOU, ME, AND SKELETOR ARE COUSINS? AND THE THREE OF US NEED TO SAVE THE WORLD FROM THE MONSTERS WHO SET ME UP?
PRETTY MUCH.
EXCEPT SHE ISN'T.
I'M A LITTLE TOO BUSY FOR THIS. SEE YOU AT THE NEXT FAMILY PICNIC.
LOOK. MAYBE WE NEED TO SAY THIS AGAIN: THOSE BIG SCARY &^@#% HAVE HIS LITTLE BROTHER, AND WE'RE THE ONLY ONES WHO CAN GET HIM BACK.
YEAH. YOU DITCHING US IS NOT AN OPTION.
WELL, IT'S GOING TO HAVE TO BE, BECAUSE I'M NEEDED ELSEWHERE.
YOU'RE NOT THE ONLY ONE WITH A FAMILY MEMBER MISSING.
THAT'S WHEN IT DAWNS ON ME: SHE HASN'T FELT THE POWER.
GINA, WAIT! I FORGOT SOMETHING.
THERE'S ANOTHER KNIFE IN THIS SET. YOU'RE GOING TO WANT TO TAKE BOTH OF THESE.
YOU ALREADY SAW A SMALL GLIMPSE OF WHAT THEY CAN DO TO HELP YOU...IN CASE YOU GET IN TROUBLE AGAIN.

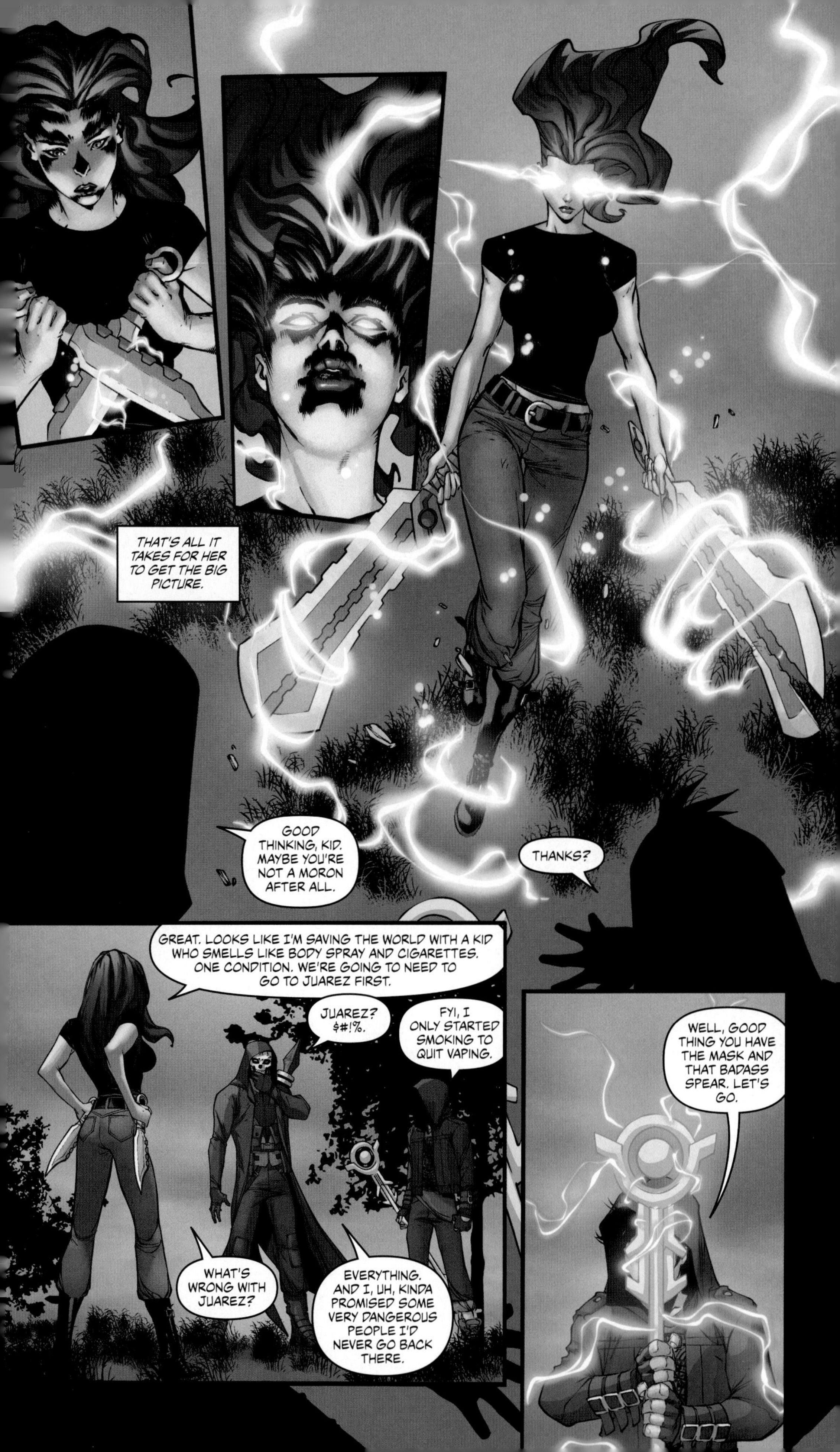
THAT'S ALL IT TAKES FOR HER TO GET THE BIG PICTURE.
GOOD THINKING, KID. MAYBE YOU'RE NOT A MORON AFTER ALL.
THANKS?
GREAT. LOOKS LIKE I'M SAVING THE WORLD WITH A KID WHO SMELLS LIKE BODY SPRAY AND CIGARETTES. ONE CONDITION. WE'RE GOING TO NEED TO GO TO JUAREZ FIRST.
JUAREZ? $#!%.
FYI, I ONLY STARTED SMOKING TO QUIT VAPING.
WHAT'S WRONG WITH JUAREZ?
EVERYTHING. AND I, UH, KINDA PROMISED SOME VERY DANGEROUS PEOPLE I'D NEVER GO BACK THERE.
WELL, GOOD THING YOU HAVE THE MASK AND THAT BADASS SPEAR. LET'S GO.

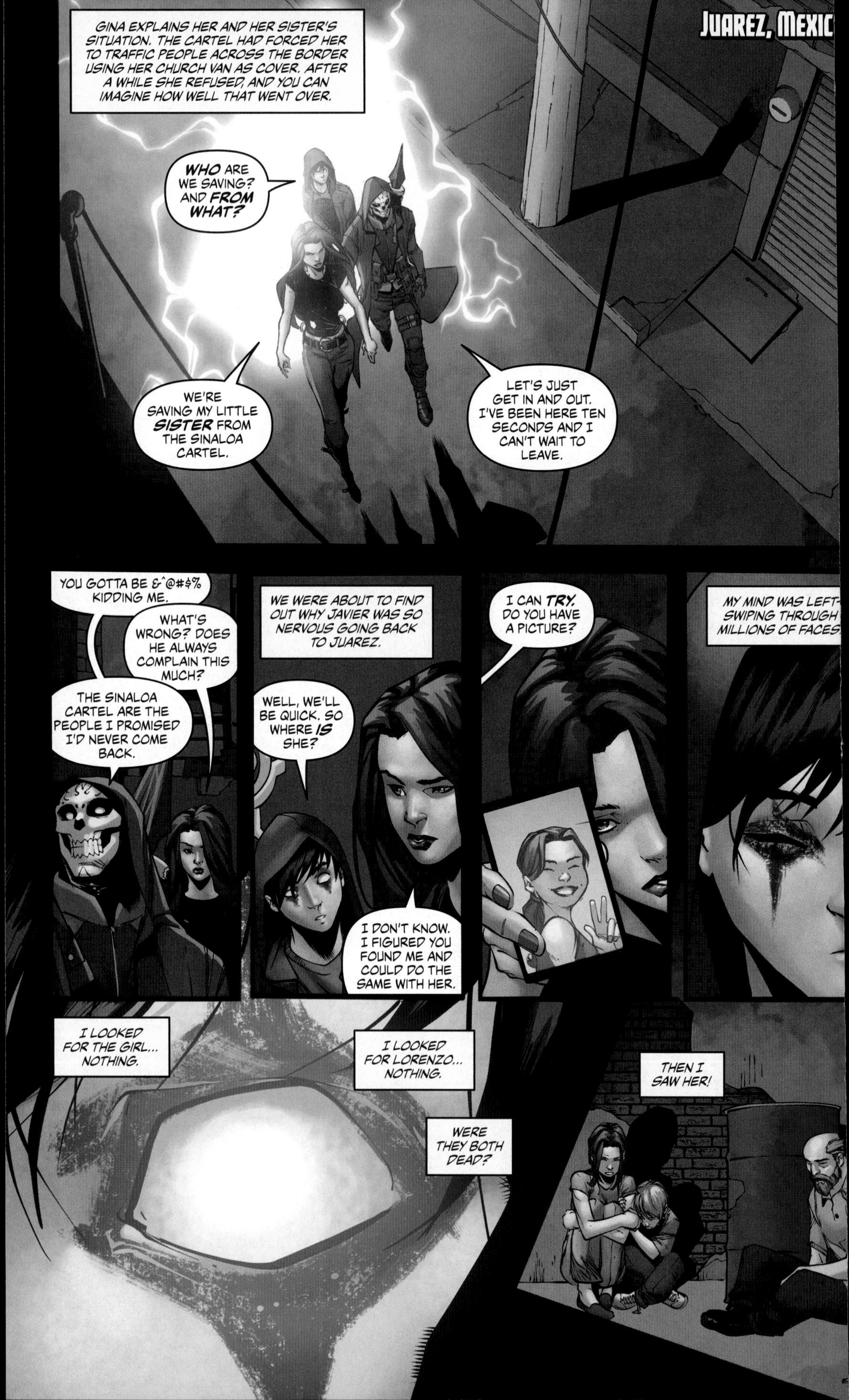

JUAREZ, MEXIC
GINA EXPLAINS HER AND HER SISTER'S SITUATION. THE CARTEL HAD FORCED HER TO TRAFFIC PEOPLE ACROSS THE BORDER USING HER CHURCH VAN AS COVER. AFTER A WHILE SHE REFUSED, AND YOU CAN IMAGINE HOW WELL THAT WENT OVER.
WHO ARE WE SAVING? AND FROM WHAT?
WE'RE SAVING MY LITTLE SISTER FROM THE SINALOA CARTEL.
LET'S JUST GET IN AND OUT. I'VE BEEN HERE TEN SECONDS AND I CAN'T WAIT TO LEAVE.
YOU GOTTA BE &^@#$% KIDDING ME.
WHAT'S WRONG? DOES HE ALWAYS COMPLAIN THIS MUCH?
THE SINALOA CARTEL ARE THE PEOPLE I PROMISED I'D NEVER COME BACK.
WE WERE ABOUT TO FIND OUT WHY JAVIER WAS SO NERVOUS GOING BACK TO JUAREZ.
WELL, WE'LL BE QUICK. SO WHERE IS SHE?
I DON'T KNOW. I FIGURED YOU FOUND ME AND COULD DO THE SAME WITH HER.
I CAN TRY. DO YOU HAVE A PICTURE?
MY MIND WAS LEFT-SWIPING THROUGH MILLIONS OF FACES.
I LOOKED FOR THE GIRL... NOTHING.
I LOOKED FOR LORENZO... NOTHING.
WERE THEY BOTH DEAD?
THEN I SAW HER!

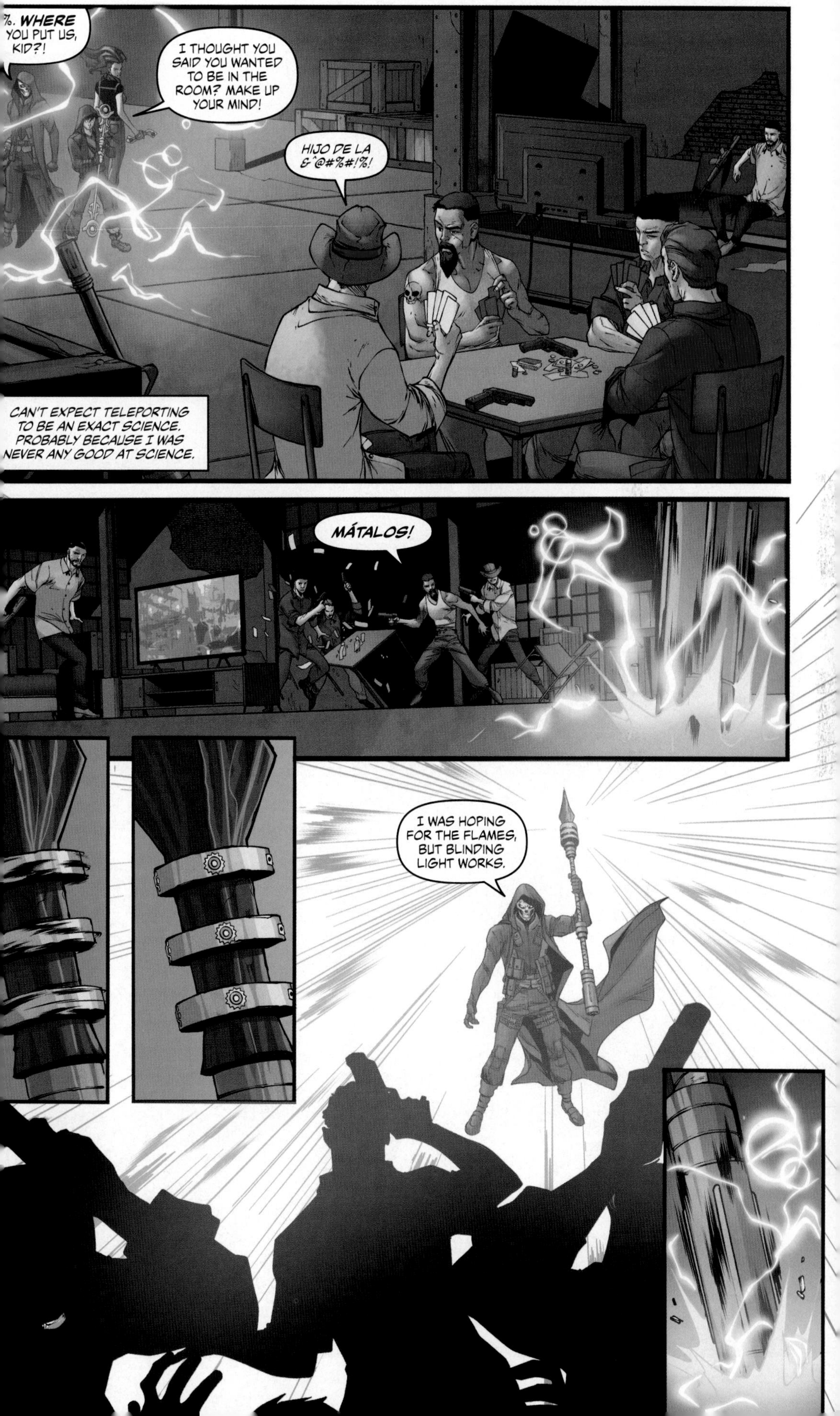
%. WHERE YOU PUT US, KID?!
I THOUGHT YOU SAID YOU WANTED TO BE IN THE ROOM? MAKE UP YOUR MIND!
HIJO DE LA &^@#%#!%!
CAN'T EXPECT TELEPORTING TO BE AN EXACT SCIENCE. PROBABLY BECAUSE I WAS NEVER ANY GOOD AT SCIENCE.
MÁTALOS!
I WAS HOPING FOR THE FLAMES, BUT BLINDING LIGHT WORKS.

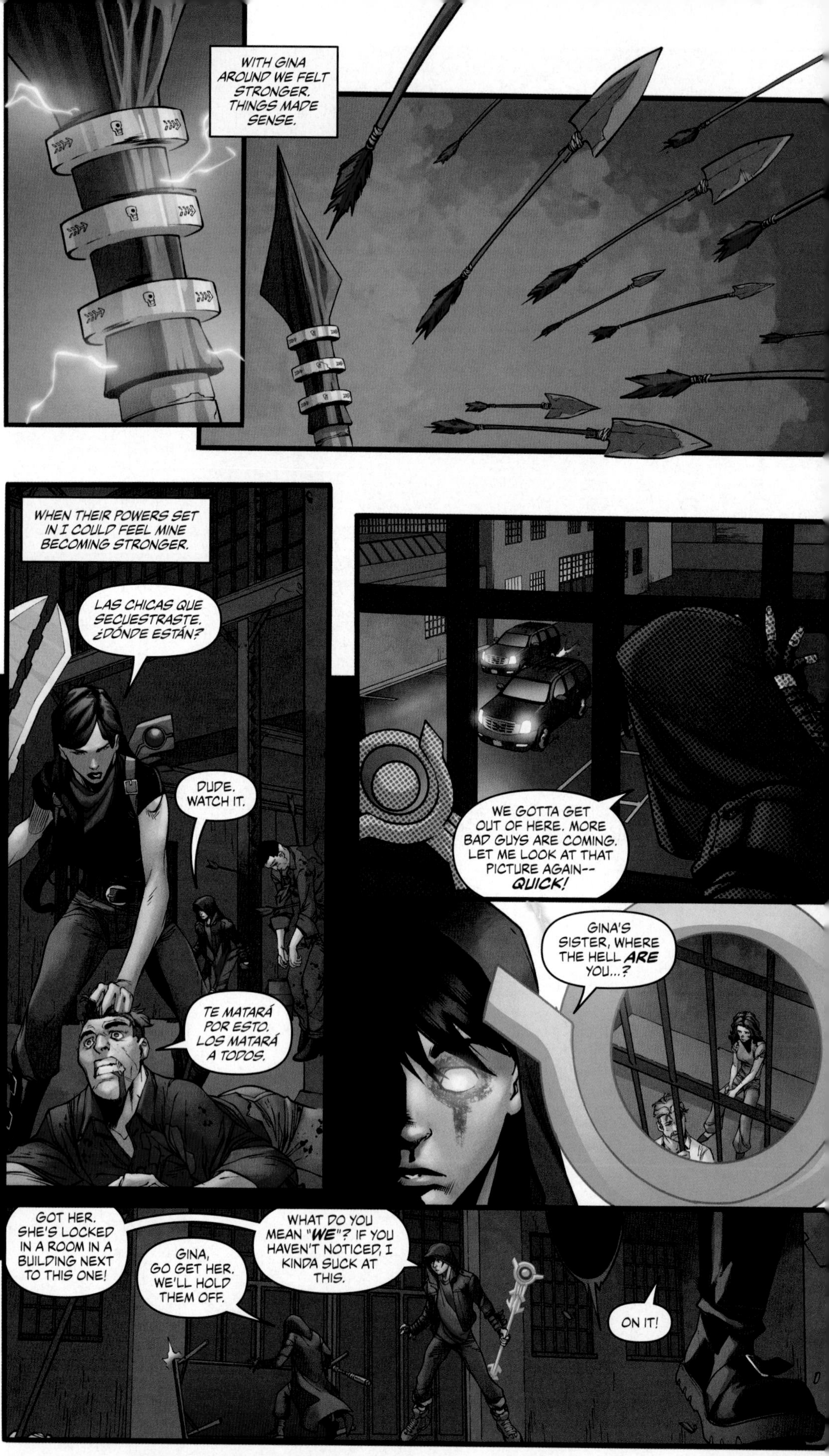

WITH GINA AROUND WE FELT STRONGER. THINGS MADE SENSE.
WHEN THEIR POWERS SET IN I COULD FEEL MINE BECOMING STRONGER.
LAS CHICAS QUE SECUESTRASTE. ¿DÓNDE ESTÁN?
DUDE. WATCH IT.
TE MATARÁ POR ESTO. LOS MATARÁ A TODOS.
WE GOTTA GET OUT OF HERE. MORE BAD GUYS ARE COMING. LET ME LOOK AT THAT PICTURE AGAIN-- QUICK!
GINA'S SISTER, WHERE THE HELL ARE YOU...?
GOT HER. SHE'S LOCKED IN A ROOM IN A BUILDING NEXT TO THIS ONE!
GINA, GO GET HER. WE'LL HOLD THEM OFF.
WHAT DO YOU MEAN "WE"? IF YOU HAVEN'T NOTICED, I KINDA SUCK AT THIS.
ON IT!

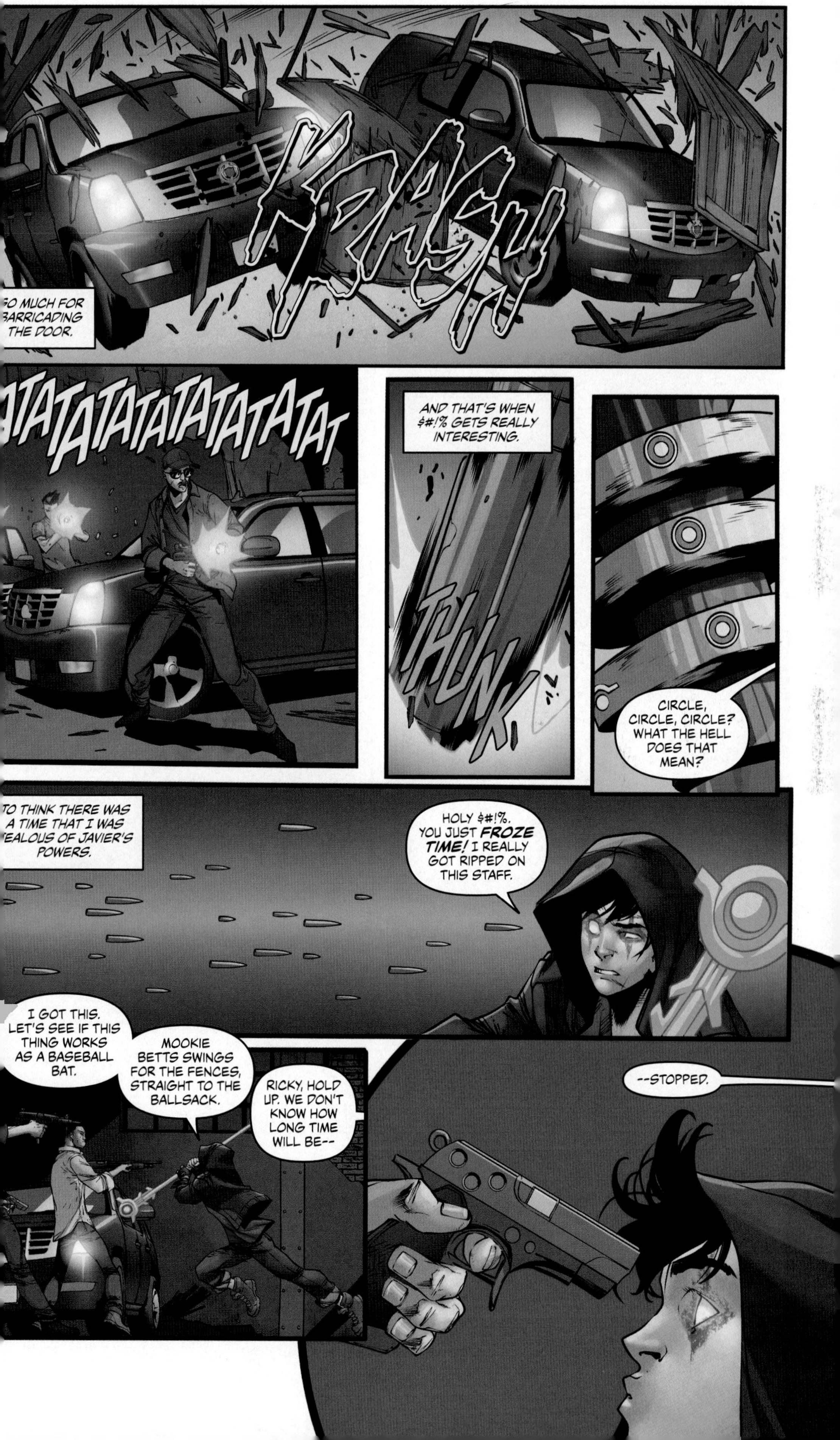
SO MUCH FOR BARRICADING THE DOOR.
KRASH
TATATATATATATATATATAT
AND THAT'S WHEN $#!% GETS REALLY INTERESTING.
THUNK
CIRCLE, CIRCLE, CIRCLE? WHAT THE HELL DOES THAT MEAN?
TO THINK THERE WAS A TIME THAT I WAS JEALOUS OF JAVIER'S POWERS.
HOLY $#!%. YOU JUST FROZE TIME! I REALLY GOT RIPPED ON THIS STAFF.
I GOT THIS. LET'S SEE IF THIS THING WORKS AS A BASEBALL BAT.
MOOKIE BETTS SWINGS FOR THE FENCES, STRAIGHT TO THE BALLSACK.
RICKY, HOLD UP. WE DON'T KNOW HOW LONG TIME WILL BE--
--STOPPED.

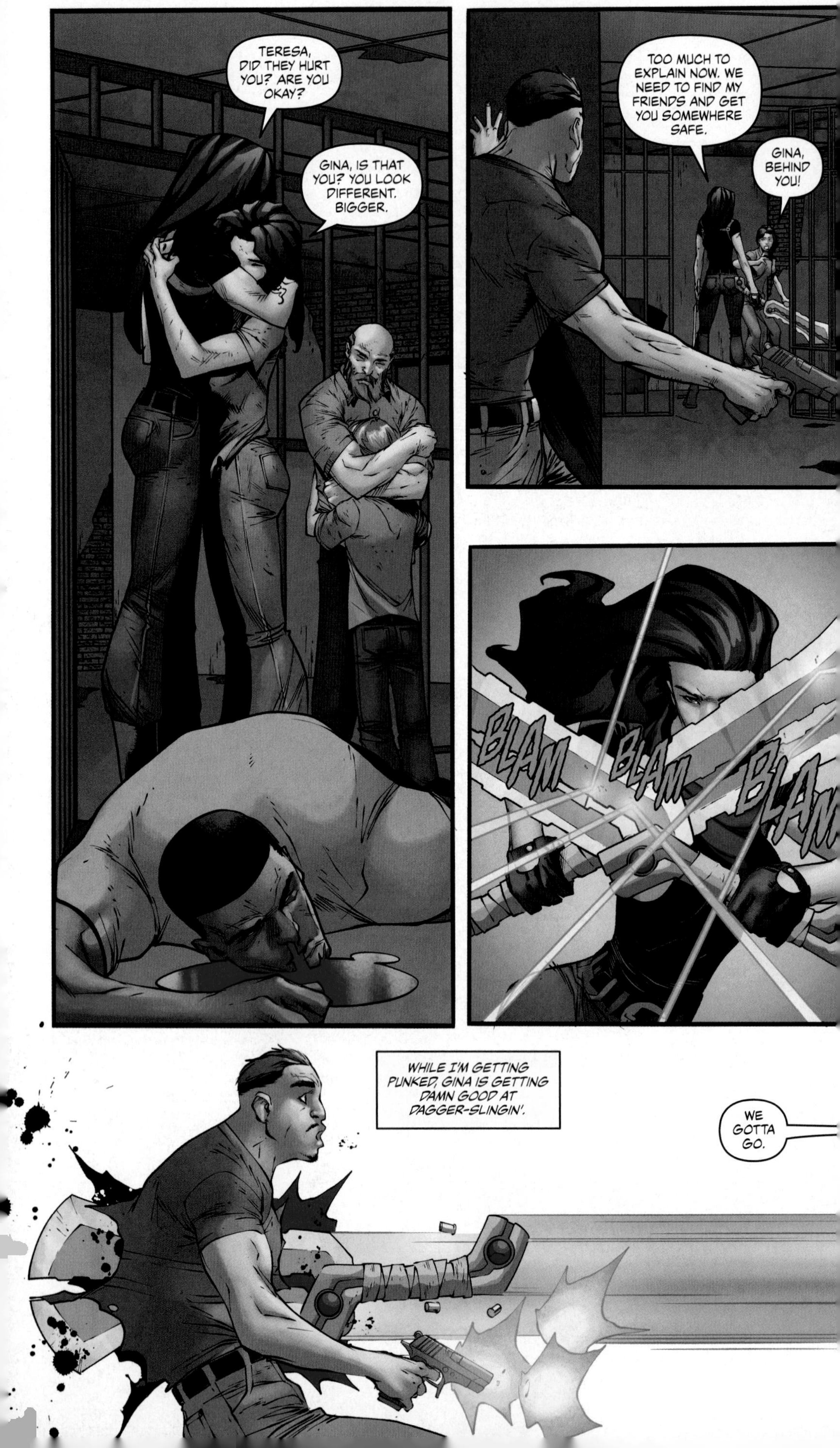
TERESA, DID THEY HURT YOU? ARE YOU OKAY?
GINA, IS THAT YOU? YOU LOOK DIFFERENT. BIGGER.
TOO MUCH TO EXPLAIN NOW. WE NEED TO FIND MY FRIENDS AND GET YOU SOMEWHERE SAFE.
GINA, BEHIND YOU!
BLAM BLAM BLAM
WHILE I'M GETTING PUNKED, GINA IS GETTING DAMN GOOD AT DAGGER-SLINGIN'.
WE GOTTA GO.

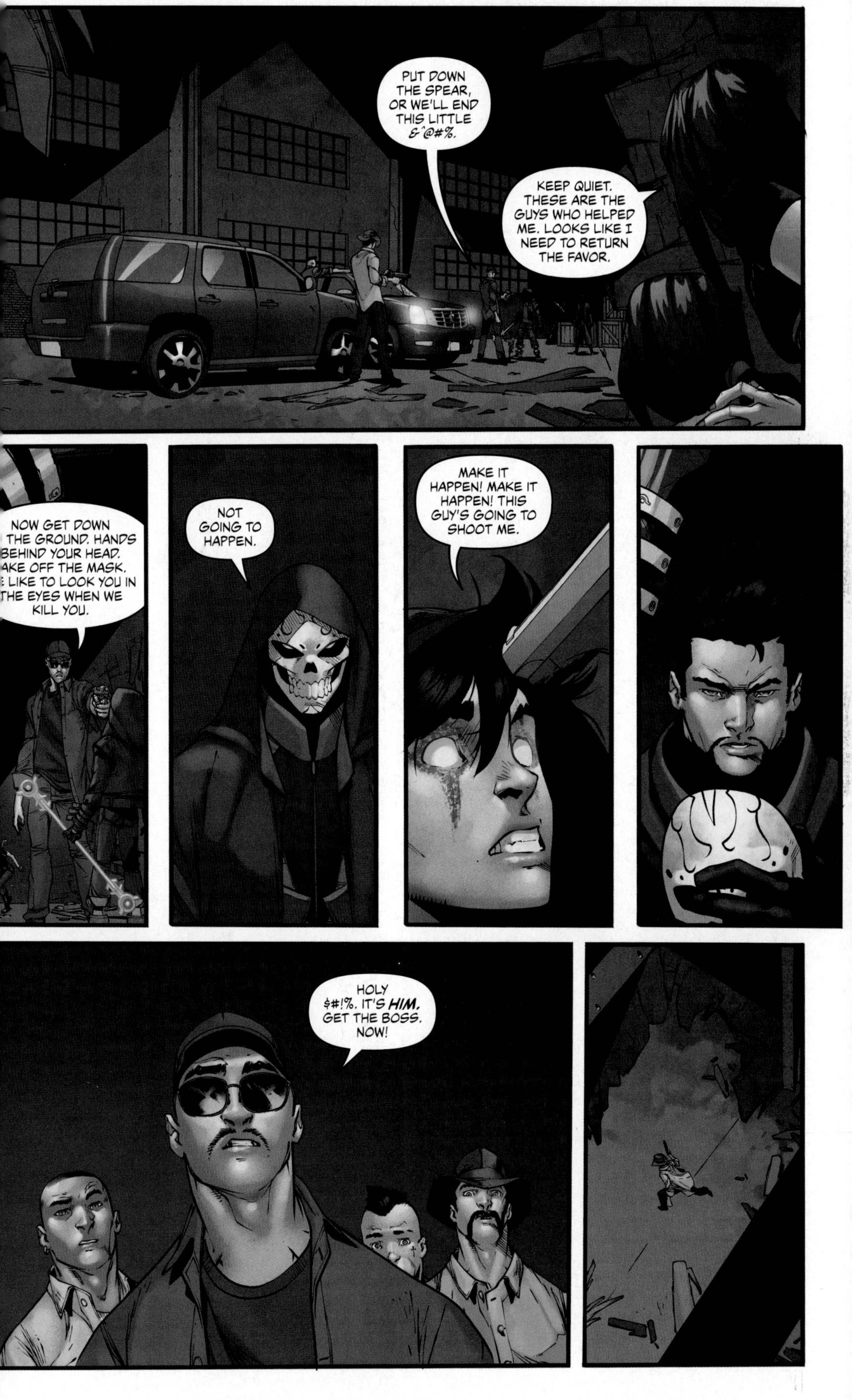
PUT DOWN THE SPEAR, OR WE'LL END THIS LITTLE &^@#%.
KEEP QUIET. THESE ARE THE GUYS WHO HELPED ME. LOOKS LIKE I NEED TO RETURN THE FAVOR.
NOW GET DOWN THE GROUND. HANDS BEHIND YOUR HEAD. AKE OFF THE MASK. E LIKE TO LOOK YOU IN THE EYES WHEN WE KILL YOU.
NOT GOING TO HAPPEN.
MAKE IT HAPPEN! MAKE IT HAPPEN! THIS GUY'S GOING TO SHOOT ME.
HOLY $#!%. IT'S HIM. GET THE BOSS. NOW!

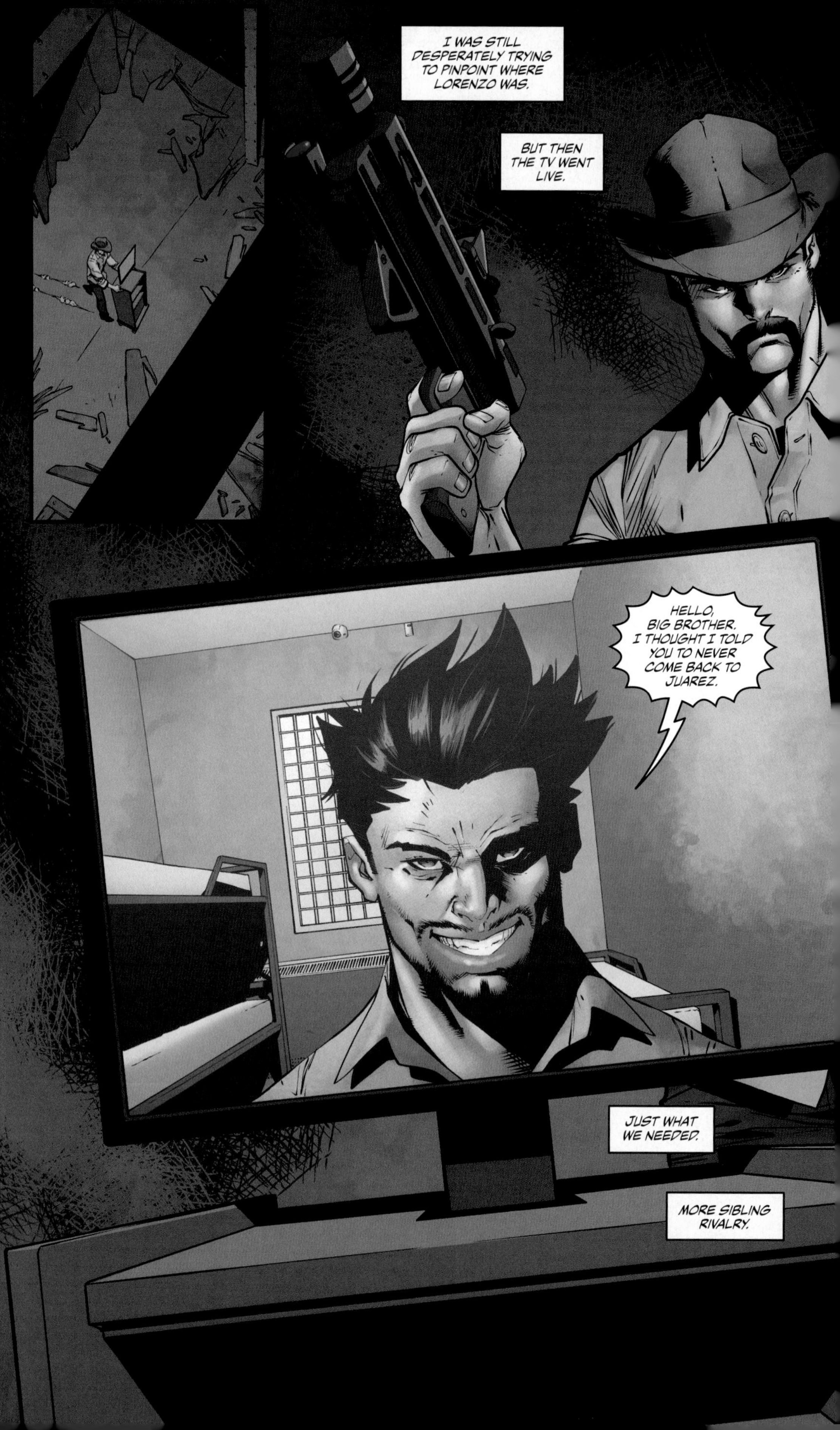

I WAS STILL DESPERATELY TRYING TO PINPOINT WHERE LORENZO WAS.
BUT THEN THE TV WENT LIVE.
HELLO, BIG BROTHER. I THOUGHT I TOLD YOU TO NEVER COME BACK TO JUAREZ.
JUST WHAT WE NEEDED.
MORE SIBLING RIVALRY.

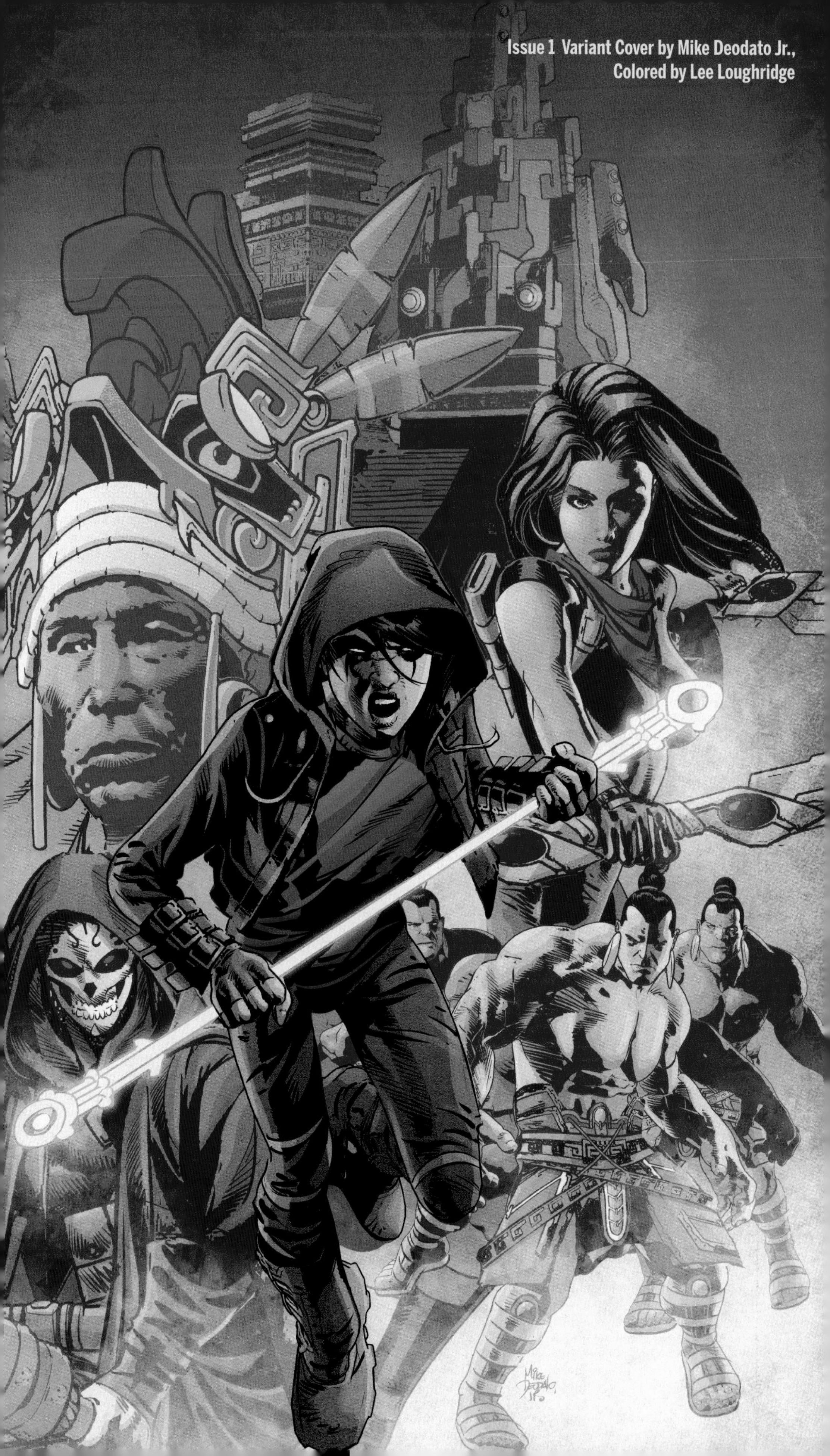

Issue 1 Variant Cover by Mike Deodato Jr.,
Colored by Lee Loughridge

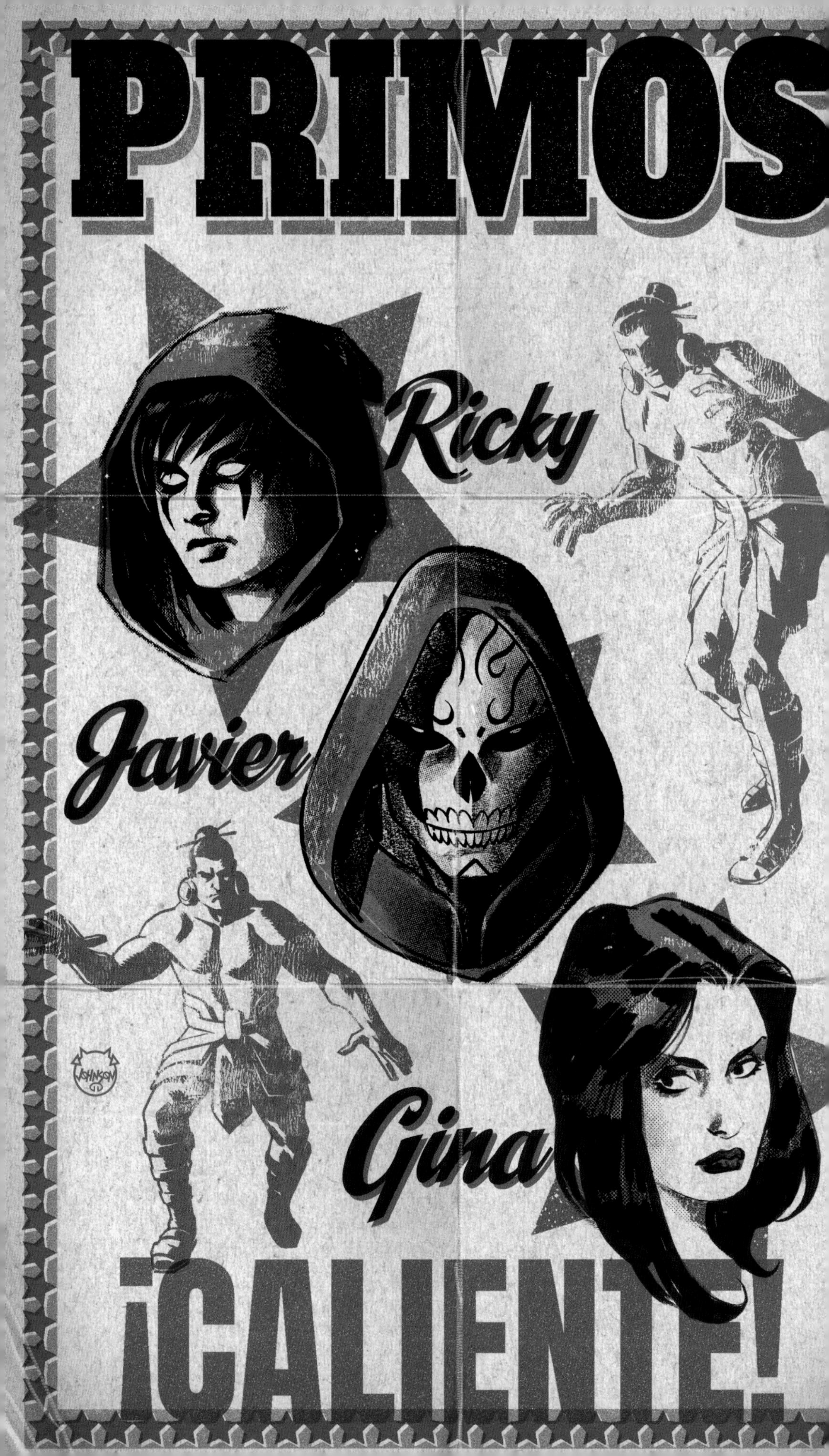
PRIMOS
Ricky
Javier
Gina
JOHNSON
¡CALIENTE!

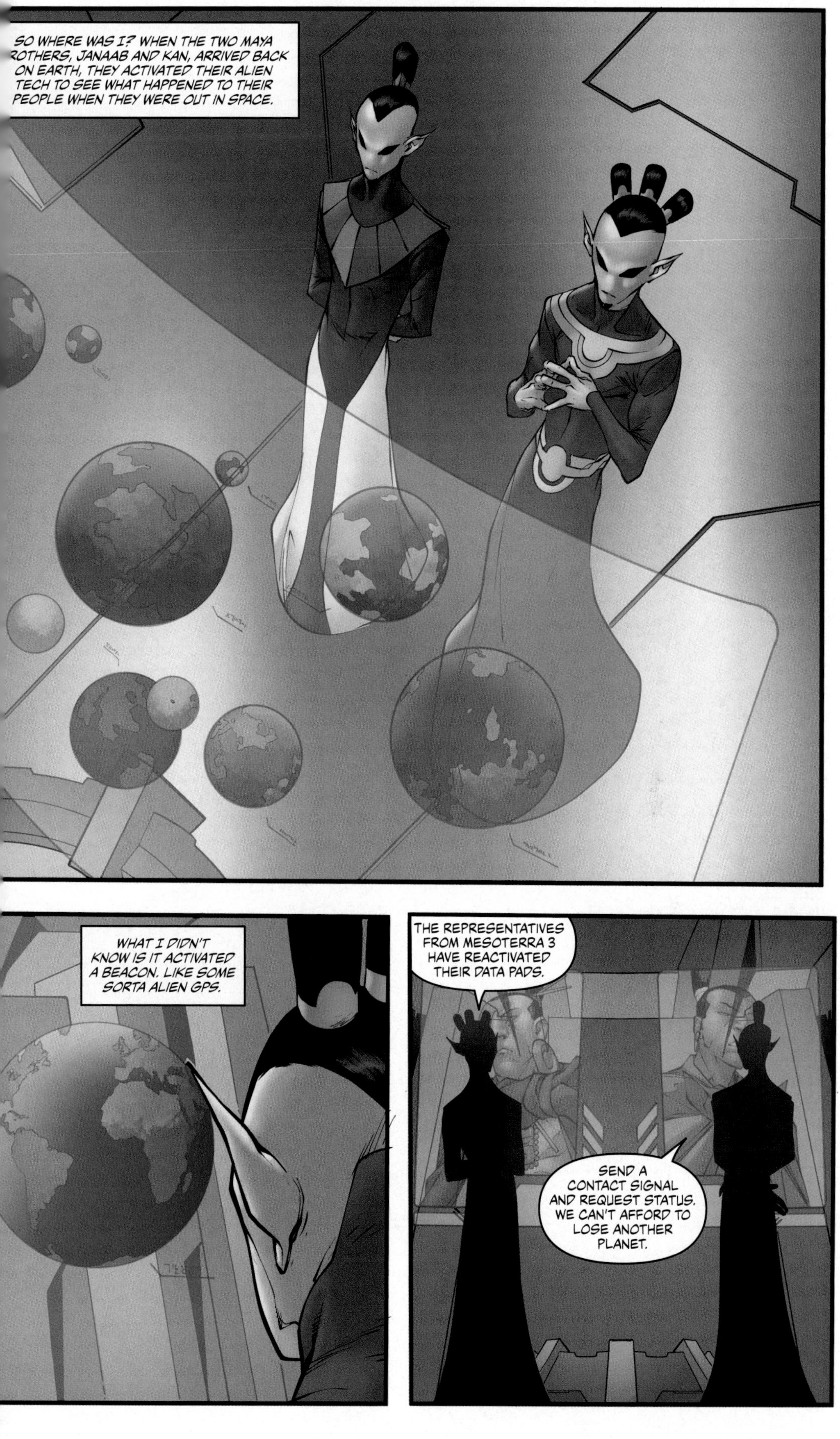
SO WHERE WAS I? WHEN THE TWO MAYA BROTHERS, JANAAB AND KAN, ARRIVED BACK ON EARTH, THEY ACTIVATED THEIR ALIEN TECH TO SEE WHAT HAPPENED TO THEIR PEOPLE WHEN THEY WERE OUT IN SPACE.
WHAT I DIDN'T KNOW IS IT ACTIVATED A BEACON. LIKE SOME SORTA ALIEN GPS.
THE REPRESENTATIVES FROM MESOTERRA 3 HAVE REACTIVATED THEIR DATA PADS.
SEND A CONTACT SIGNAL AND REQUEST STATUS. WE CAN'T AFFORD TO LOSE ANOTHER PLANET.

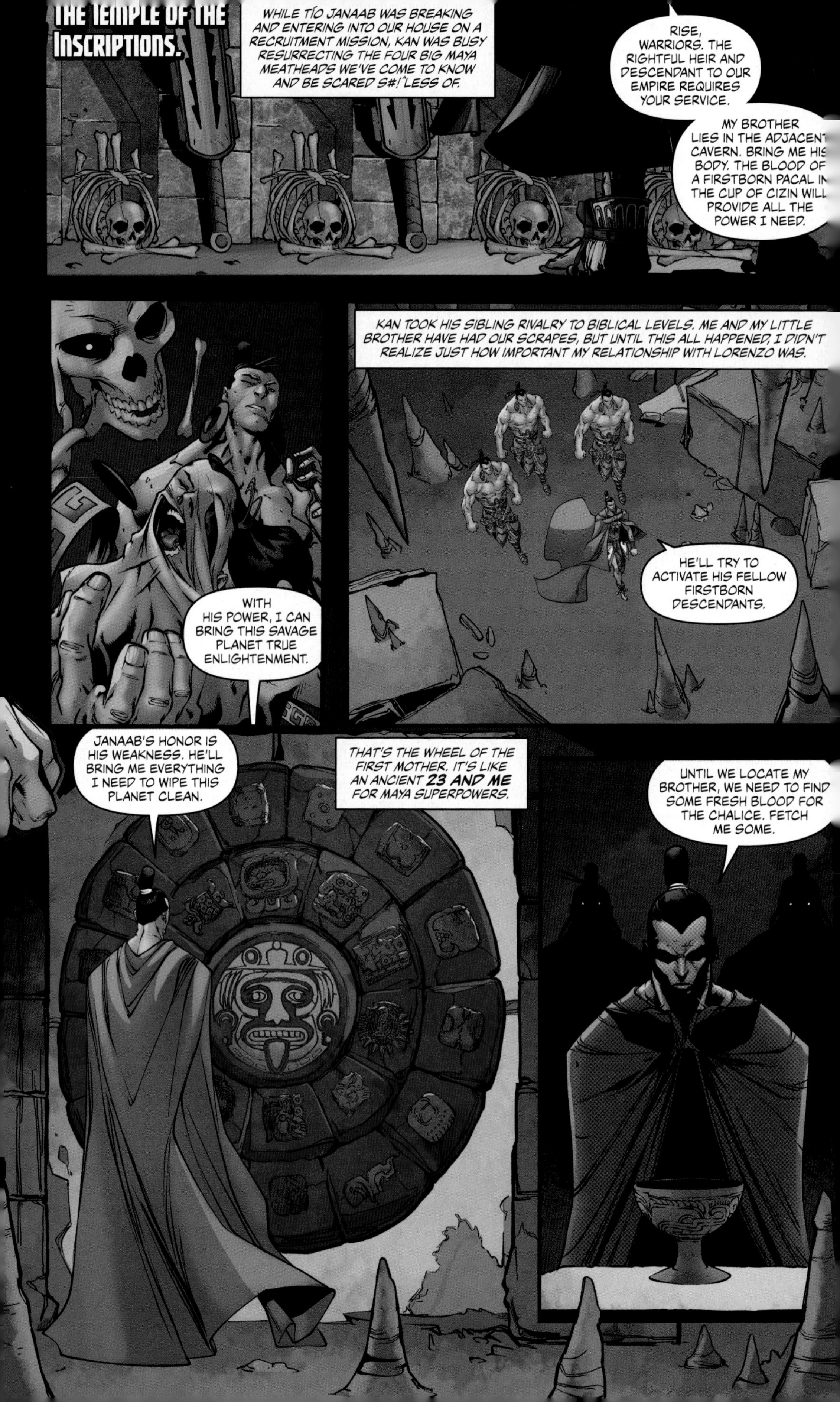

THE TEMPLE OF THE INSCRIPTIONS.
WHILE TÍO JANAAB WAS BREAKING AND ENTERING INTO OUR HOUSE ON A RECRUITMENT MISSION, KAN WAS BUSY RESURRECTING THE FOUR BIG MAYA MEATHEADS WE'VE COME TO KNOW AND BE SCARED S#!'LESS OF.
RISE, WARRIORS. THE RIGHTFUL HEIR AND DESCENDANT TO OUR EMPIRE REQUIRES YOUR SERVICE.
MY BROTHER LIES IN THE ADJACENT CAVERN. BRING ME HIS BODY. THE BLOOD OF A FIRSTBORN PACAL IN THE CUP OF CIZIN WILL PROVIDE ALL THE POWER I NEED.
WITH HIS POWER, I CAN BRING THIS SAVAGE PLANET TRUE ENLIGHTENMENT.
KAN TOOK HIS SIBLING RIVALRY TO BIBLICAL LEVELS. ME AND MY LITTLE BROTHER HAVE HAD OUR SCRAPES, BUT UNTIL THIS ALL HAPPENED, I DIDN'T REALIZE JUST HOW IMPORTANT MY RELATIONSHIP WITH LORENZO WAS.
HE'LL TRY TO ACTIVATE HIS FELLOW FIRSTBORN DESCENDANTS.
JANAAB'S HONOR IS HIS WEAKNESS. HE'LL BRING ME EVERYTHING I NEED TO WIPE THIS PLANET CLEAN.
THAT'S THE WHEEL OF THE FIRST MOTHER. IT'S LIKE AN ANCIENT 23 AND ME FOR MAYA SUPERPOWERS.
UNTIL WE LOCATE MY BROTHER, WE NEED TO FIND SOME FRESH BLOOD FOR THE CHALICE. FETCH ME SOME.

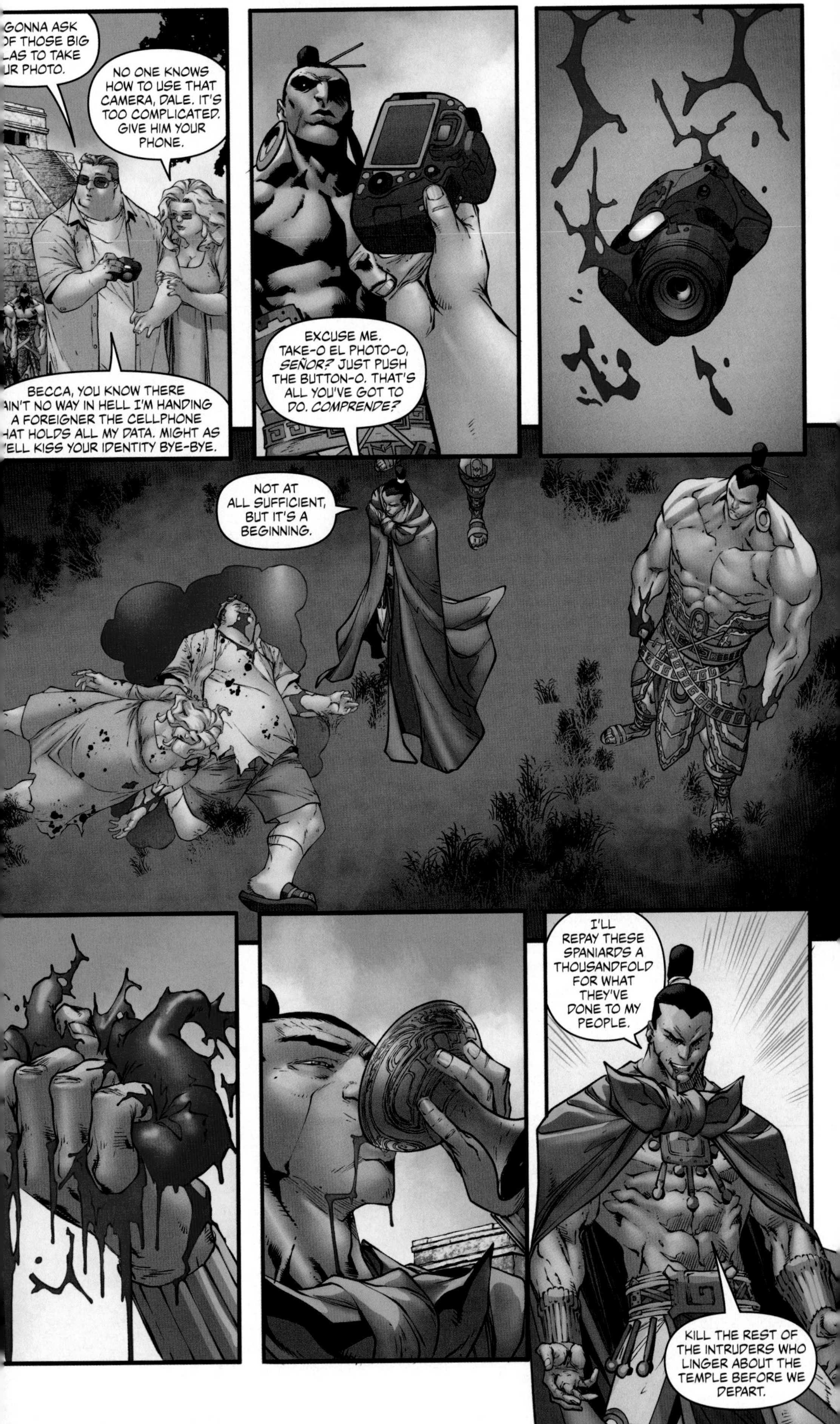
GONNA ASK
OF THOSE BIG
LAS TO TAKE
UR PHOTO.
NO ONE KNOWS HOW TO USE THAT CAMERA, DALE. IT'S TOO COMPLICATED. GIVE HIM YOUR PHONE.
BECCA, YOU KNOW THERE
AIN'T NO WAY IN HELL I'M HANDING
A FOREIGNER THE CELLPHONE
HAT HOLDS ALL MY DATA. MIGHT AS
ELL KISS YOUR IDENTITY BYE-BYE.
EXCUSE ME. TAKE-O EL PHOTO-O, *SEÑOR?* JUST PUSH THE BUTTON-O. THAT'S ALL YOU'VE GOT TO DO. *COMPRENDE?*
NOT AT ALL SUFFICIENT, BUT IT'S A BEGINNING.
I'LL REPAY THESE SPANIARDS A THOUSANDFOLD FOR WHAT THEY'VE DONE TO MY PEOPLE.
KILL THE REST OF THE INTRUDERS WHO LINGER ABOUT THE TEMPLE BEFORE WE DEPART.

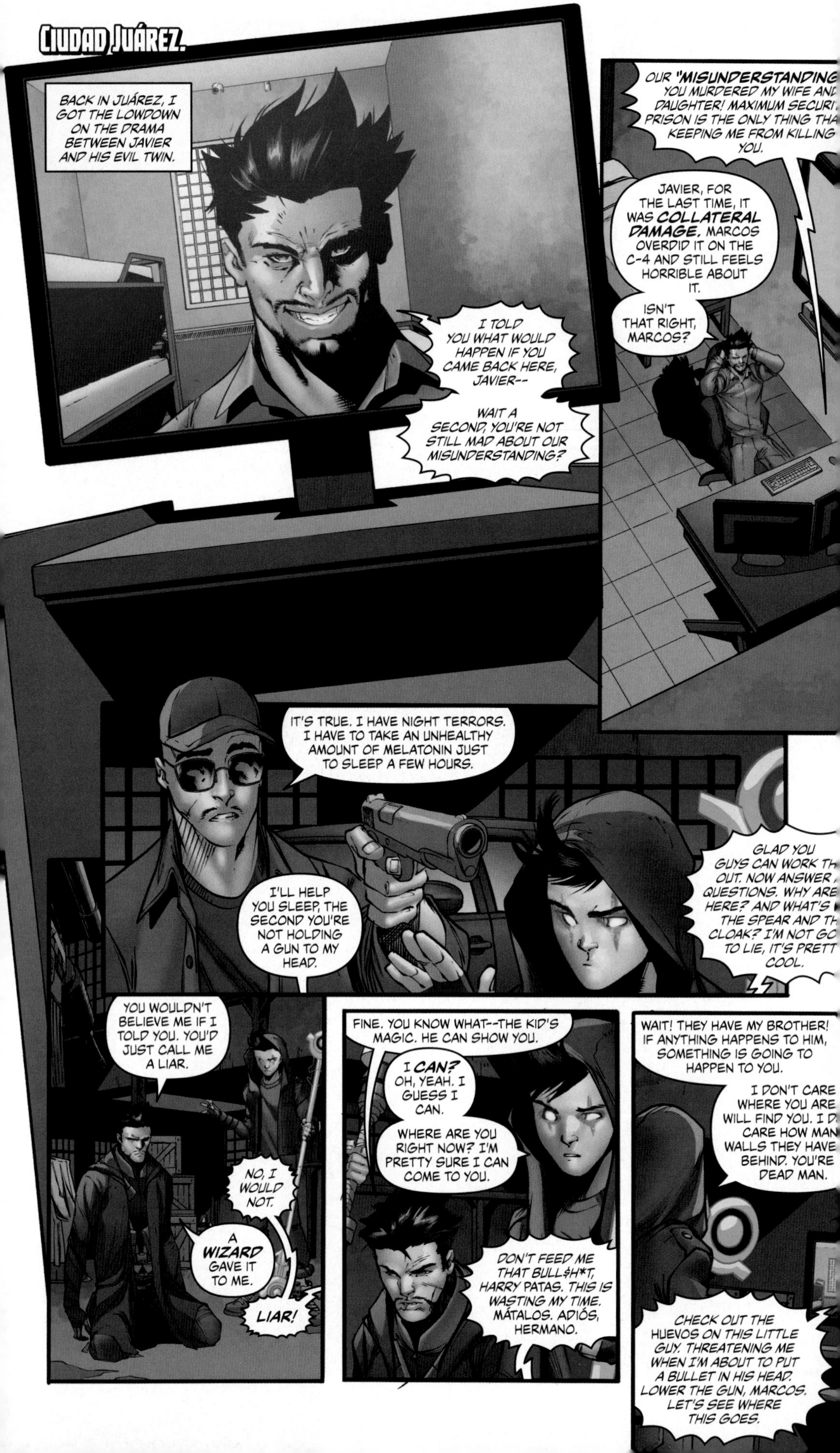

CIUDAD JUÁREZ.
BACK IN JUÁREZ, I GOT THE LOWDOWN ON THE DRAMA BETWEEN JAVIER AND HIS EVIL TWIN.
I TOLD YOU WHAT WOULD HAPPEN IF YOU CAME BACK HERE, JAVIER--
WAIT A SECOND, YOU'RE NOT STILL MAD ABOUT OUR MISUNDERSTANDING?
OUR "MISUNDERSTANDING YOU MURDERED MY WIFE AND DAUGHTER! MAXIMUM SECURI PRISON IS THE ONLY THING THA KEEPING ME FROM KILLING YOU.
JAVIER, FOR THE LAST TIME, IT WAS COLLATERAL DAMAGE. MARCOS OVERDID IT ON THE C-4 AND STILL FEELS HORRIBLE ABOUT IT.
ISN'T THAT RIGHT, MARCOS?
IT'S TRUE. I HAVE NIGHT TERRORS. I HAVE TO TAKE AN UNHEALTHY AMOUNT OF MELATONIN JUST TO SLEEP A FEW HOURS.
I'LL HELP YOU SLEEP, THE SECOND YOU'RE NOT HOLDING A GUN TO MY HEAD.
GLAD YOU GUYS CAN WORK TH OUT. NOW ANSWER QUESTIONS. WHY ARE HERE? AND WHAT'S THE SPEAR AND TH CLOAK? I'M NOT GO TO LIE, IT'S PRETT COOL.
YOU WOULDN'T BELIEVE ME IF I TOLD YOU. YOU'D JUST CALL ME A LIAR.
NO, I WOULD NOT.
A WIZARD GAVE IT TO ME.
LIAR!
FINE. YOU KNOW WHAT--THE KID'S MAGIC. HE CAN SHOW YOU.
I CAN? OH, YEAH. I GUESS I CAN.
WHERE ARE YOU RIGHT NOW? I'M PRETTY SURE I CAN COME TO YOU.
DON'T FEED ME THAT BULL$H*T, HARRY PATAS. THIS IS WASTING MY TIME. MÁTALOS. ADIÓS, HERMANO.
WAIT! THEY HAVE MY BROTHER! IF ANYTHING HAPPENS TO HIM, SOMETHING IS GOING TO HAPPEN TO YOU.
I DON'T CARE WHERE YOU ARE WILL FIND YOU. I D CARE HOW MAN WALLS THEY HAVE BEHIND. YOU'RE DEAD MAN.
CHECK OUT THE HUEVOS ON THIS LITTLE GUY. THREATENING ME WHEN I'M ABOUT TO PUT A BULLET IN HIS HEAD. LOWER THE GUN, MARCOS. LET'S SEE WHERE THIS GOES.

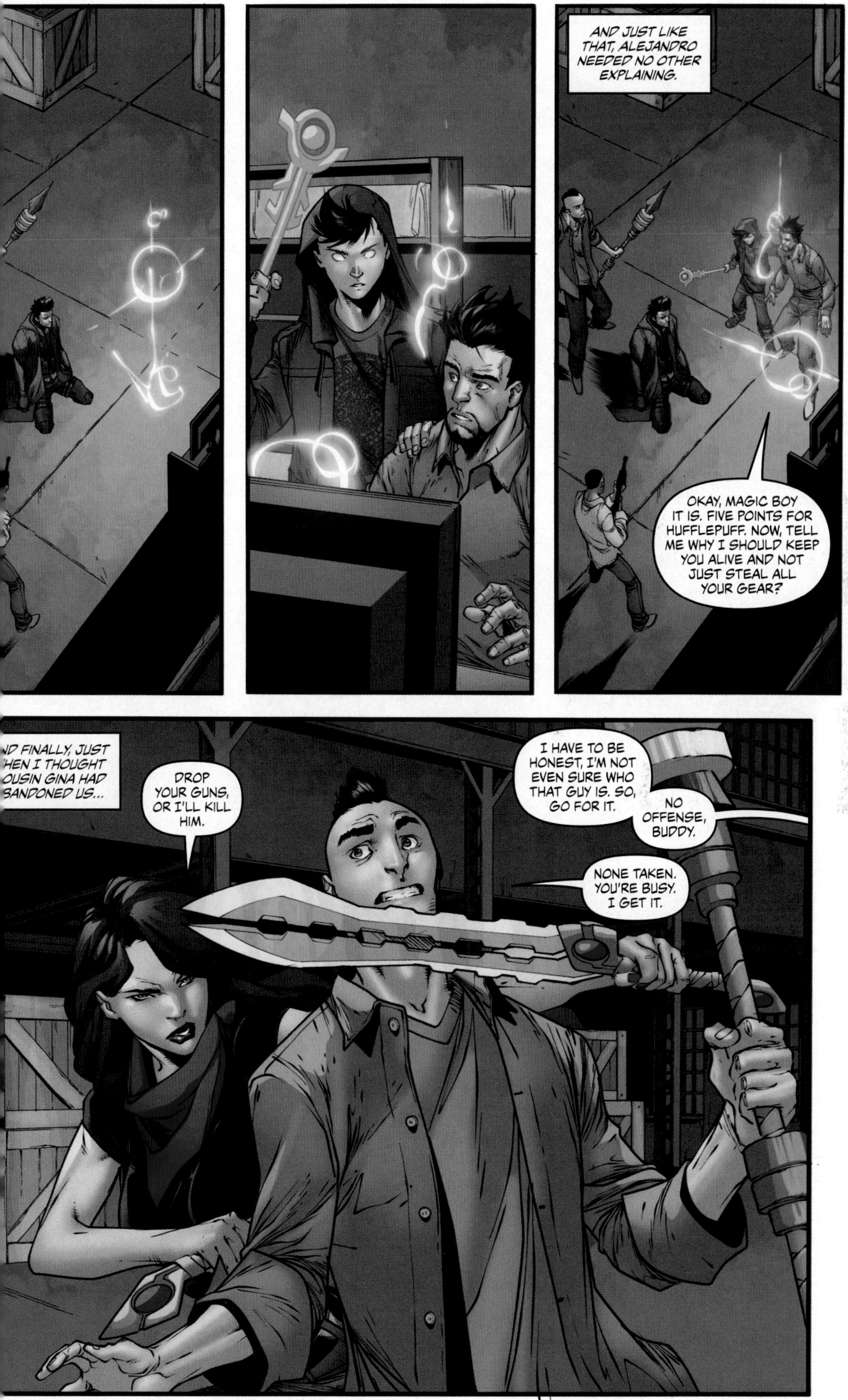
AND JUST LIKE THAT, ALEJANDRO NEEDED NO OTHER EXPLAINING.
OKAY, MAGIC BOY IT IS. FIVE POINTS FOR HUFFLEPUFF. NOW, TELL ME WHY I SHOULD KEEP YOU ALIVE AND NOT JUST STEAL ALL YOUR GEAR?
ND FINALLY, JUST HEN I THOUGHT OUSIN GINA HAD BANDONED US...
DROP YOUR GUNS, OR I'LL KILL HIM.
I HAVE TO BE HONEST, I'M NOT EVEN SURE WHO THAT GUY IS. SO, GO FOR IT.
NO OFFENSE, BUDDY.
NONE TAKEN. YOU'RE BUSY. I GET IT.

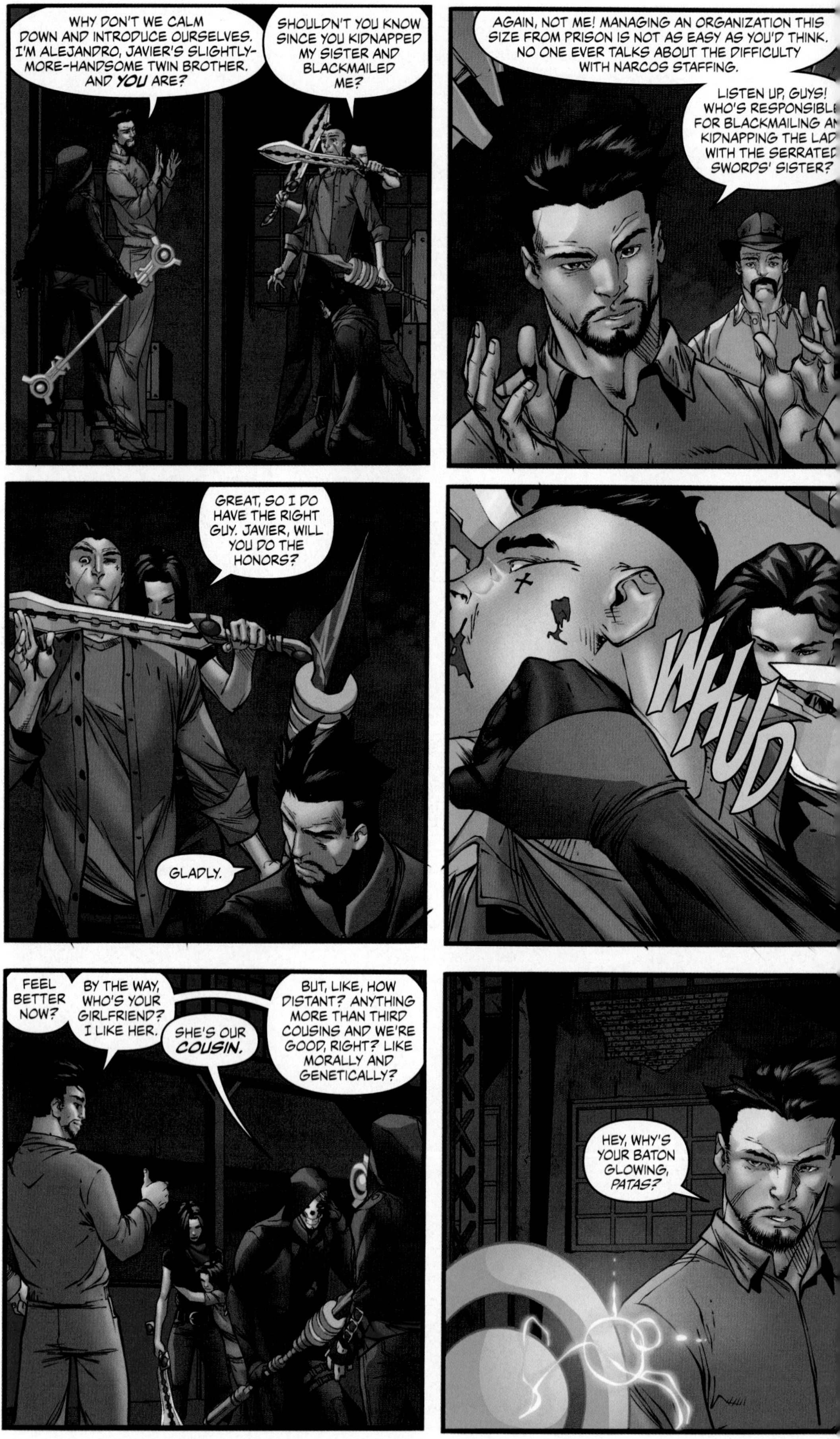
WHY DON'T WE CALM DOWN AND INTRODUCE OURSELVES. I'M ALEJANDRO, JAVIER'S SLIGHTLY-MORE-HANDSOME TWIN BROTHER. AND YOU ARE?
SHOULDN'T YOU KNOW SINCE YOU KIDNAPPED MY SISTER AND BLACKMAILED ME?
AGAIN, NOT ME! MANAGING AN ORGANIZATION THIS SIZE FROM PRISON IS NOT AS EASY AS YOU'D THINK. NO ONE EVER TALKS ABOUT THE DIFFICULTY WITH NARCOS STAFFING.
LISTEN UP, GUYS! WHO'S RESPONSIBLE FOR BLACKMAILING AN KIDNAPPING THE LAD WITH THE SERRATED SWORDS' SISTER?
GREAT, SO I DO HAVE THE RIGHT GUY. JAVIER, WILL YOU DO THE HONORS?
GLADLY.
WHUD
FEEL BETTER NOW?
BY THE WAY, WHO'S YOUR GIRLFRIEND? I LIKE HER.
SHE'S OUR COUSIN.
BUT, LIKE, HOW DISTANT? ANYTHING MORE THAN THIRD COUSINS AND WE'RE GOOD, RIGHT? LIKE MORALLY AND GENETICALLY?
HEY, WHY'S YOUR BATON GLOWING, PATAS?

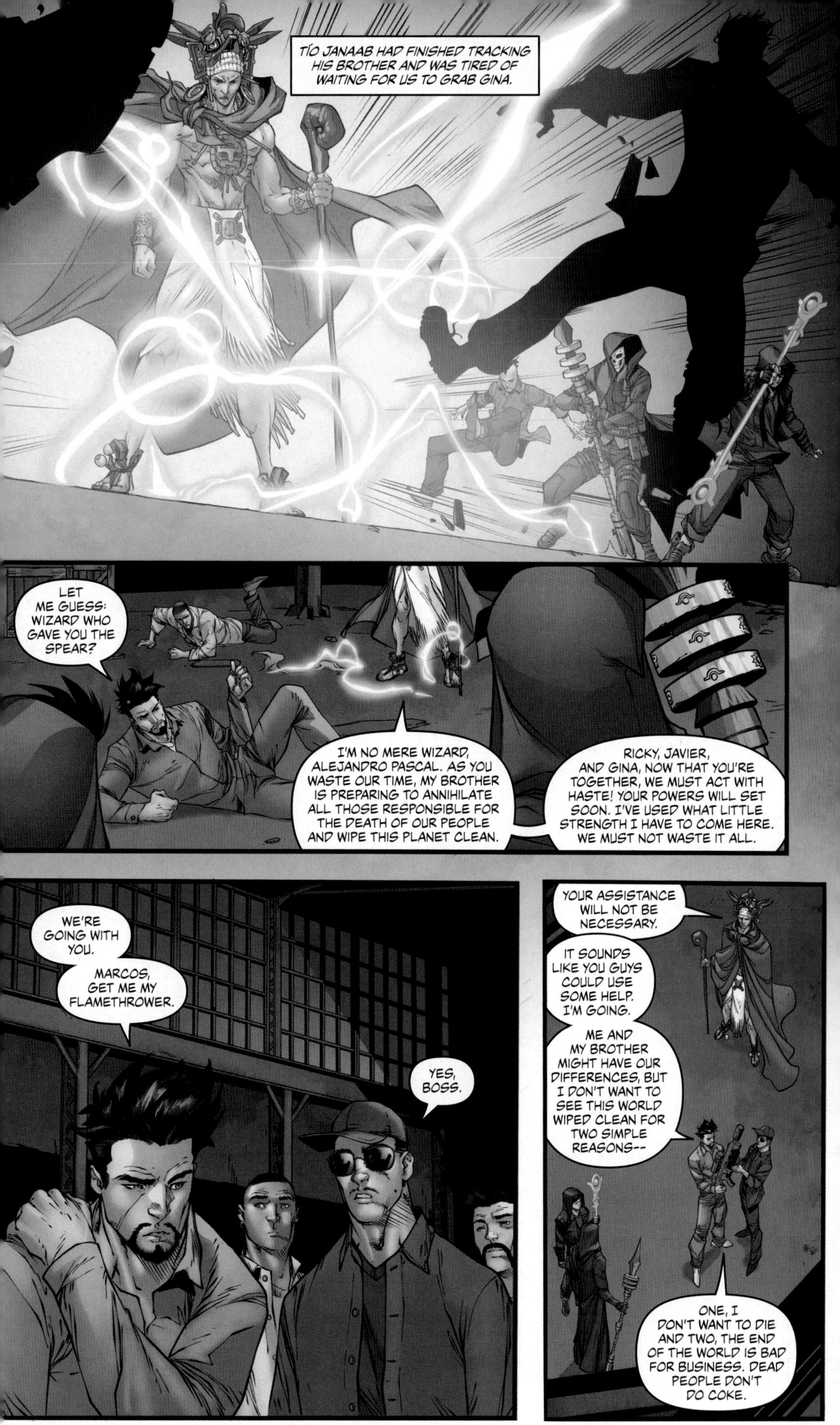
TÍO JANAAB HAD FINISHED TRACKING HIS BROTHER AND WAS TIRED OF WAITING FOR US TO GRAB GINA.
LET ME GUESS: WIZARD WHO GAVE YOU THE SPEAR?
I'M NO MERE WIZARD, ALEJANDRO PASCAL. AS YOU WASTE OUR TIME, MY BROTHER IS PREPARING TO ANNIHILATE ALL THOSE RESPONSIBLE FOR THE DEATH OF OUR PEOPLE AND WIPE THIS PLANET CLEAN.
RICKY, JAVIER, AND GINA, NOW THAT YOU'RE TOGETHER, WE MUST ACT WITH HASTE! YOUR POWERS WILL SET SOON. I'VE USED WHAT LITTLE STRENGTH I HAVE TO COME HERE. WE MUST NOT WASTE IT ALL.
WE'RE GOING WITH YOU.
MARCOS, GET ME MY FLAMETHROWER.
YES, BOSS.
YOUR ASSISTANCE WILL NOT BE NECESSARY.
IT SOUNDS LIKE YOU GUYS COULD USE SOME HELP. I'M GOING.
ME AND MY BROTHER MIGHT HAVE OUR DIFFERENCES, BUT I DON'T WANT TO SEE THIS WORLD WIPED CLEAN FOR TWO SIMPLE REASONS--
ONE, I DON'T WANT TO DIE AND TWO, THE END OF THE WORLD IS BAD FOR BUSINESS. DEAD PEOPLE DON'T DO COKE.

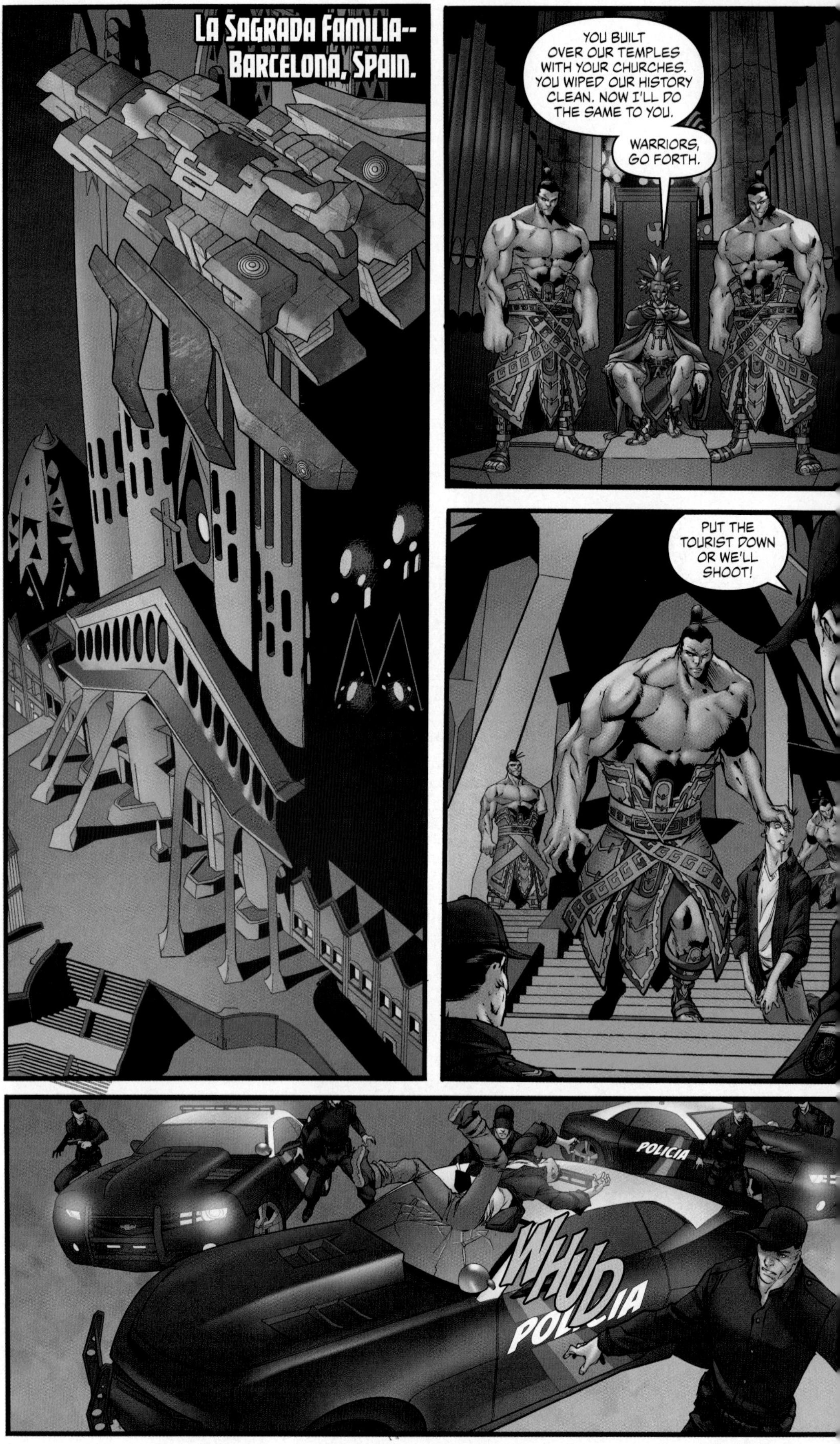
La Sagrada Familia--
Barcelona, Spain.
YOU BUILT OVER OUR TEMPLES WITH YOUR CHURCHES. YOU WIPED OUR HISTORY CLEAN. NOW I'LL DO THE SAME TO YOU.
WARRIORS, GO FORTH.
PUT THE TOURIST DOWN OR WE'LL SHOOT!
POLICIA
WHUD
POLICIA

GOOD JOB, RICKY.

I'M JUST HAPPY I DIDN'T PUT US IN THE POOL.

THIS SHOULD BE A SAFE PLACE FOR YOUR SISTER.

NOT NG HER ONE.

ME AND THE GUYS CAN WATCH HER. ANYONE GETS CLOSE, THEY'RE TOAST.
GET IT? YOU KNOW, BECAUSE OF MY *FLAMETHROWER.*

THERE'S NO WAY IN HELL I'M LEAVING MY SISTER WITH YOU.
TERESA, STAY HERE AND BARRICADE THE DOOR. ONLY OPEN IT FOR ME.

EVERYONE READY? RICKY, PUT US DOWN THERE.

ALRIGHT. LET'S *DO* THIS!

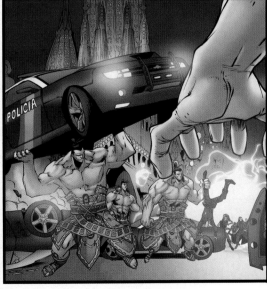

POLICIA

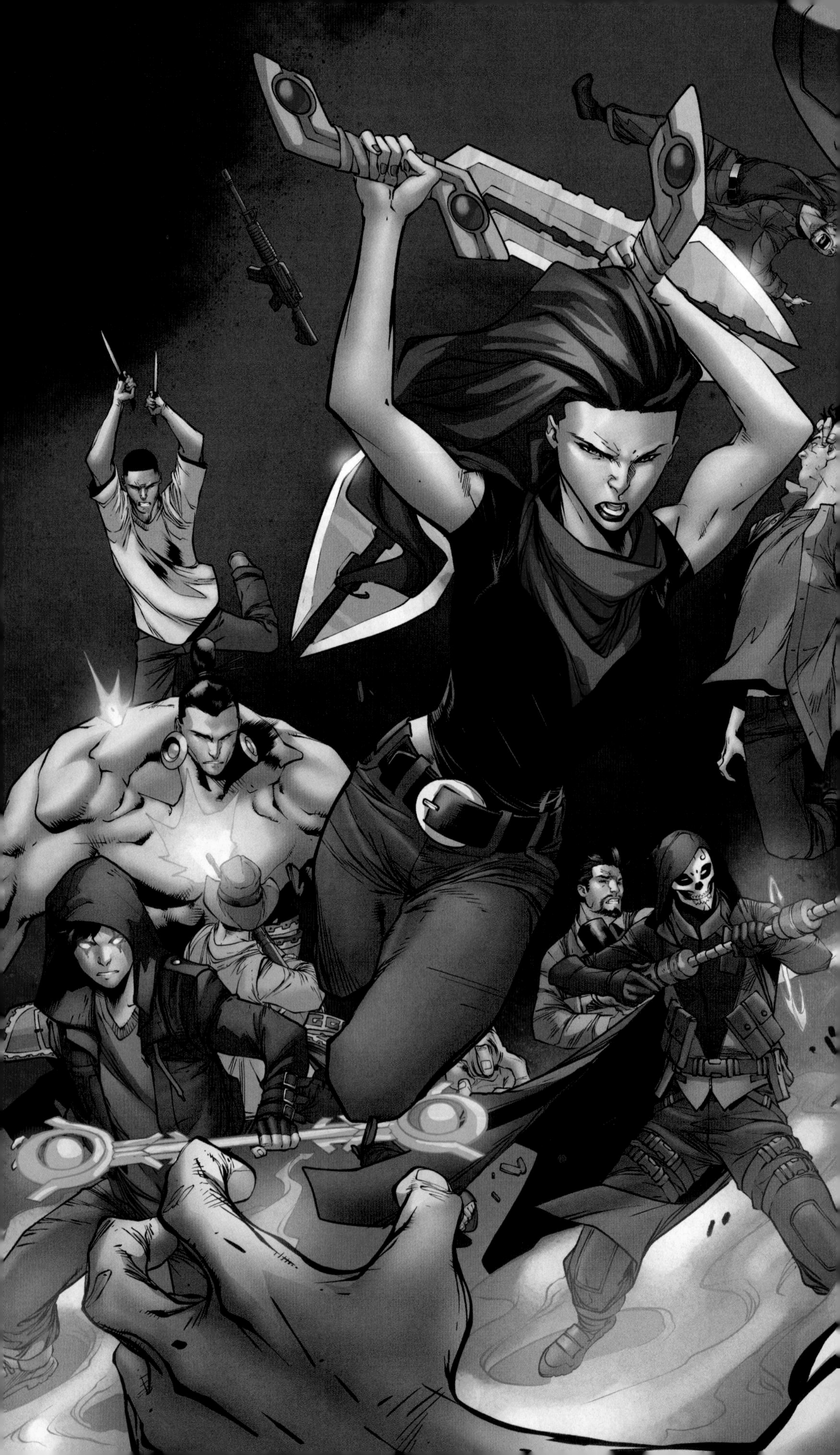

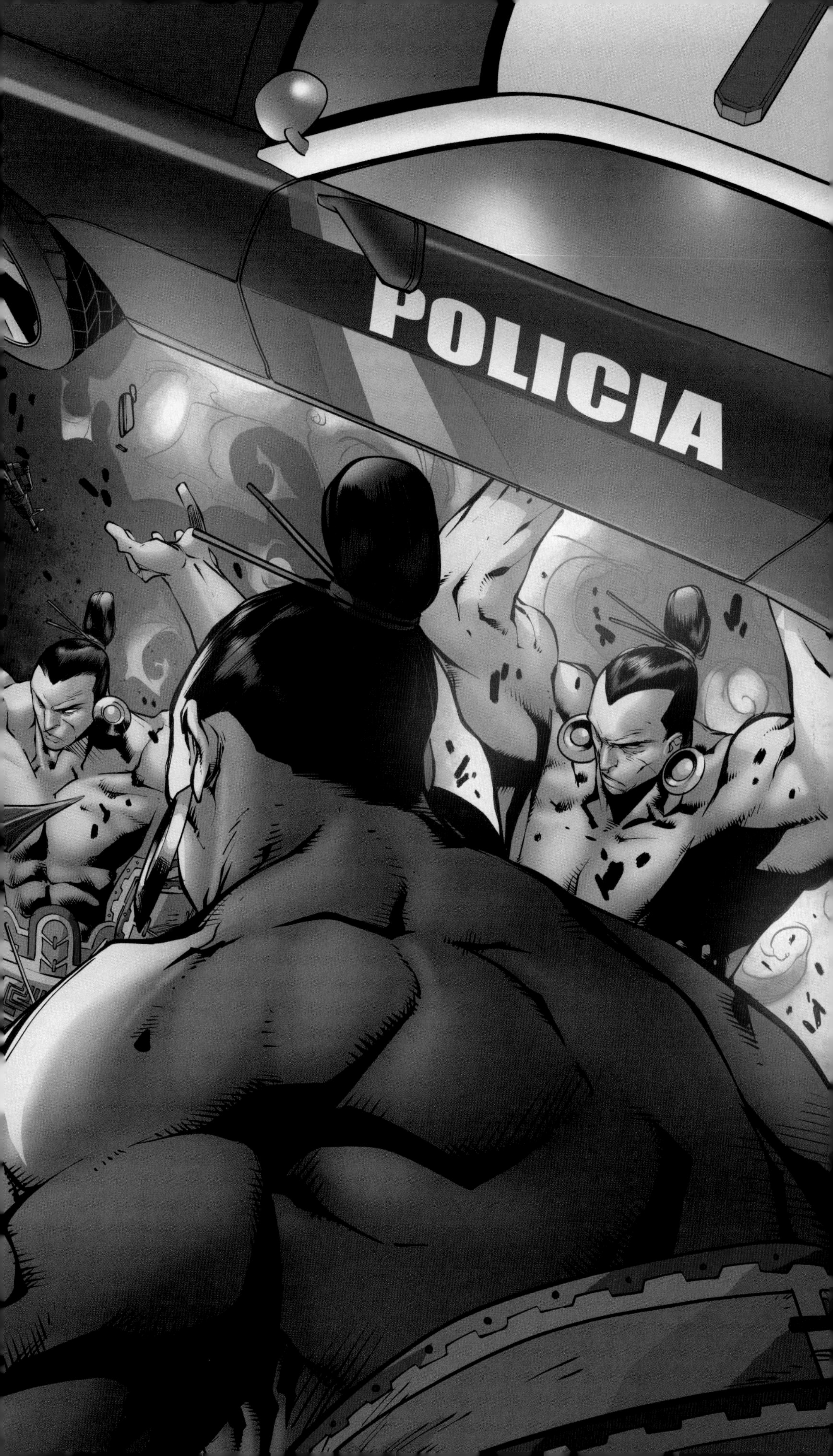
POLICIA

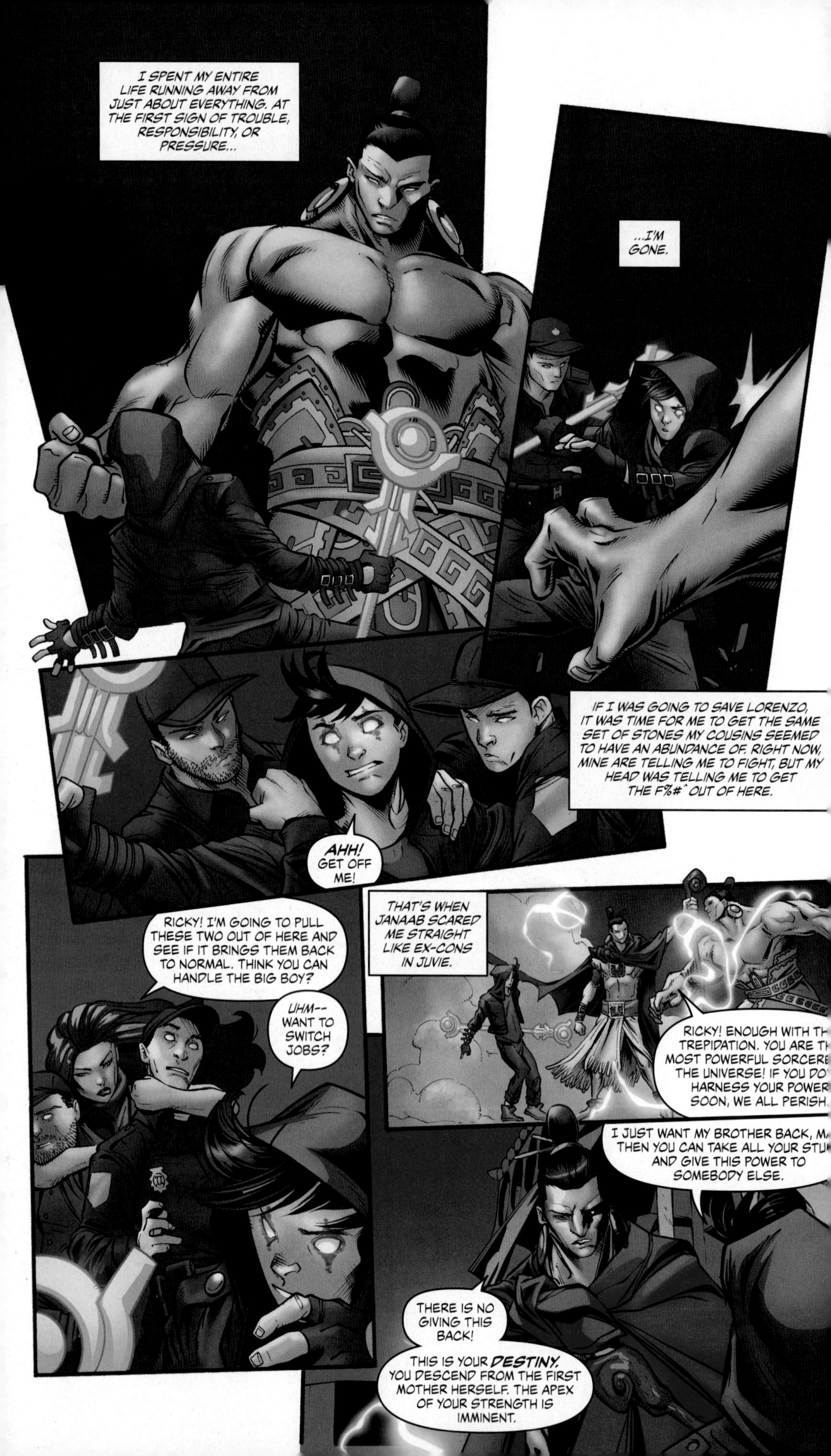
I SPENT MY ENTIRE LIFE RUNNING AWAY FROM JUST ABOUT EVERYTHING. AT THE FIRST SIGN OF TROUBLE, RESPONSIBILITY, OR PRESSURE...
...I'M GONE.
IF I WAS GOING TO SAVE LORENZO, IT WAS TIME FOR ME TO GET THE SAME SET OF STONES MY COUSINS SEEMED TO HAVE AN ABUNDANCE OF. RIGHT NOW, MINE ARE TELLING ME TO FIGHT, BUT MY HEAD WAS TELLING ME TO GET THE F%#^ OUT OF HERE.
AHH! GET OFF ME!
RICKY! I'M GOING TO PULL THESE TWO OUT OF HERE AND SEE IF IT BRINGS THEM BACK TO NORMAL. THINK YOU CAN HANDLE THE BIG BOY?
UHM-- WANT TO SWITCH JOBS?
THAT'S WHEN JANAAB SCARED ME STRAIGHT LIKE EX-CONS IN JUVIE.
RICKY! ENOUGH WITH TH TREPIDATION. YOU ARE TH MOST POWERFUL SORCERE THE UNIVERSE! IF YOU DO HARNESS YOUR POWER SOON, WE ALL PERISH.
I JUST WANT MY BROTHER BACK, M THEN YOU CAN TAKE ALL YOUR STU AND GIVE THIS POWER TO SOMEBODY ELSE.
THERE IS NO GIVING THIS BACK!
THIS IS YOUR DESTINY. YOU DESCEND FROM THE FIRST MOTHER HERSELF. THE APEX OF YOUR STRENGTH IS IMMINENT.

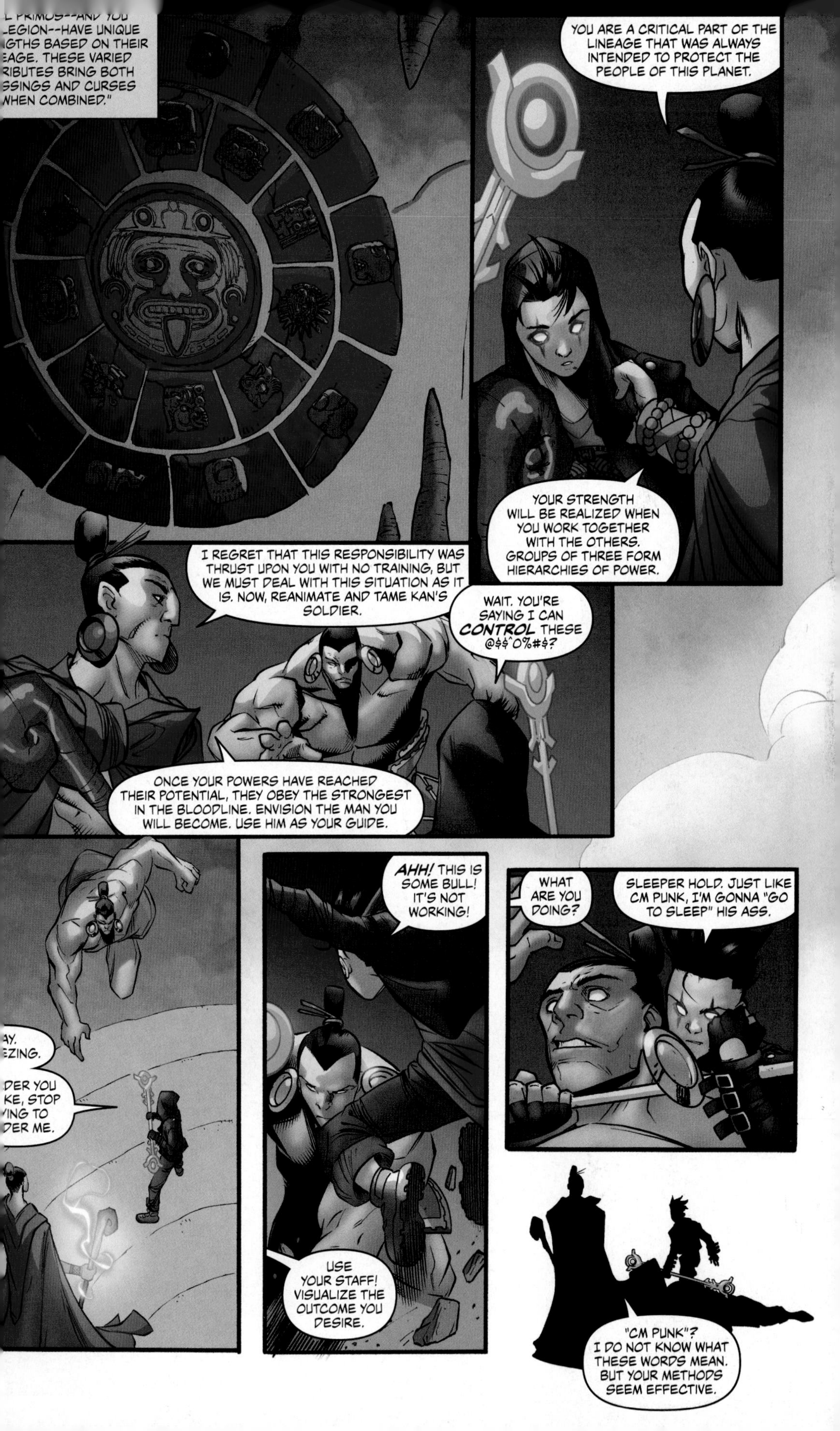

L PRIMOS--AND YOU
LEGION--HAVE UNIQUE
NGTHS BASED ON THEIR
EAGE. THESE VARIED
RIBUTES BRING BOTH
SSINGS AND CURSES
WHEN COMBINED."
YOU ARE A CRITICAL PART OF THE LINEAGE THAT WAS ALWAYS INTENDED TO PROTECT THE PEOPLE OF THIS PLANET.
YOUR STRENGTH WILL BE REALIZED WHEN YOU WORK TOGETHER WITH THE OTHERS. GROUPS OF THREE FORM HIERARCHIES OF POWER.
I REGRET THAT THIS RESPONSIBILITY WAS THRUST UPON YOU WITH NO TRAINING, BUT WE MUST DEAL WITH THIS SITUATION AS IT IS. NOW, REANIMATE AND TAME KAN'S SOLDIER.
WAIT. YOU'RE SAYING I CAN **CONTROL** THESE @$$^0%#$?
ONCE YOUR POWERS HAVE REACHED THEIR POTENTIAL, THEY OBEY THE STRONGEST IN THE BLOODLINE. ENVISION THE MAN YOU WILL BECOME. USE HIM AS YOUR GUIDE.
AY.
EZING.
DER YOU
KE, STOP
YING TO
DER ME.
AHH! THIS IS SOME BULL! IT'S NOT WORKING!
USE YOUR STAFF! VISUALIZE THE OUTCOME YOU DESIRE.
WHAT ARE YOU DOING?
SLEEPER HOLD. JUST LIKE CM PUNK, I'M GONNA "GO TO SLEEP" HIS ASS.
"CM PUNK"? I DO NOT KNOW WHAT THESE WORDS MEAN. BUT YOUR METHODS SEEM EFFECTIVE.

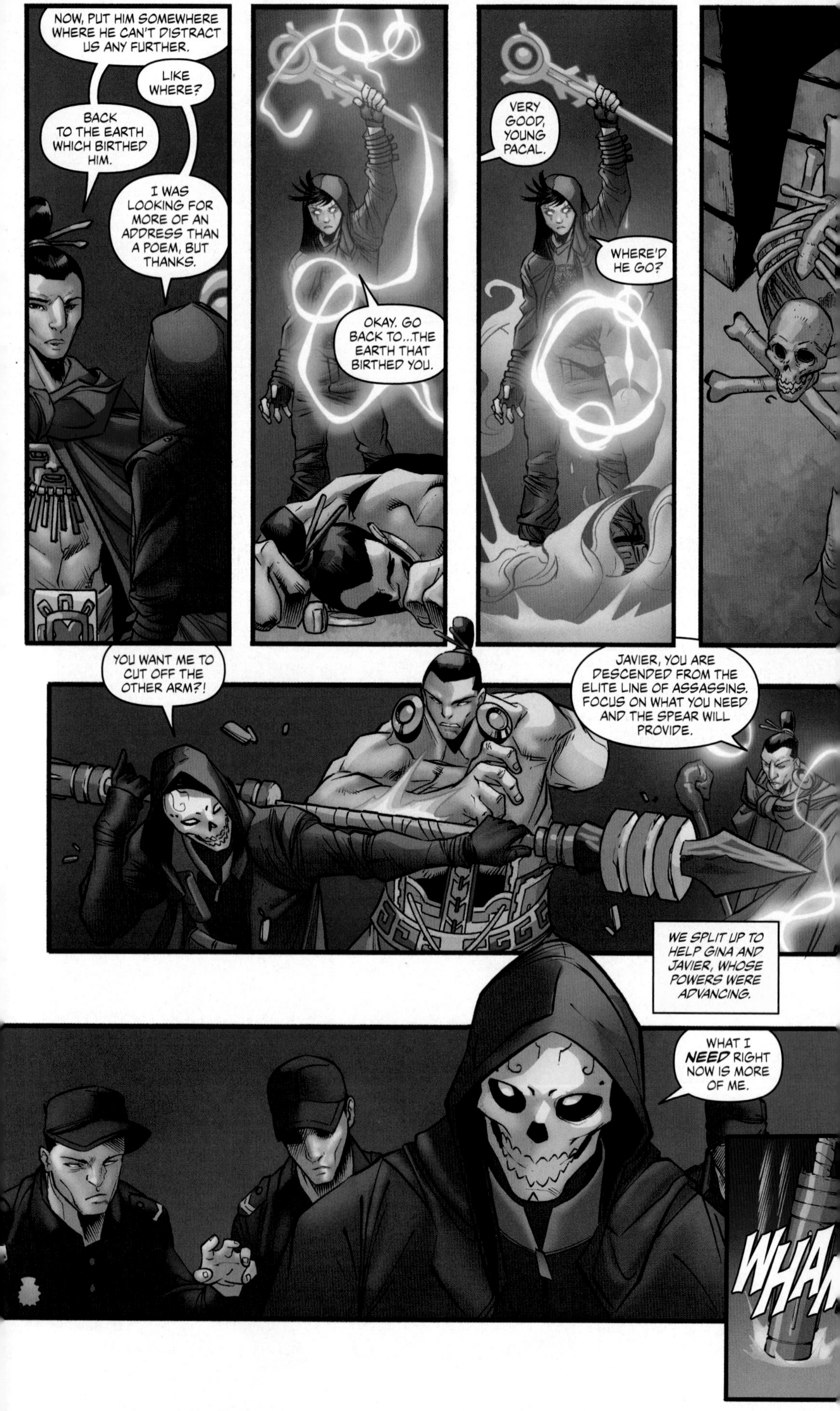
NOW, PUT HIM SOMEWHERE WHERE HE CAN'T DISTRACT US ANY FURTHER.
LIKE WHERE?
BACK TO THE EARTH WHICH BIRTHED HIM.
I WAS LOOKING FOR MORE OF AN ADDRESS THAN A POEM, BUT THANKS.
OKAY. GO BACK TO...THE EARTH THAT BIRTHED YOU.
VERY GOOD, YOUNG PACAL.
WHERE'D HE GO?
YOU WANT ME TO CUT OFF THE OTHER ARM?!
JAVIER, YOU ARE DESCENDED FROM THE ELITE LINE OF ASSASSINS. FOCUS ON WHAT YOU NEED AND THE SPEAR WILL PROVIDE.
WE SPLIT UP TO HELP GINA AND JAVIER, WHOSE POWERS WERE ADVANCING.
WHAT I **NEED** RIGHT NOW IS MORE OF ME.
WHAM

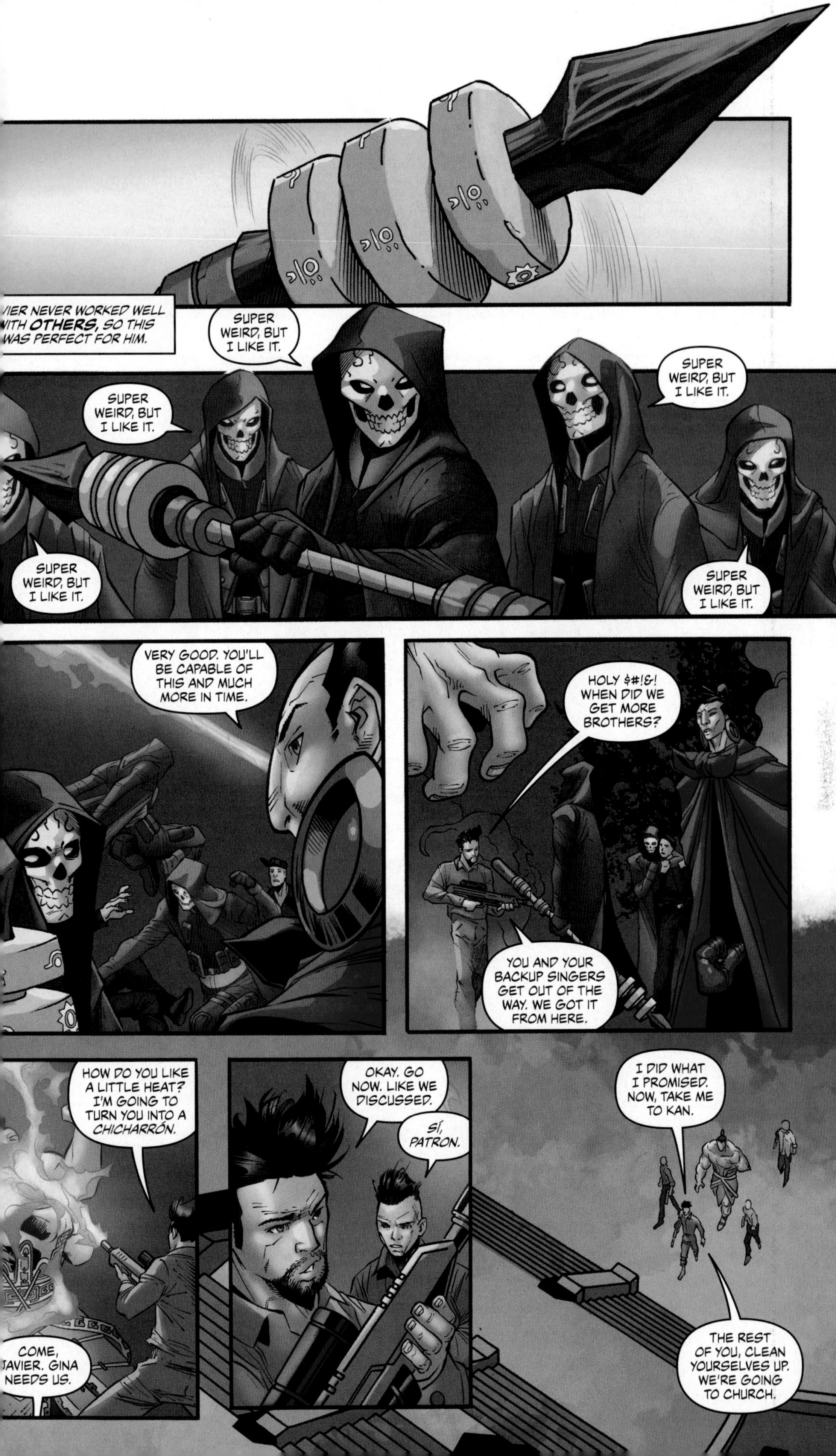
VIER NEVER WORKED WELL WITH OTHERS, SO THIS WAS PERFECT FOR HIM.
SUPER WEIRD, BUT I LIKE IT.
SUPER WEIRD, BUT I LIKE IT.
SUPER WEIRD, BUT I LIKE IT.
SUPER WEIRD, BUT I LIKE IT.
SUPER WEIRD, BUT I LIKE IT.
VERY GOOD. YOU'LL BE CAPABLE OF THIS AND MUCH MORE IN TIME.
HOLY $#!&! WHEN DID WE GET MORE BROTHERS?
YOU AND YOUR BACKUP SINGERS GET OUT OF THE WAY. WE GOT IT FROM HERE.
HOW DO YOU LIKE A LITTLE HEAT? I'M GOING TO TURN YOU INTO A CHICHARRÓN.
COME, JAVIER. GINA NEEDS US.
OKAY. GO NOW. LIKE WE DISCUSSED.
SÍ, PATRON.
I DID WHAT I PROMISED. NOW, TAKE ME TO KAN.
THE REST OF YOU, CLEAN YOURSELVES UP. WE'RE GOING TO CHURCH.

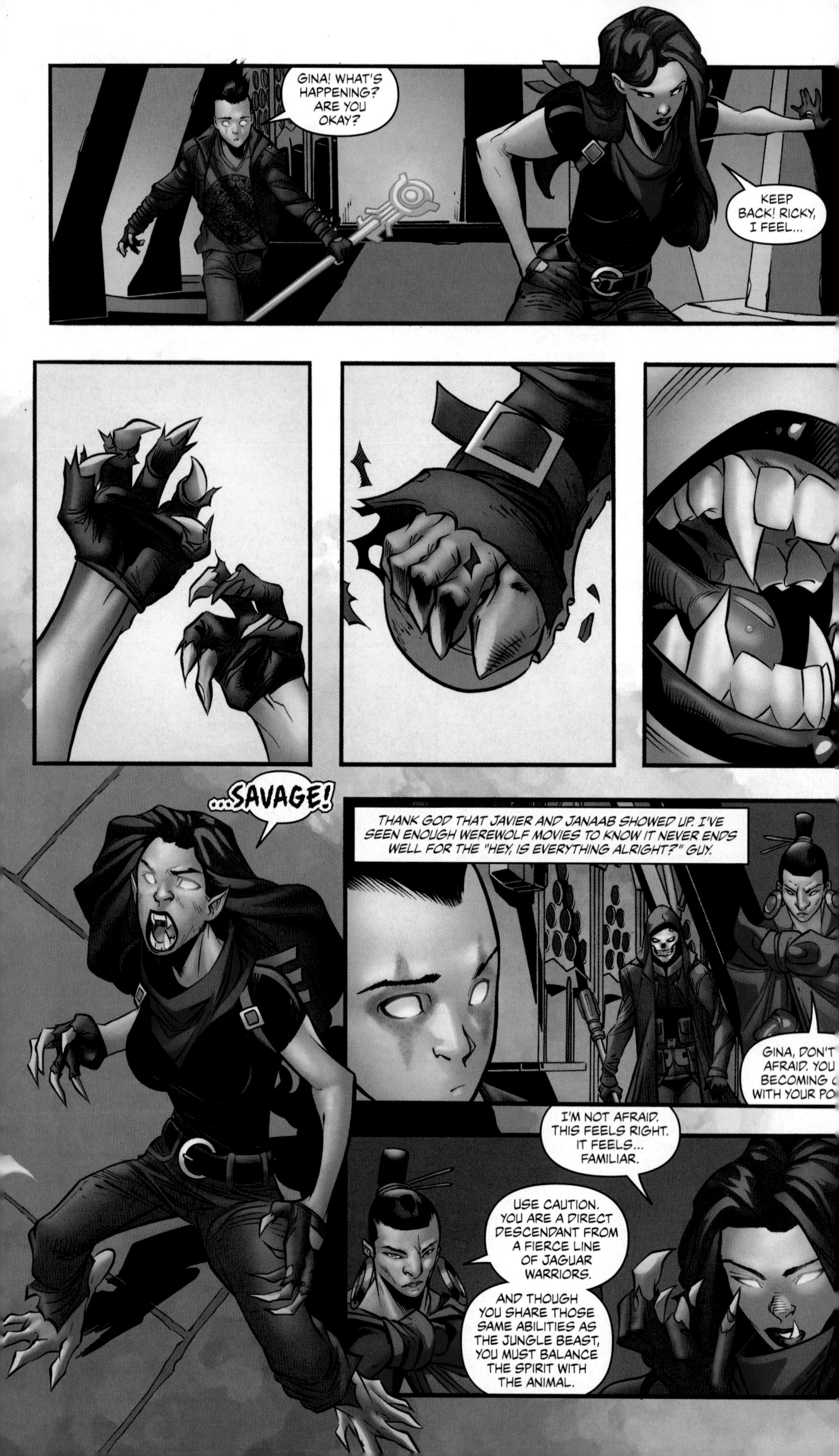

GINA! WHAT'S HAPPENING? ARE YOU OKAY?
KEEP BACK! RICKY, I FEEL...
...SAVAGE!
THANK GOD THAT JAVIER AND JANAAB SHOWED UP. I'VE SEEN ENOUGH WEREWOLF MOVIES TO KNOW IT NEVER ENDS WELL FOR THE "HEY, IS EVERYTHING ALRIGHT?" GUY.
GINA, DON'T AFRAID. YOU BECOMING WITH YOUR PO
I'M NOT AFRAID. THIS FEELS RIGHT. IT FEELS... FAMILIAR.
USE CAUTION. YOU ARE A DIRECT DESCENDANT FROM A FIERCE LINE OF JAGUAR WARRIORS.
AND THOUGH YOU SHARE THOSE SAME ABILITIES AS THE JUNGLE BEAST, YOU MUST BALANCE THE SPIRIT WITH THE ANIMAL.

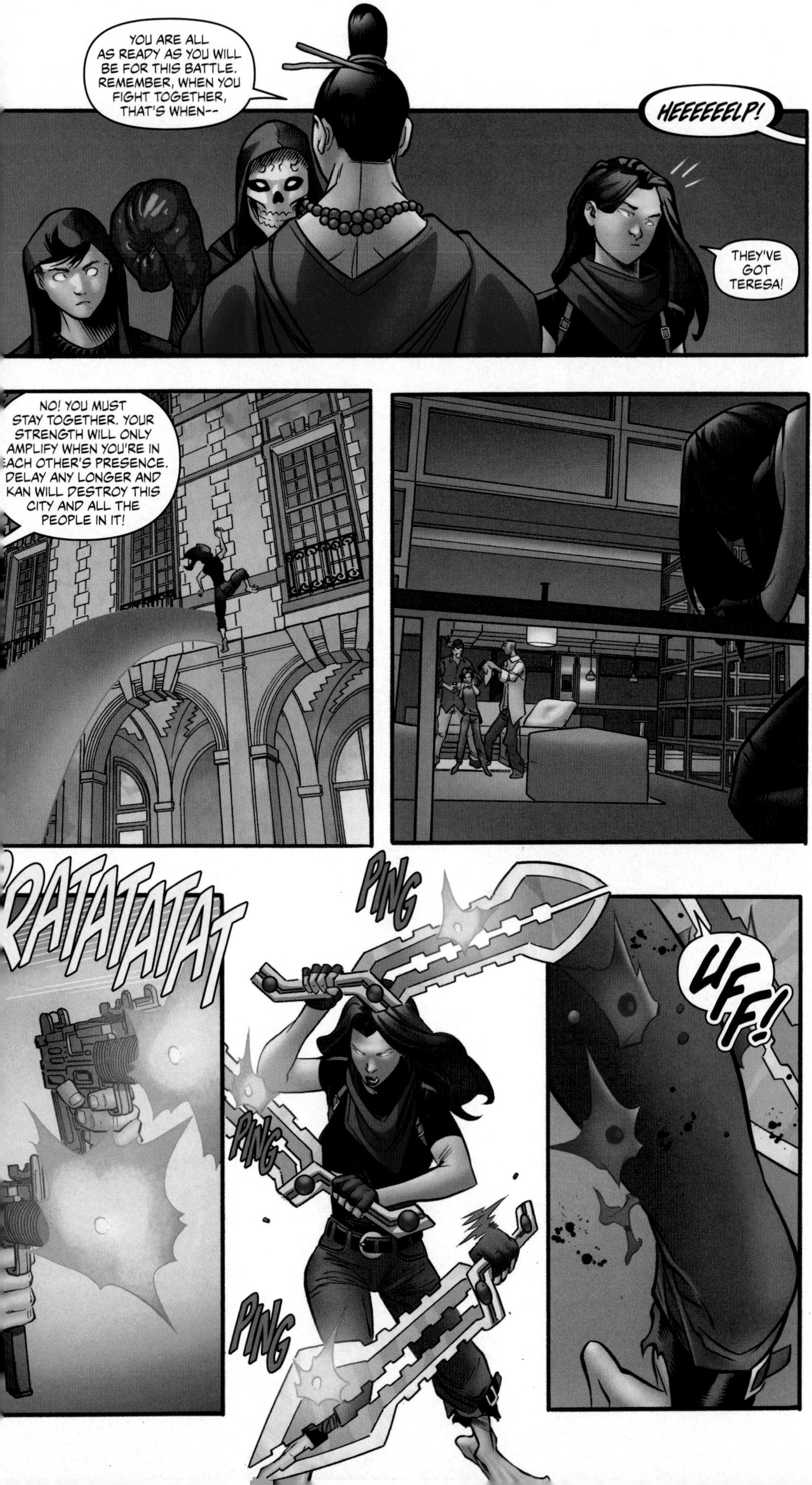
YOU ARE ALL AS READY AS YOU WILL BE FOR THIS BATTLE. REMEMBER, WHEN YOU FIGHT TOGETHER, THAT'S WHEN--
HEEEEEELP!
THEY'VE GOT TERESA!
NO! YOU MUST STAY TOGETHER. YOUR STRENGTH WILL ONLY AMPLIFY WHEN YOU'RE IN EACH OTHER'S PRESENCE. DELAY ANY LONGER AND KAN WILL DESTROY THIS CITY AND ALL THE PEOPLE IN IT!
RATATATAT
PING
PING
PING
UFF!

FWOOSH

TERESA!

ZZZZZZZ

GINA, YOU'RE HURT!

I'M FINE. THEY TOOK TERESA! GO AFTER THEM!

ALEJANDRO TAKING YOUR SISTER WAS NO COINCIDENCE. THAT EVIL $#@%´ MUST HAVE CUT SOME SORT OF SIDE DEAL WITH KAN.

ARE YOU OKAY TO WALK?

I'M SURE AS HELL NOT STAYING HERE. SO, YES.

GOOD. IT'S TIME TO END THIS. LET'S GO.

WHATEVER HAPPENS DOWN THE[RE] FROM NOW ON WE NEED TO ST[AY] TOGETHER AT ALL TIMES.

WOW. I'M IMPRESSED. YOU ALMOST SOUND LIKE A LEADER.

THANKS.

I SAID "ALMOST."

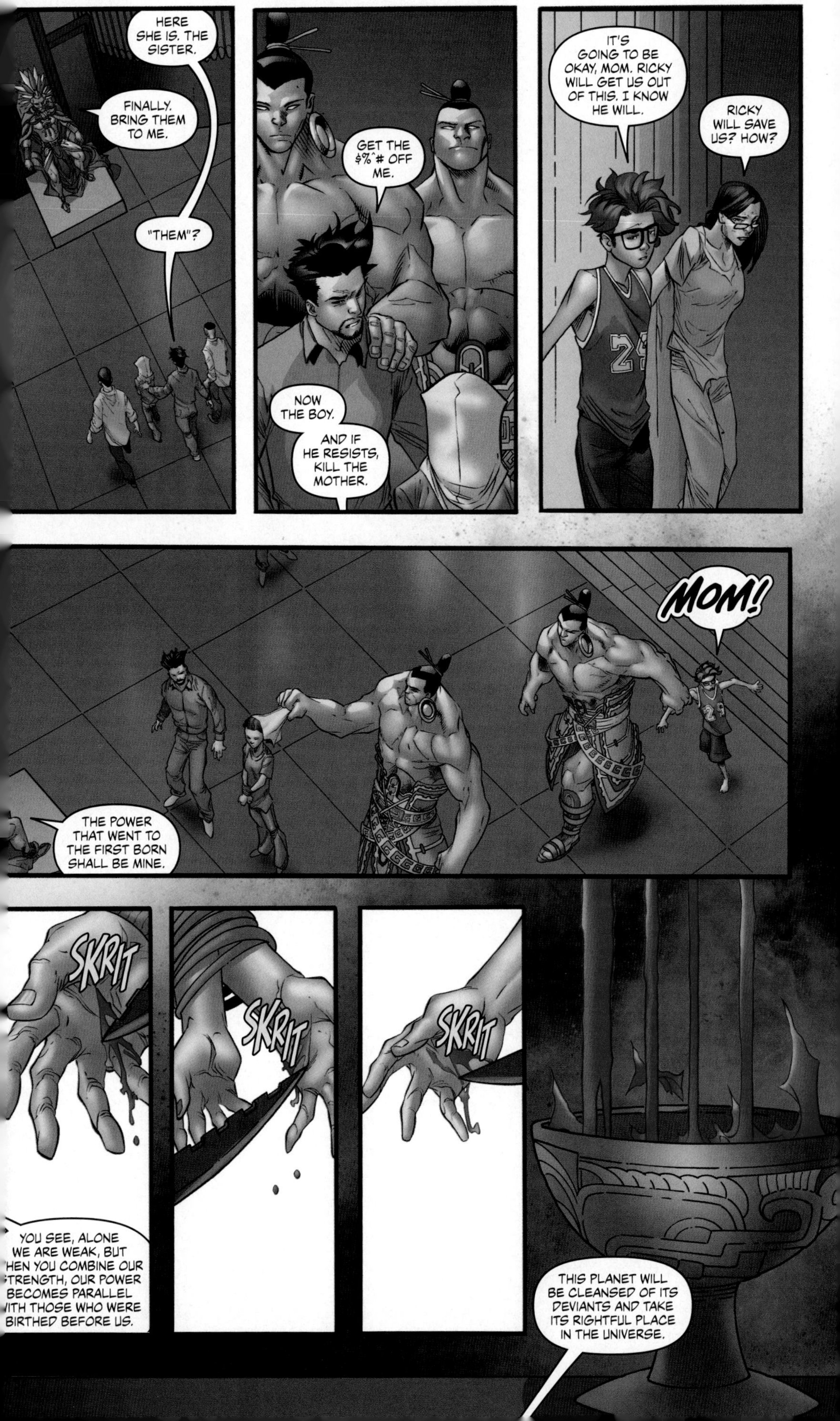
HERE SHE IS. THE SISTER.
FINALLY. BRING THEM TO ME.
"THEM"?
GET THE $%^# OFF ME.
NOW THE BOY.
AND IF HE RESISTS, KILL THE MOTHER.
IT'S GOING TO BE OKAY, MOM. RICKY WILL GET US OUT OF THIS. I KNOW HE WILL.
RICKY WILL SAVE US? HOW?
MOM!
THE POWER THAT WENT TO THE FIRST BORN SHALL BE MINE.
SKRIT
SKRIT
SKRIT
YOU SEE, ALONE WE ARE WEAK, BUT HEN YOU COMBINE OUR TRENGTH, OUR POWER BECOMES PARALLEL WITH THOSE WHO WERE BIRTHED BEFORE US.
THIS PLANET WILL BE CLEANSED OF ITS DEVIANTS AND TAKE ITS RIGHTFUL PLACE IN THE UNIVERSE.

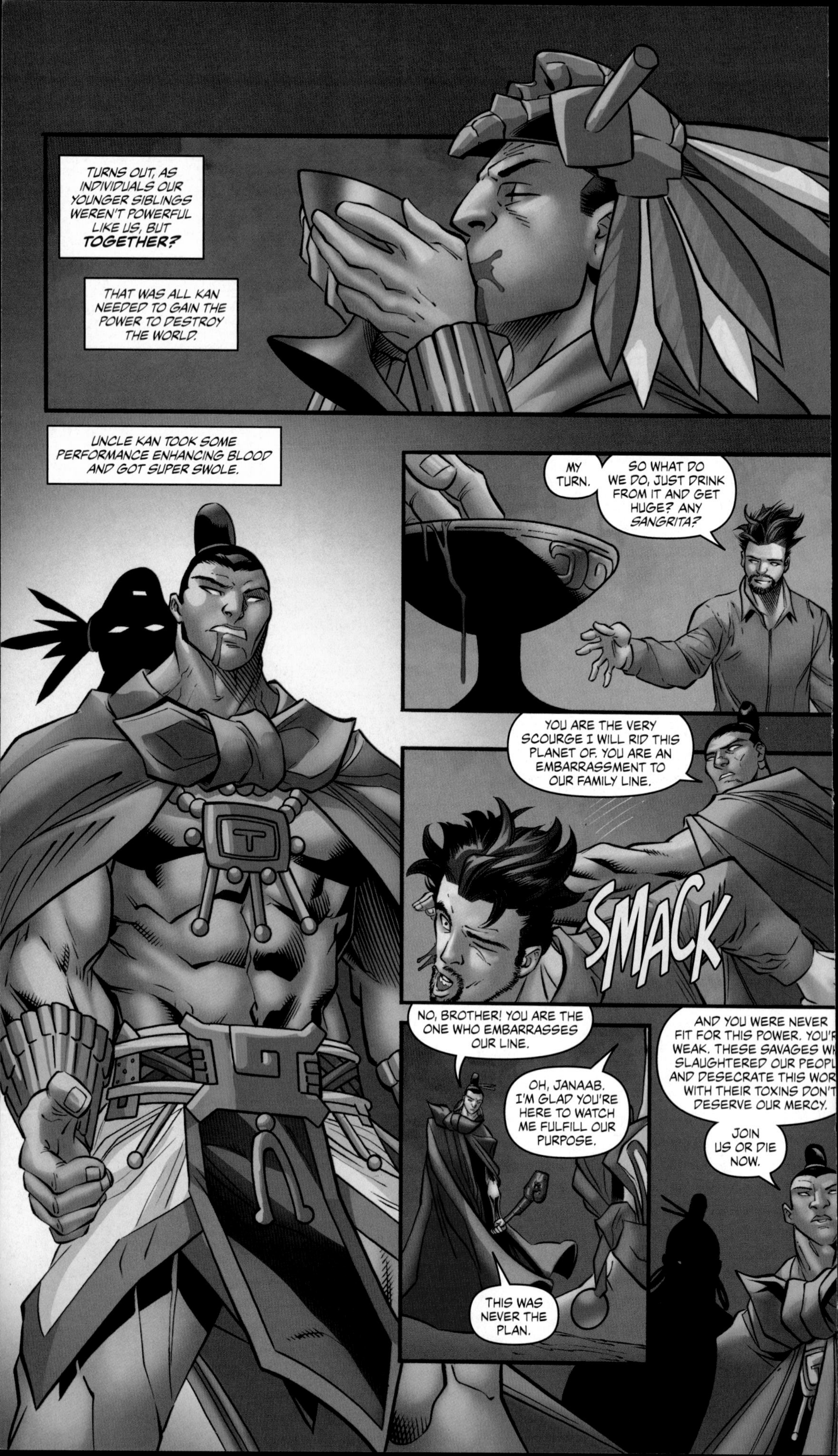

TURNS OUT, AS INDIVIDUALS OUR YOUNGER SIBLINGS WEREN'T POWERFUL LIKE US, BUT **TOGETHER?**
THAT WAS ALL KAN NEEDED TO GAIN THE POWER TO DESTROY THE WORLD.
UNCLE KAN TOOK SOME PERFORMANCE ENHANCING BLOOD AND GOT SUPER SWOLE.
MY TURN.
SO WHAT DO WE DO, JUST DRINK FROM IT AND GET HUGE? ANY SANGRITA?
YOU ARE THE VERY SCOURGE I WILL RID THIS PLANET OF. YOU ARE AN EMBARRASSMENT TO OUR FAMILY LINE.
SMACK
NO, BROTHER! YOU ARE THE ONE WHO EMBARRASSES OUR LINE.
OH, JANAAB. I'M GLAD YOU'RE HERE TO WATCH ME FULFILL OUR PURPOSE.
AND YOU WERE NEVER FIT FOR THIS POWER. YOU'R WEAK. THESE SAVAGES WH SLAUGHTERED OUR PEOPL AND DESECRATE THIS WOR WITH THEIR TOXINS DON'T DESERVE OUR MERCY.
JOIN US OR DIE NOW.
THIS WAS NEVER THE PLAN.

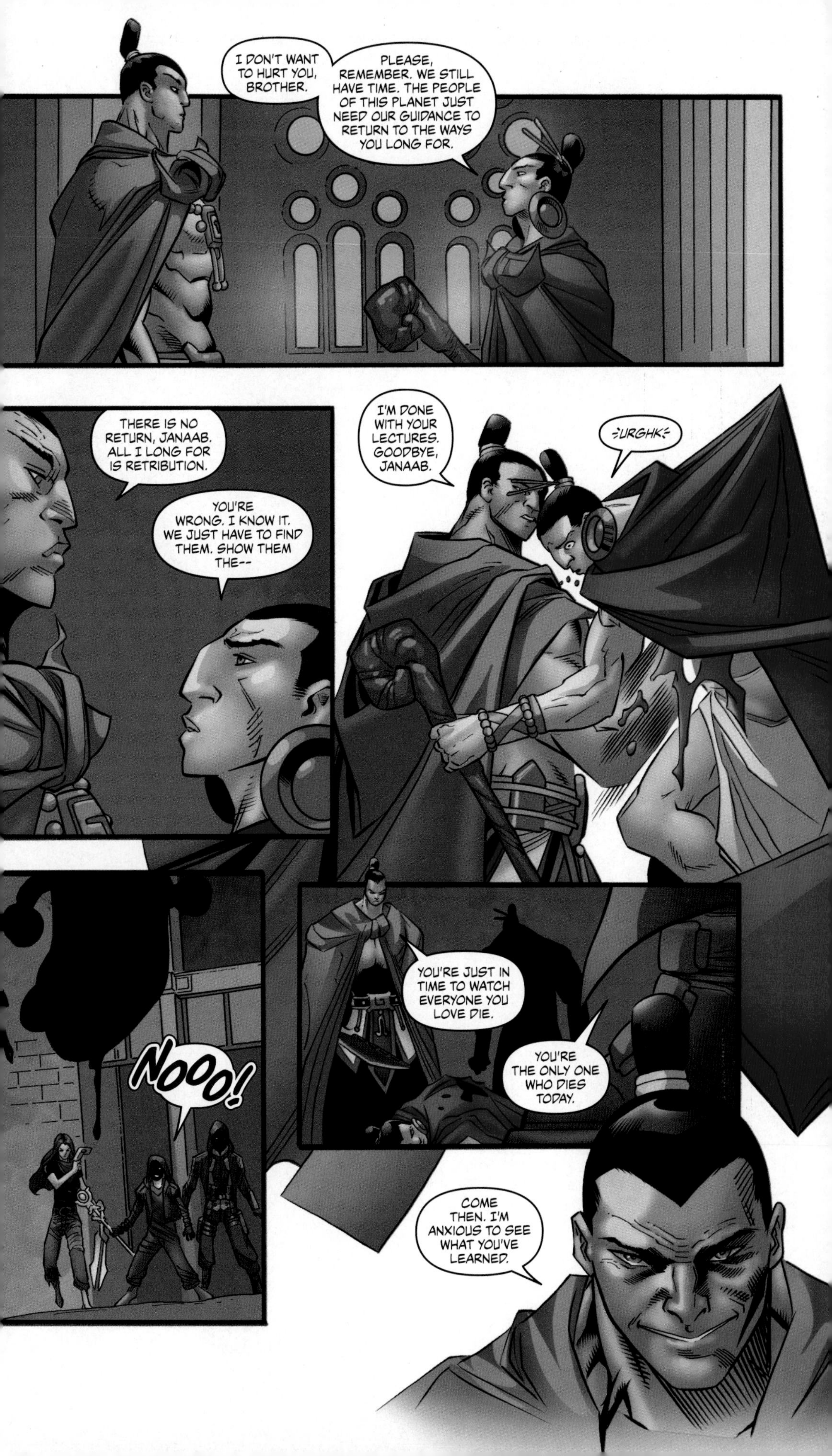
I DON'T WANT TO HURT YOU, BROTHER.
PLEASE, REMEMBER. WE STILL HAVE TIME. THE PEOPLE OF THIS PLANET JUST NEED OUR GUIDANCE TO RETURN TO THE WAYS YOU LONG FOR.
THERE IS NO RETURN, JANAAB. ALL I LONG FOR IS RETRIBUTION.
YOU'RE WRONG. I KNOW IT. WE JUST HAVE TO FIND THEM. SHOW THEM THE--
I'M DONE WITH YOUR LECTURES. GOODBYE, JANAAB.
URGHK
NOOO!
YOU'RE JUST IN TIME TO WATCH EVERYONE YOU LOVE DIE.
YOU'RE THE ONLY ONE WHO DIES TODAY.
COME THEN. I'M ANXIOUS TO SEE WHAT YOU'VE LEARNED.

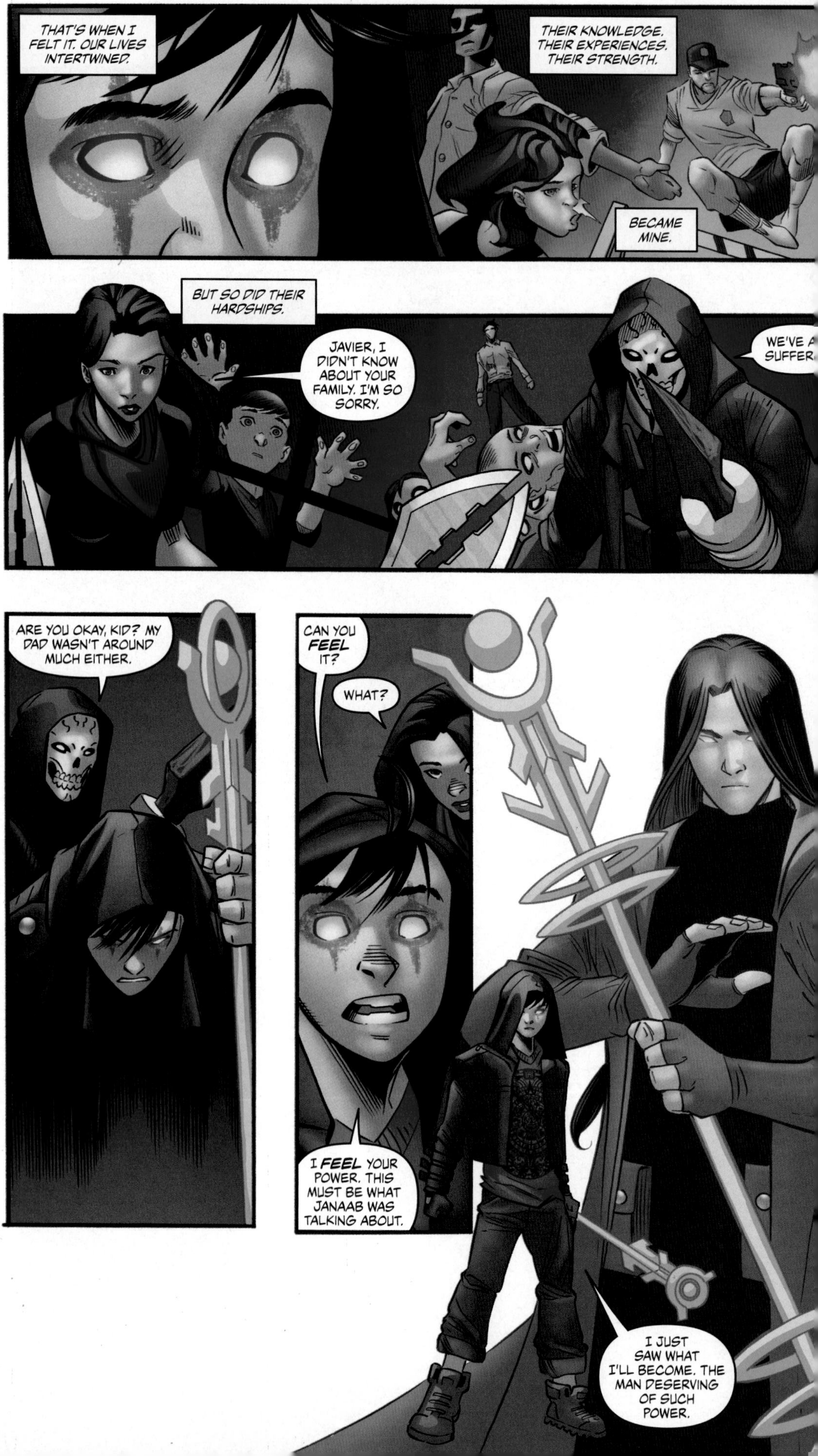
THAT'S WHEN I FELT IT. OUR LIVES INTERTWINED.
THEIR KNOWLEDGE. THEIR EXPERIENCES. THEIR STRENGTH.
BECAME MINE.
BUT SO DID THEIR HARDSHIPS.
JAVIER, I DIDN'T KNOW ABOUT YOUR FAMILY. I'M SO SORRY.
WE'VE A SUFFER
ARE YOU OKAY, KID? MY DAD WASN'T AROUND MUCH EITHER.
CAN YOU FEEL IT?
WHAT?
I FEEL YOUR POWER. THIS MUST BE WHAT JANAAB WAS TALKING ABOUT.
I JUST SAW WHAT I'LL BECOME. THE MAN DESERVING OF SUCH POWER.

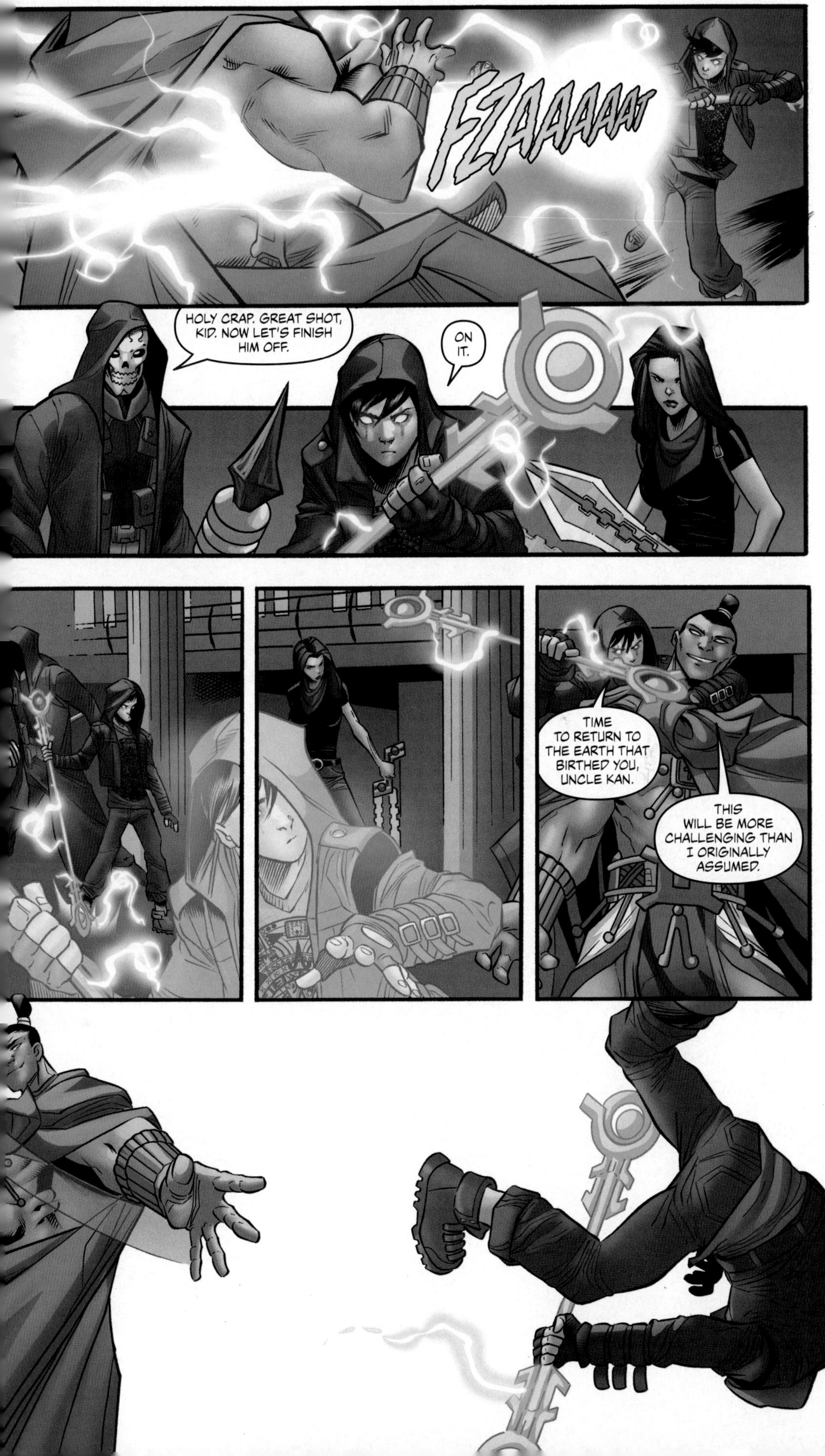
FZAAAAAAT
HOLY CRAP. GREAT SHOT, KID. NOW LET'S FINISH HIM OFF.
ON IT.
TIME TO RETURN TO THE EARTH THAT BIRTHED YOU, UNCLE KAN.
THIS WILL BE MORE CHALLENGING THAN I ORIGINALLY ASSUMED.

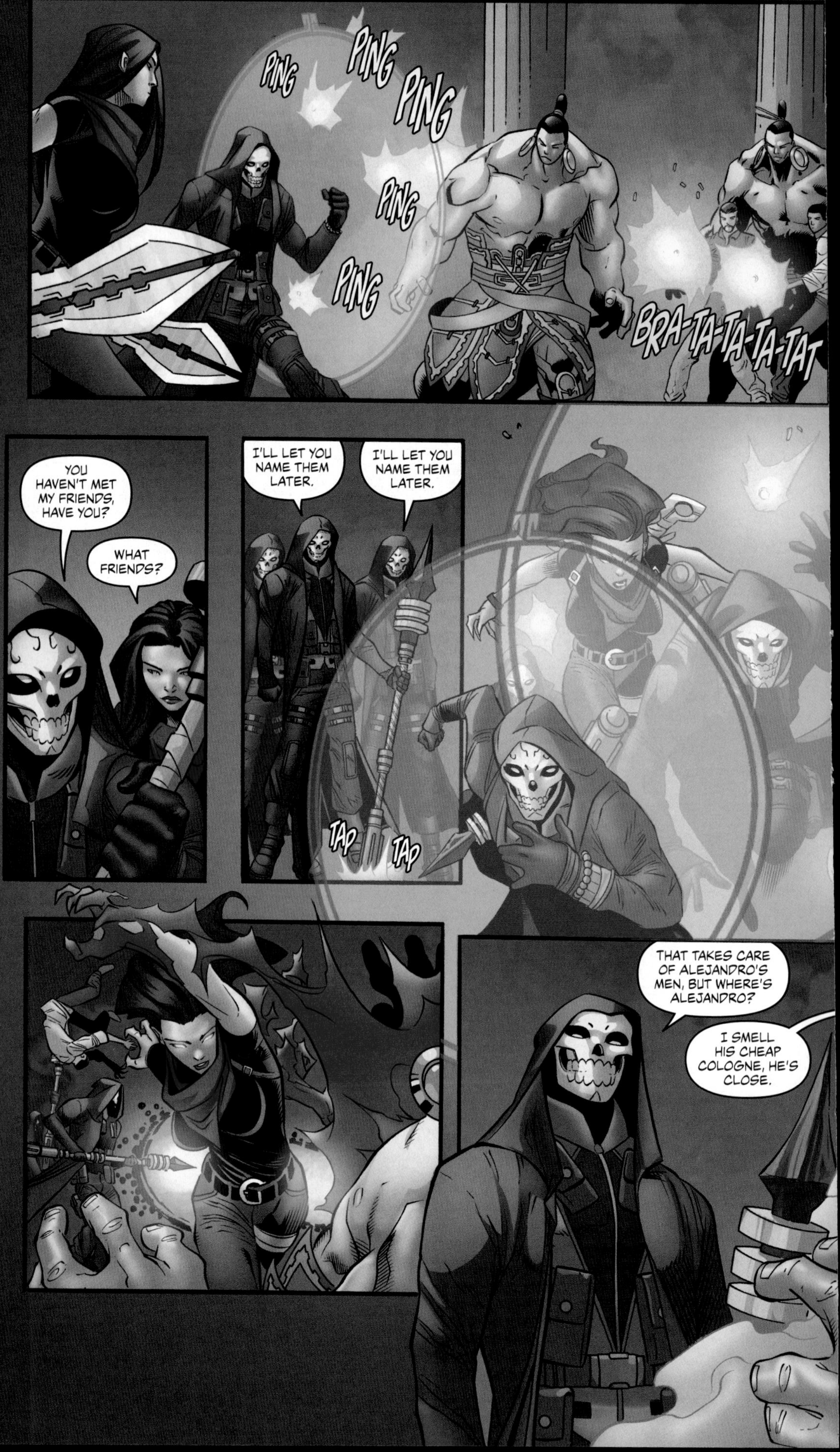
PING
PING
PING
PING
PING
BRA-TA-TA-TA-TAT
YOU HAVEN'T MET MY FRIENDS, HAVE YOU?
WHAT FRIENDS?
I'LL LET YOU NAME THEM LATER.
I'LL LET YOU NAME THEM LATER.
TAP
TAP
THAT TAKES CARE OF ALEJANDRO'S MEN, BUT WHERE'S ALEJANDRO?
I SMELL HIS CHEAP COLOGNE, HE'S CLOSE.

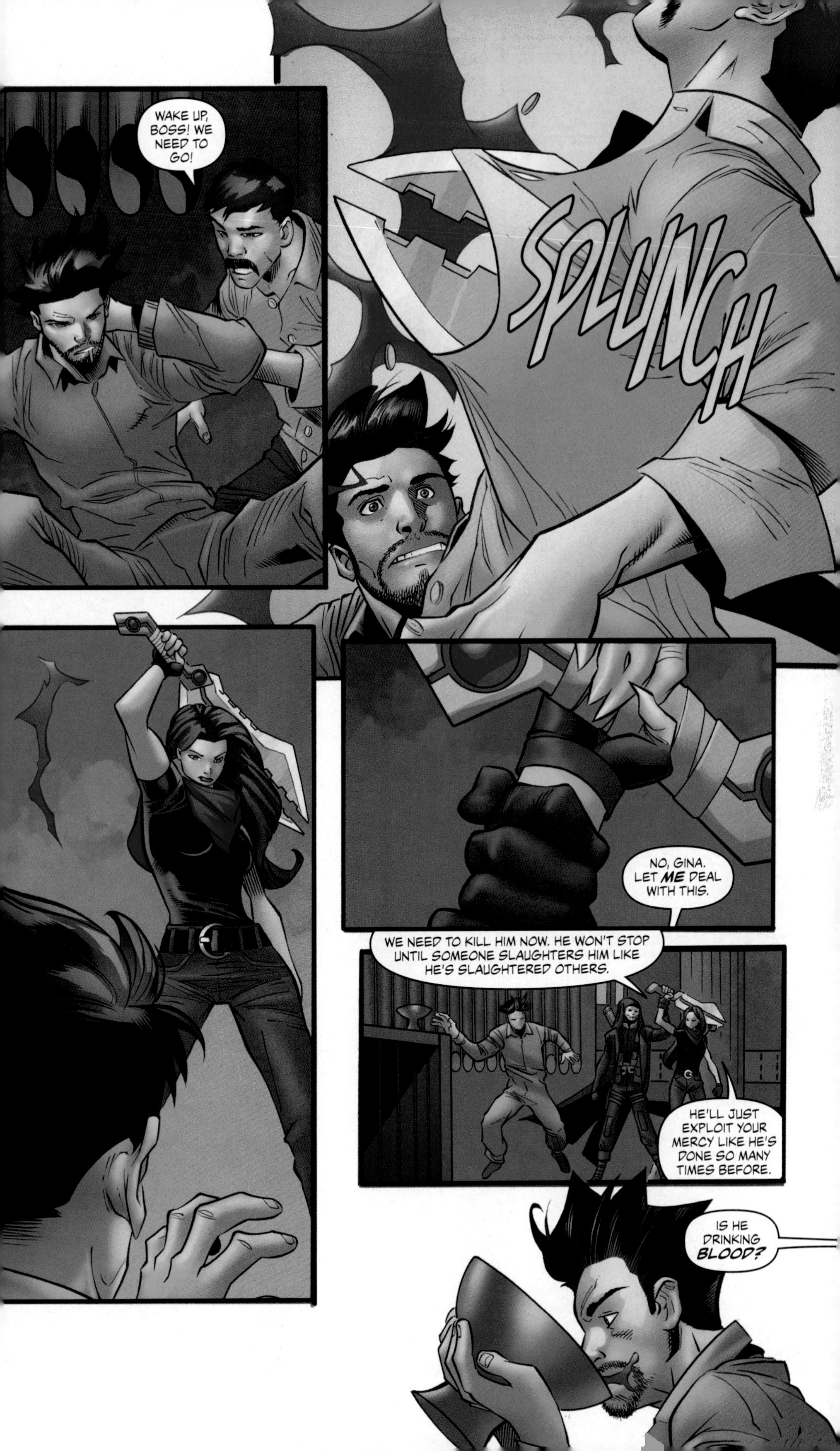
WAKE UP, BOSS! WE NEED TO GO!
SPLUNCH
NO, GINA. LET **ME** DEAL WITH THIS.
WE NEED TO KILL HIM NOW. HE WON'T STOP UNTIL SOMEONE SLAUGHTERS HIM LIKE HE'S SLAUGHTERED OTHERS.
HE'LL JUST EXPLOIT YOUR MERCY LIKE HE'S DONE SO MANY TIMES BEFORE.
IS HE DRINKING ***BLOOD?***

YOU DON'T UNDERSTAND THESE POWERS.

THERE'S NOTHING TO UNDERSTAND. I FEEL INCREDIBLE. I'M GETTING RIPPED WITHOUT YOUR STUPID WAND AND ALL THE HARRY *PATAS* BUDDIES.

RAAAAAUGH

WHAT'S UNNNGH HAPPENI TO ME

L WHA GRE D

NOOOOO!

KRASH

I SHOULD HAVE JUST LET YOU KILL HIM.

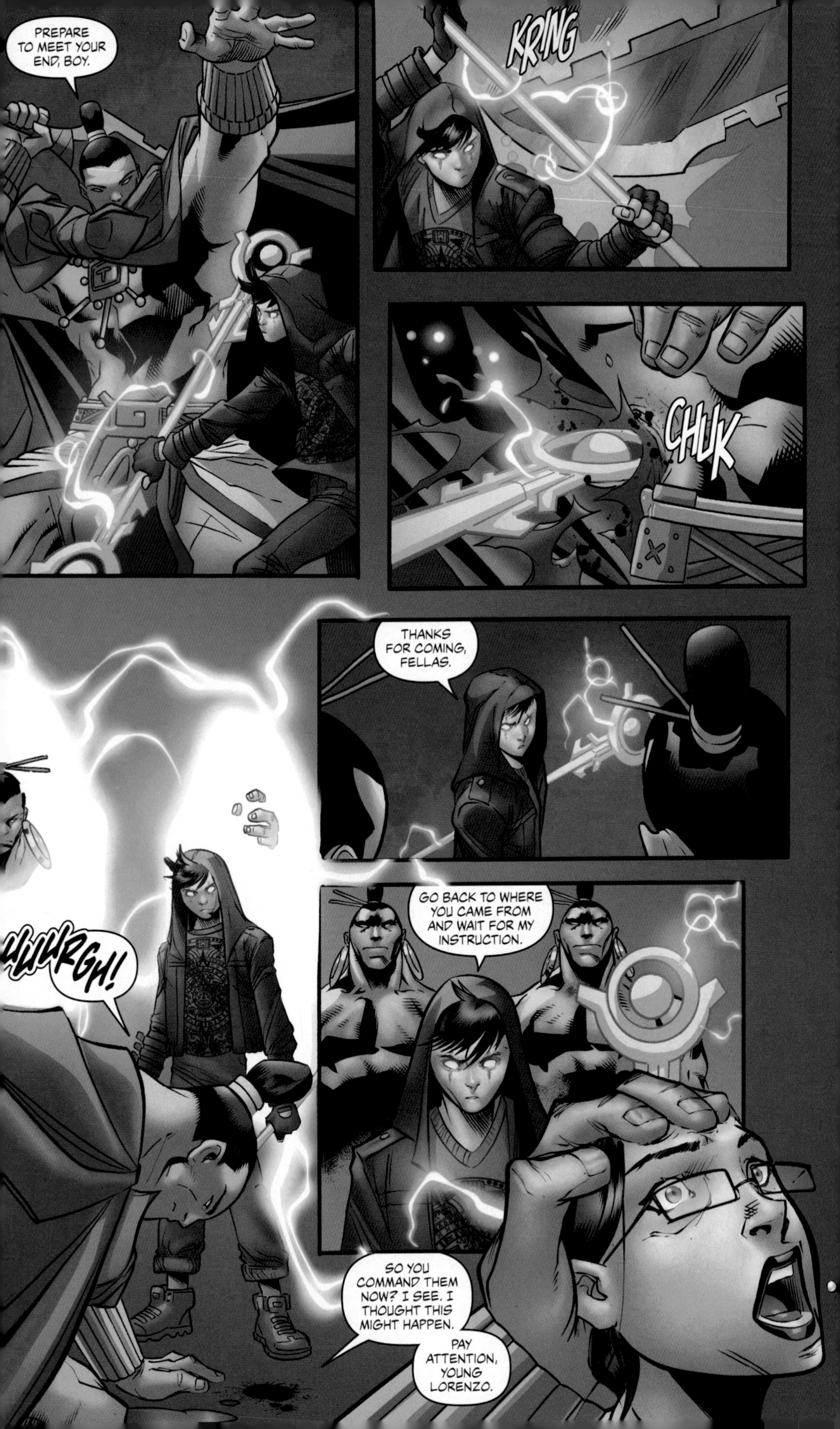
PREPARE TO MEET YOUR END, BOY.
KRING
CHUK
THANKS FOR COMING, FELLAS.
UUURGH!
GO BACK TO WHERE YOU CAME FROM AND WAIT FOR MY INSTRUCTION.
SO YOU COMMAND THEM NOW? I SEE. I THOUGHT THIS MIGHT HAPPEN.
PAY ATTENTION, YOUNG LORENZO.

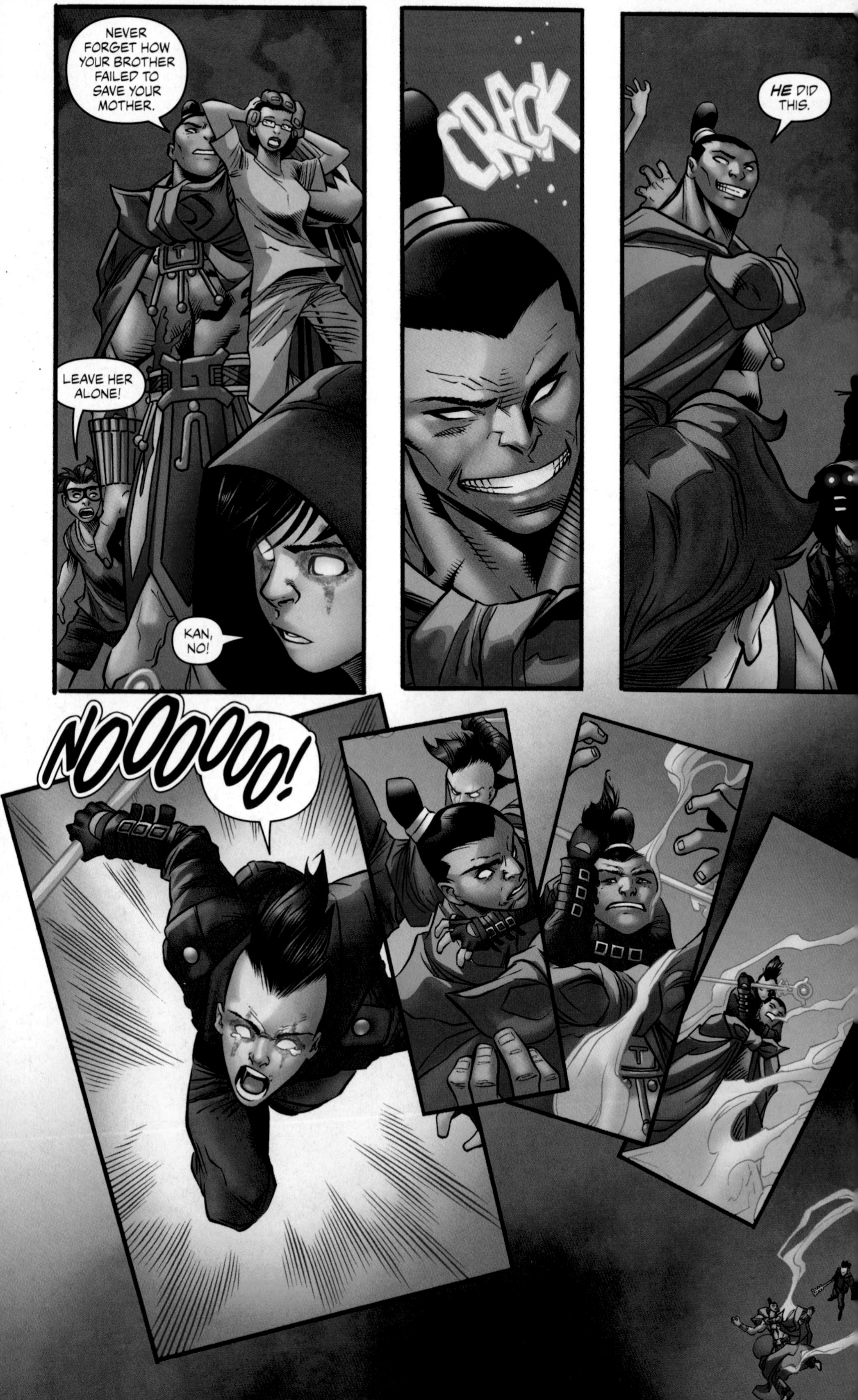
NEVER FORGET HOW YOUR BROTHER FAILED TO SAVE YOUR MOTHER.
LEAVE HER ALONE!
KAN, NO!
CRACK
HE DID THIS.
NOOOOOO!

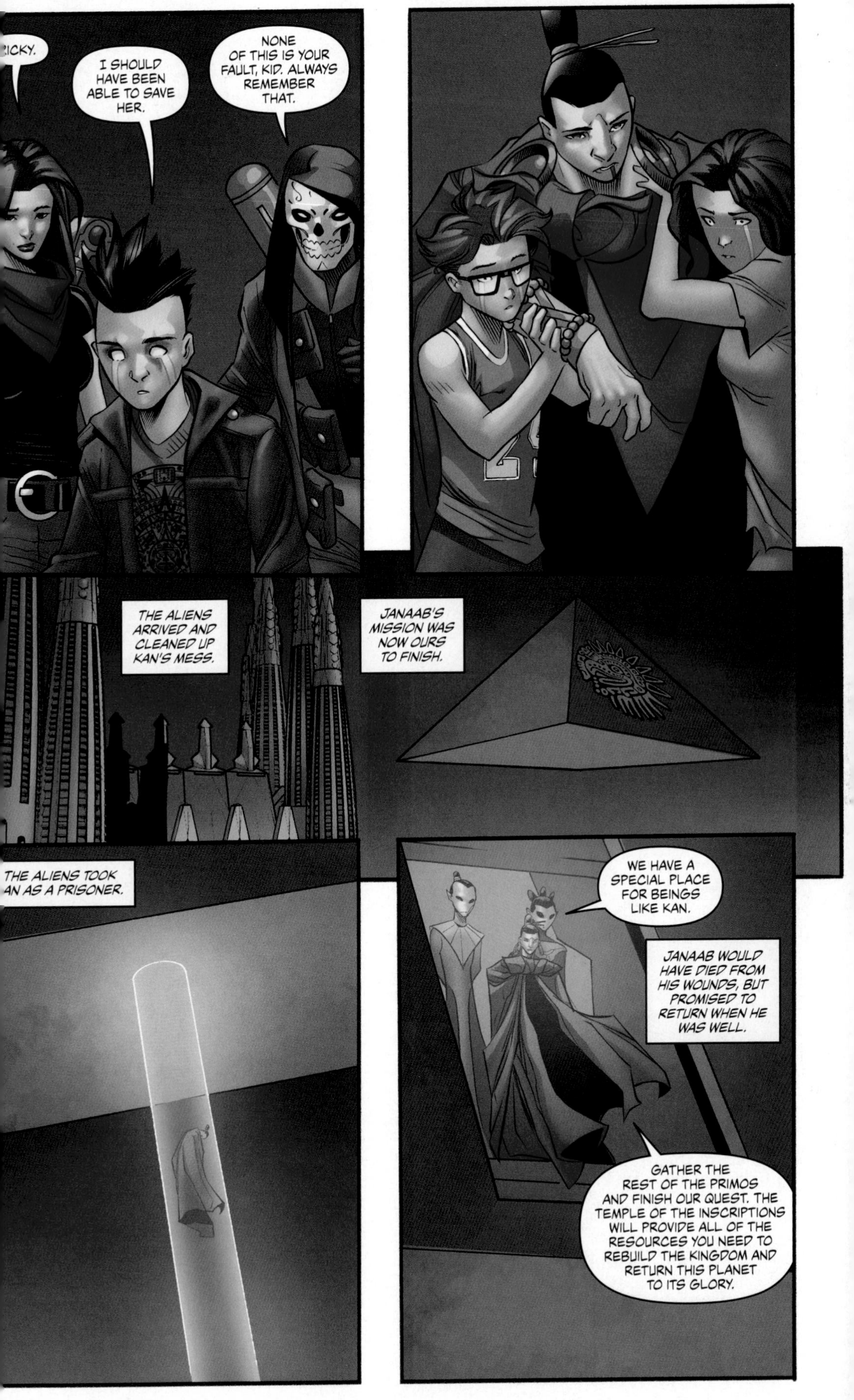

ICKY.
I SHOULD HAVE BEEN ABLE TO SAVE HER.
NONE OF THIS IS YOUR FAULT, KID. ALWAYS REMEMBER THAT.
THE ALIENS ARRIVED AND CLEANED UP KAN'S MESS.
JANAAB'S MISSION WAS NOW OURS TO FINISH.
THE ALIENS TOOK AN AS A PRISONER.
WE HAVE A SPECIAL PLACE FOR BEINGS LIKE KAN.
JANAAB WOULD HAVE DIED FROM HIS WOUNDS, BUT PROMISED TO RETURN WHEN HE WAS WELL.
GATHER THE REST OF THE PRIMOS AND FINISH OUR QUEST. THE TEMPLE OF THE INSCRIPTIONS WILL PROVIDE ALL OF THE RESOURCES YOU NEED TO REBUILD THE KINGDOM AND RETURN THIS PLANET TO ITS GLORY.

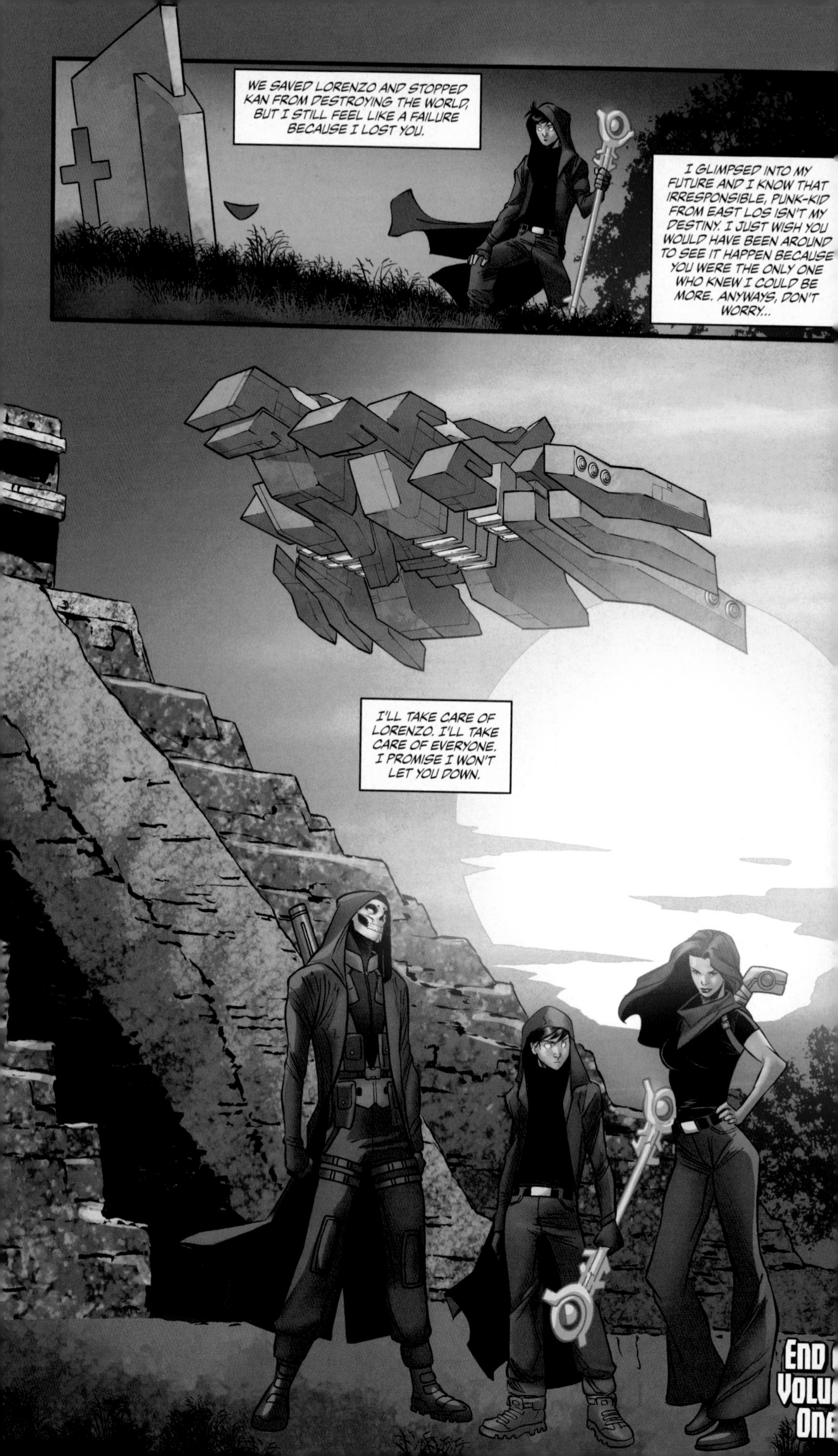
WE SAVED LORENZO AND STOPPED KAN FROM DESTROYING THE WORLD, BUT I STILL FEEL LIKE A FAILURE BECAUSE I LOST YOU.
I GLIMPSED INTO MY FUTURE AND I KNOW THAT IRRESPONSIBLE, PUNK-KID FROM EAST LOS ISN'T MY DESTINY. I JUST WISH YOU WOULD HAVE BEEN AROUND TO SEE IT HAPPEN BECAUSE YOU WERE THE ONLY ONE WHO KNEW I COULD BE MORE. ANYWAYS, DON'T WORRY...
I'LL TAKE CARE OF LORENZO. I'LL TAKE CARE OF EVERYONE. I PROMISE I WON'T LET YOU DOWN.

Pin-Up Art by Felipe Flores

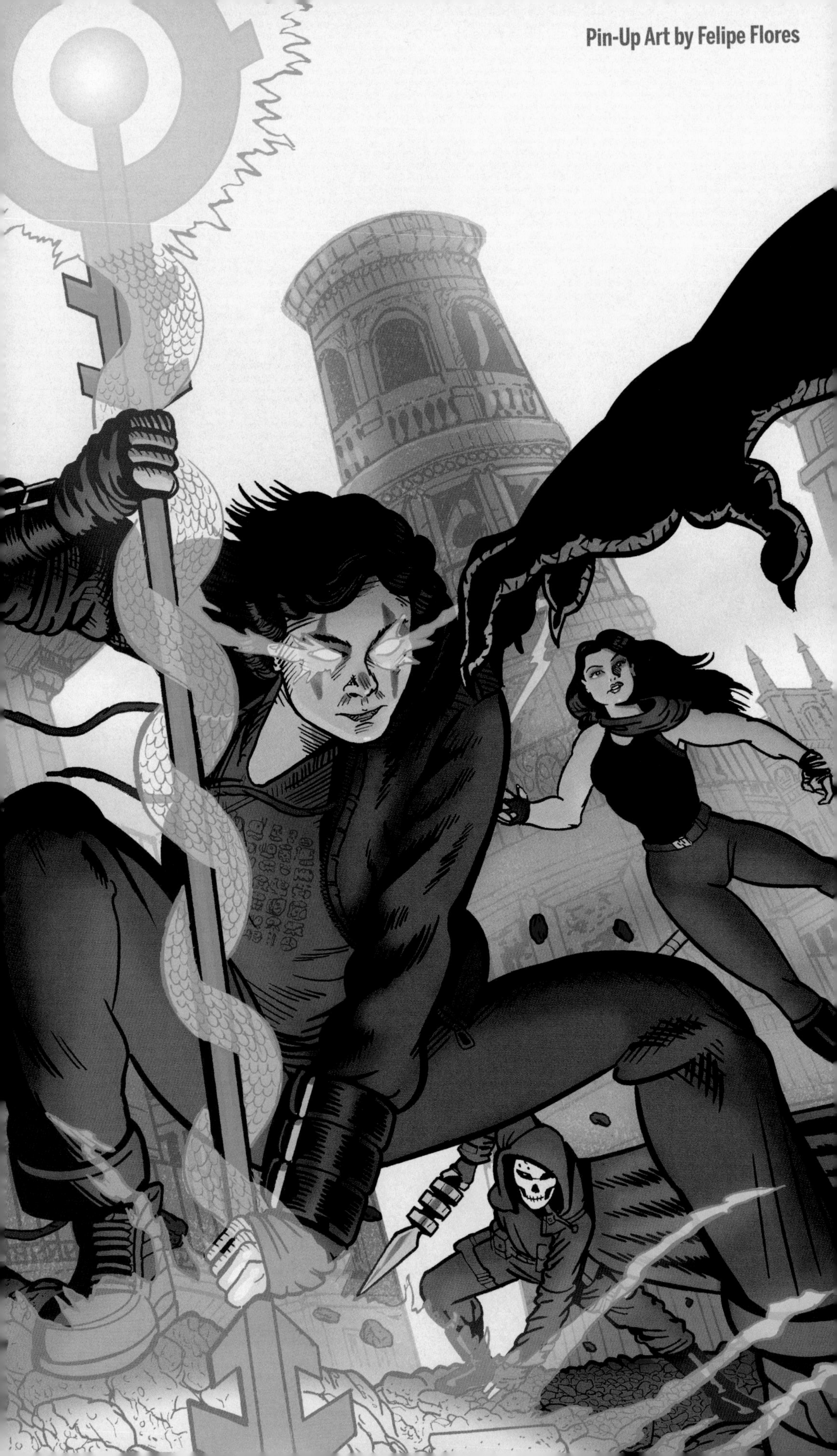

Issue 1 Variant Cover by Carlo Barberi,
Colored by Ive Svorcina

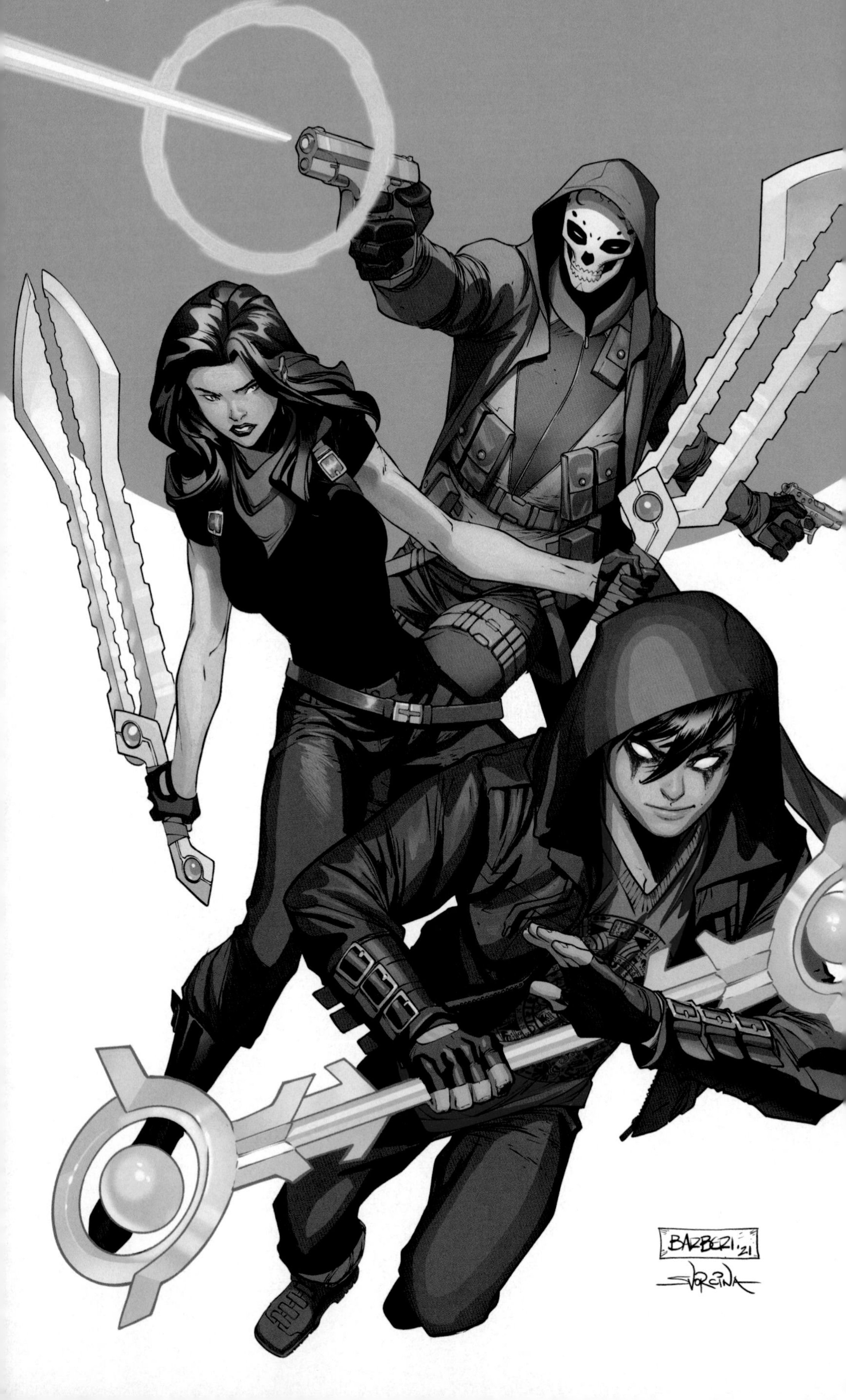
BARBERI.'21
SVORCINA

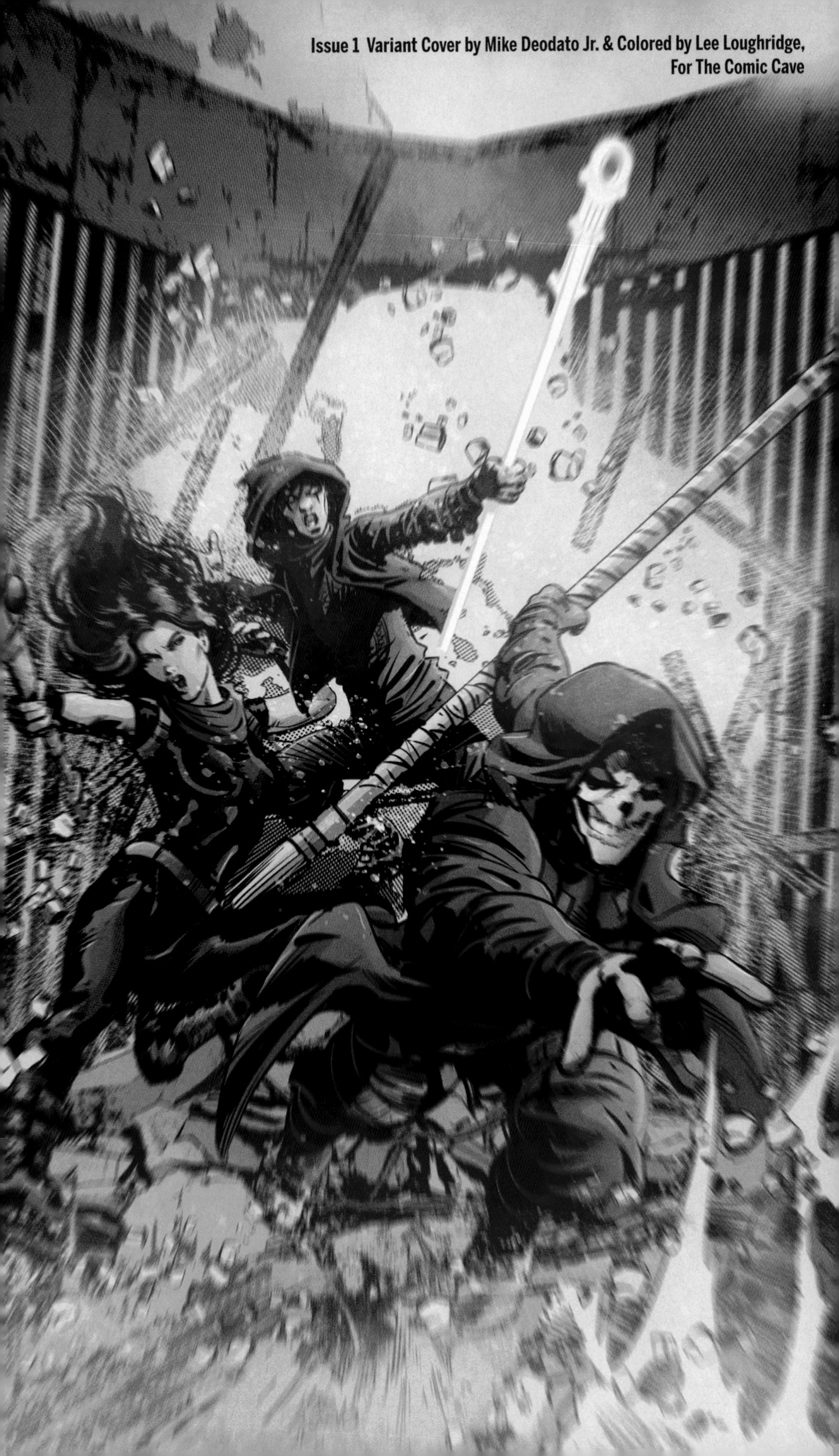

Issue 1 Variant Cover by Mike Deodato Jr. & Colored by Lee Loughridge, For The Comic Cave

Issue 1 Variant Cover by Ivan Tao, For Sad Lemon Comics

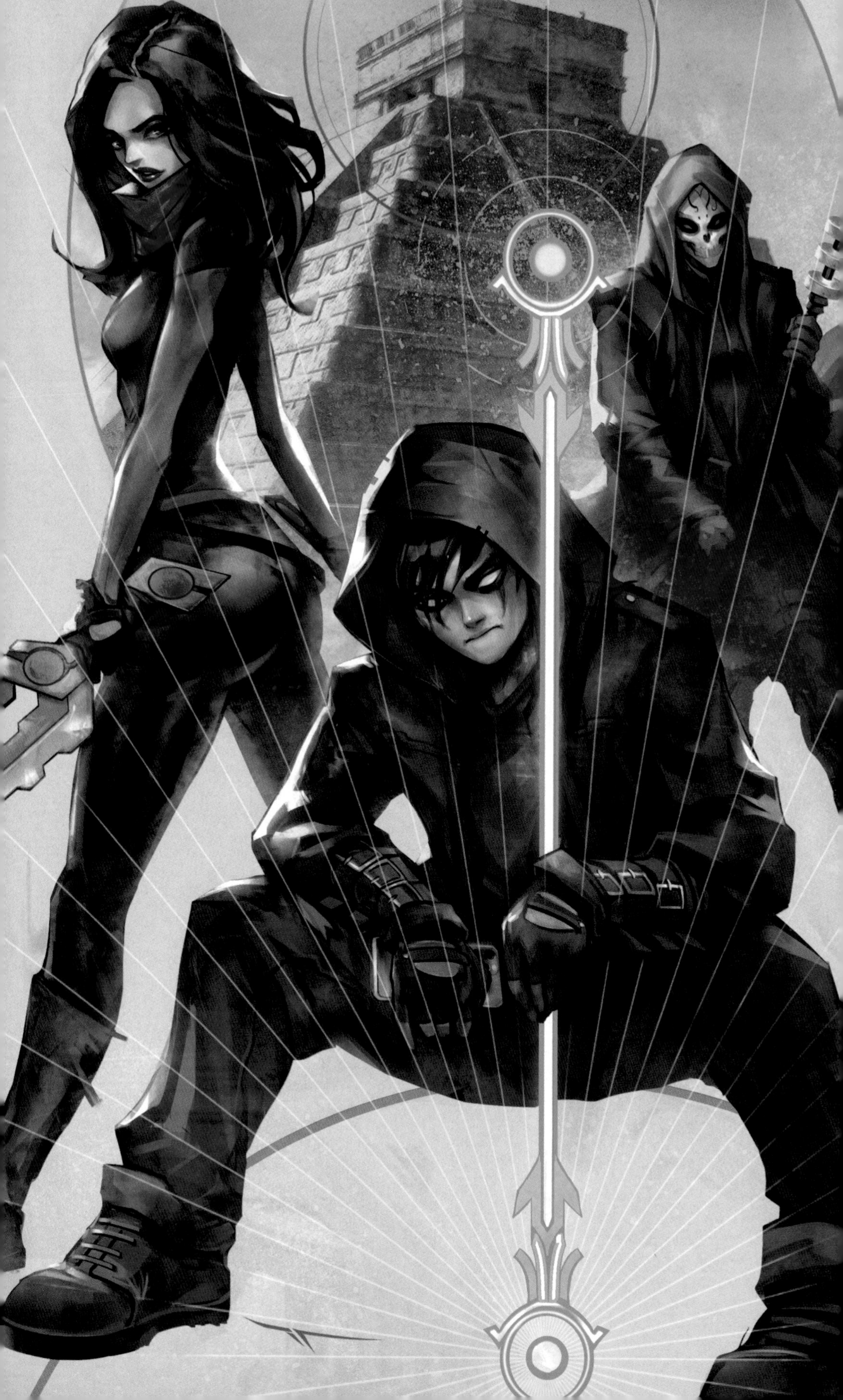

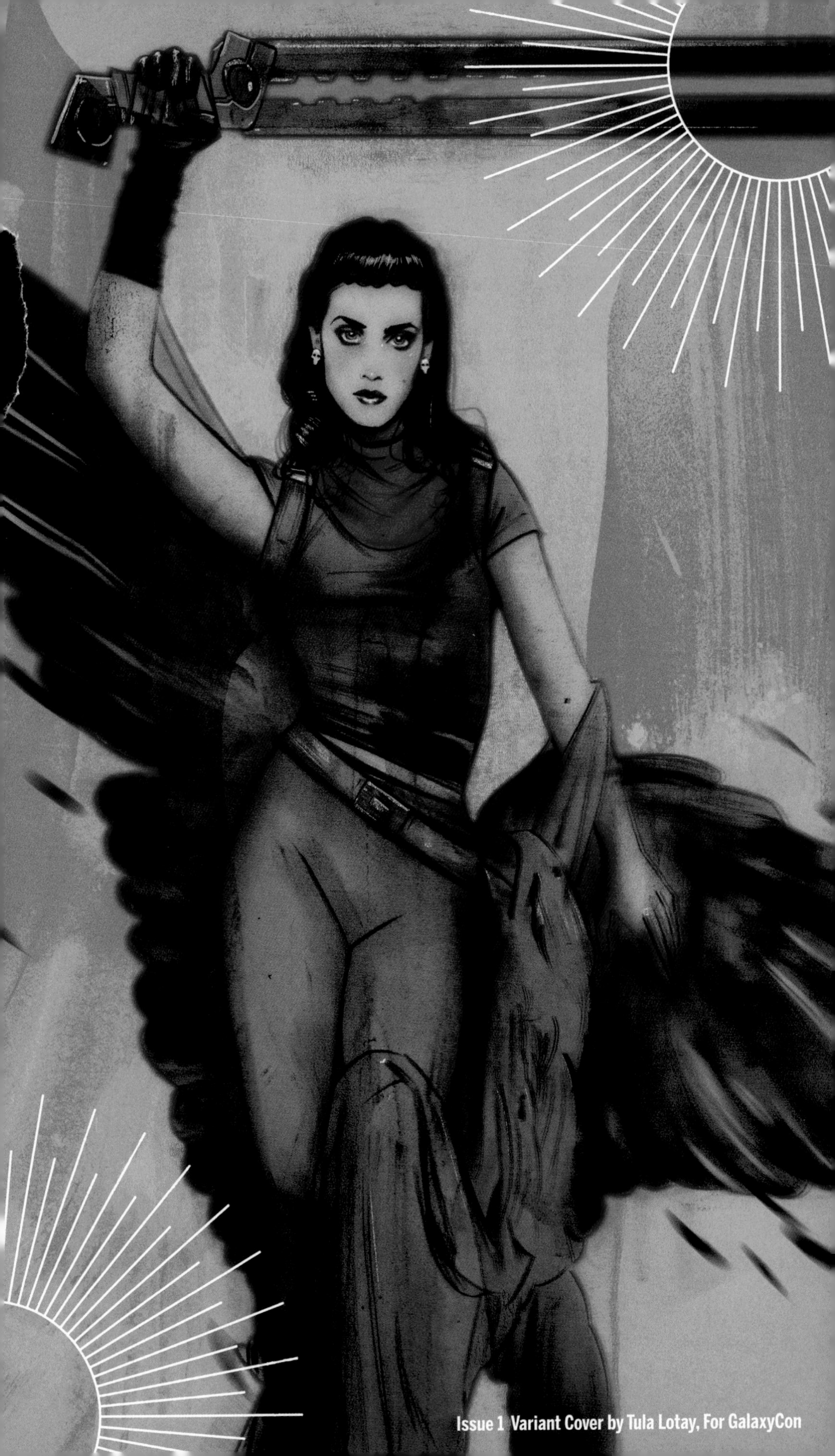

Issue 1 Variant Cover by Tula Lotay, For GalaxyCon

Issue 1 Second Printing Cover by Mike Deodato Jr.,
Colored by Lee Loughridge

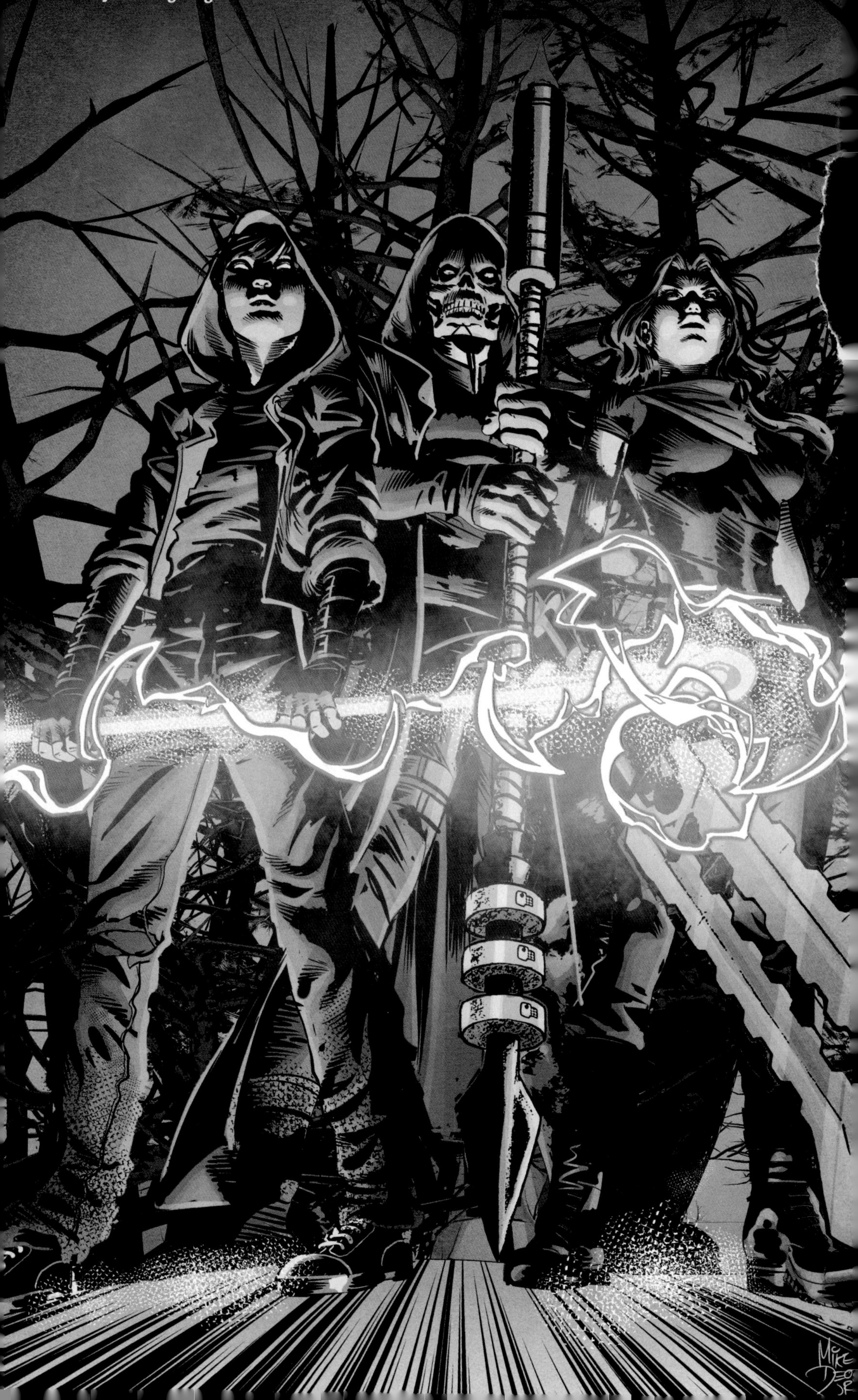

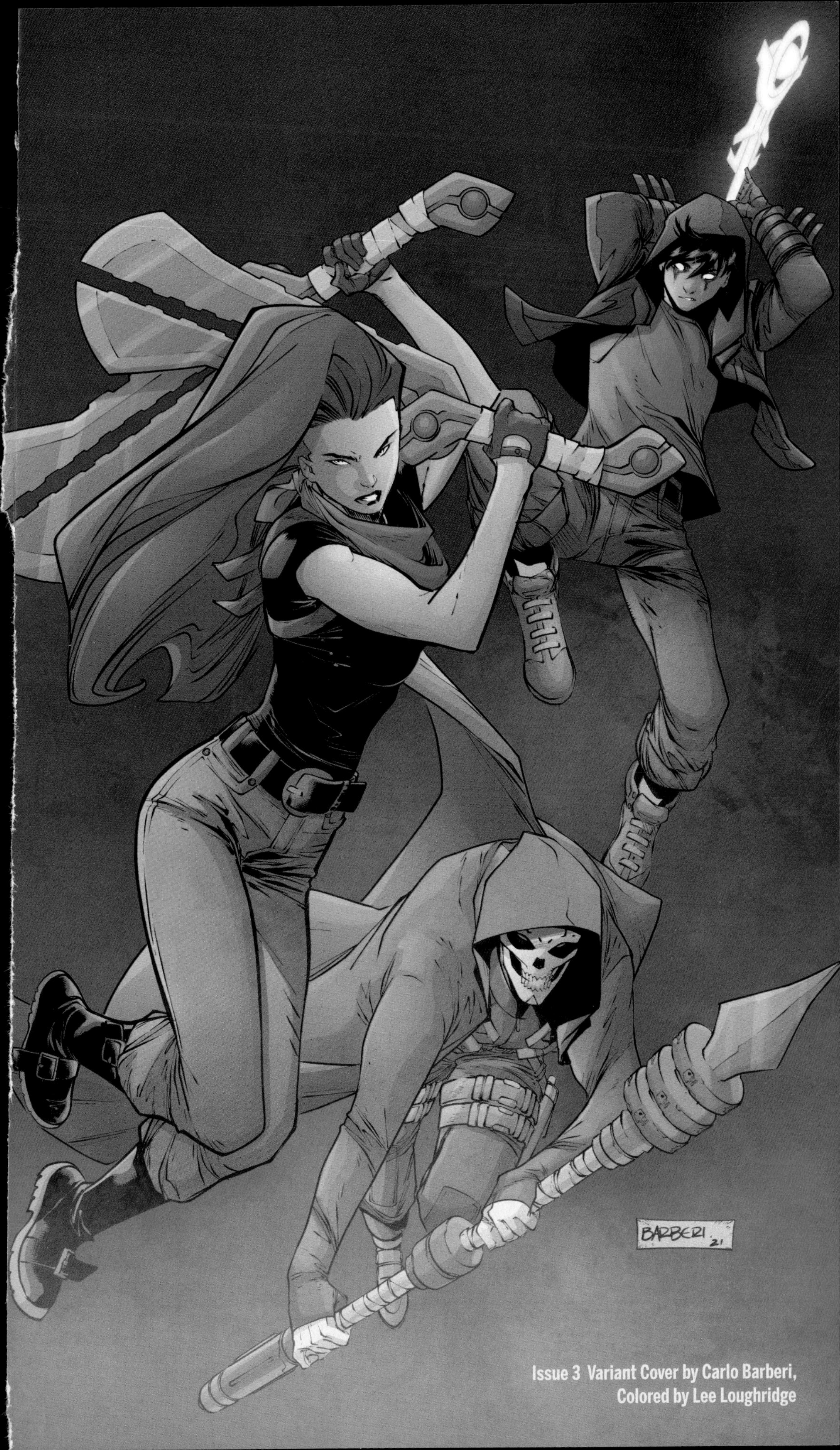
BARBERI 21

Issue 3 Variant Cover by Carlo Barberi,
Colored by Lee Loughridge

A LETTER FROM THE CREATOR OF
PRIMOS

Al Madrigal

I always had this little nagging voice in my head that told me I needed to be a standup comedian. But when I told my dad I was going to do standup, man, did I get yelled at. I mean, just constantly. My father, a first-generation Mexican, warehouse foreman, couldn't grasp why his son would drive for three hours to make $25 as the opening act for a comedian he'd never heard of. "Who the #$%^ is Louis C.K.? His last name is stupid and so are you," or "The gas costs more money than you'll make." He didn't get it. Needless to say, I ignored my dad and listened to that little nagging voice and it changed my life.

Eventually standup comedy led me to *The Daily Show with Jon Stewart* and New York, where I met fellow half-Mexican, San Franciscan Axel Alonso, who was the then Editor-in-

Chief of Marvel. We bonded over our love of the 49ers, Warriors, and Giants and our mixed-Mexican heritage, and commiserated about the lack of badass Latino superheroes. We were both always attracted to minor black characters that would show up in comics—Black Panther, Jim Rhodes/War Machine, Black Manta, Black Lightning (a lot of lazy naming in black superheroes). Latinos didn't even have that problem; we were non-existent. And it's not just comic books. We continue to be under-served in all forms of media—movies, TV, journalism, internet memes.

One of the big things I learned at *The Daily Show*: It's not enough to complain about a problem; you need to pose the solutions, as well. What are you going to do about it? With Axel's help, I started working with my friend Felipe Flores, an incredible artist and comic book fan, to come up with the *Primos* origin story that you've just read. Axel teamed us up with Carlo

Barberi (*Deadpool*), whose artistic talent amazes me at every pass. And two years later, you're holding the culmination of all that hard work. We have built a world that has deep roots in Maya history, is relevant to today's world, and, I think, manages to be unique amongst comics.

I really hope you enjoy this story, but I also hope it inspires you to write your own *Primos*. Build your own stories, create your own characters, follow your own creative dream, whatever that might be. Yes, you might get yelled at along the way, and told that you're wasting your potential/education/life/fill in the blank, but know that you'll be doing something way more fulfilling and important for yourself and your community. Listen to that little nagging voice in your head. You'll be glad you did. It'll lead you to places you never imagined.

I can't thank you enough for purchasing this first book. Stick with it. There's a lot of surprises in store for you.

Thank you,

Al Madrigal

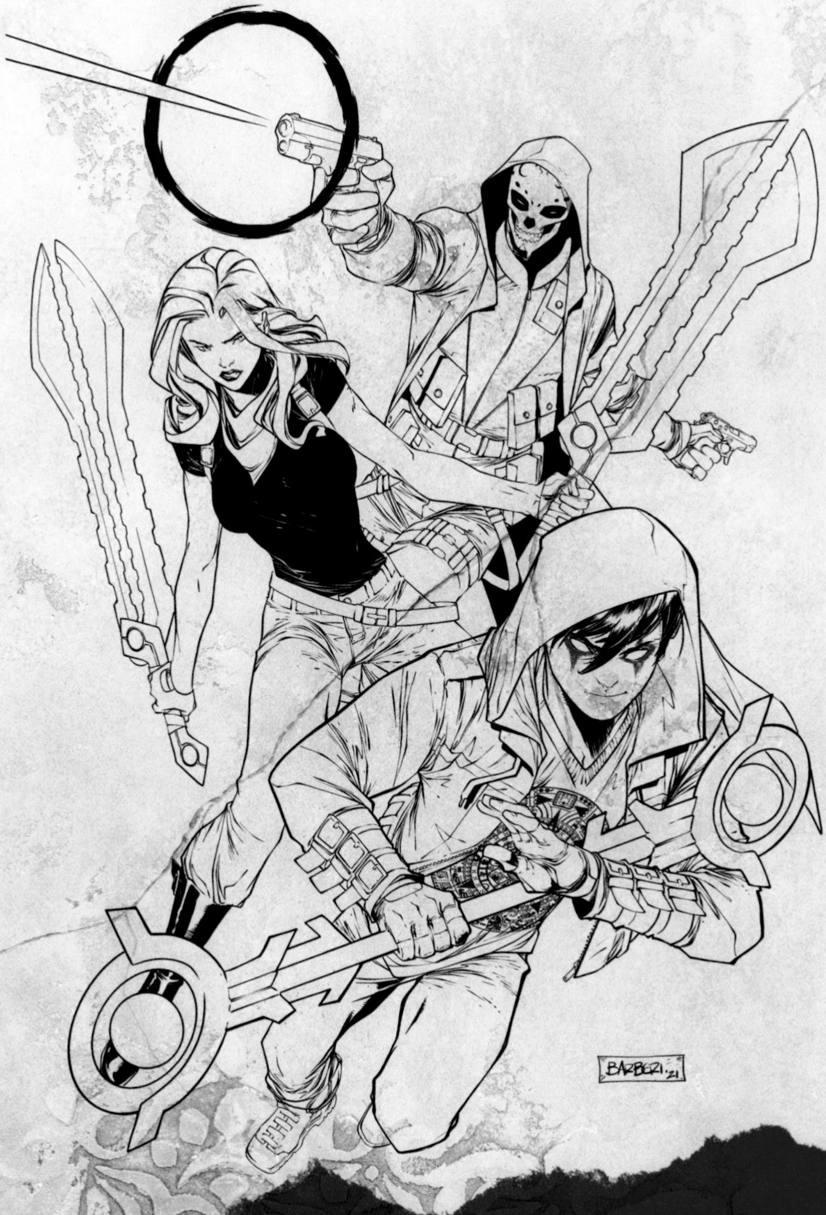
BARBERI '21

Character Sketches by Felipe Flores & Carlo Barberi

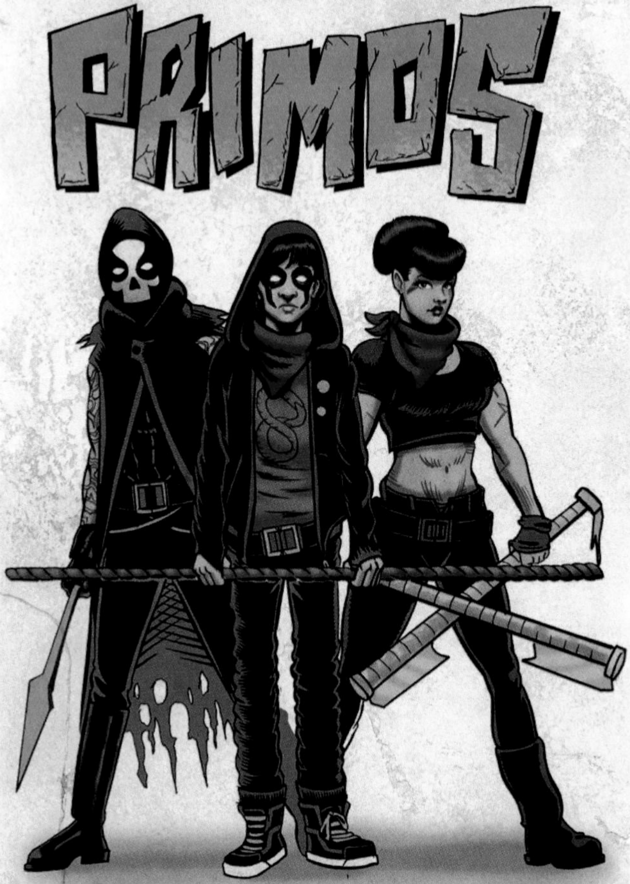
PRIMOS

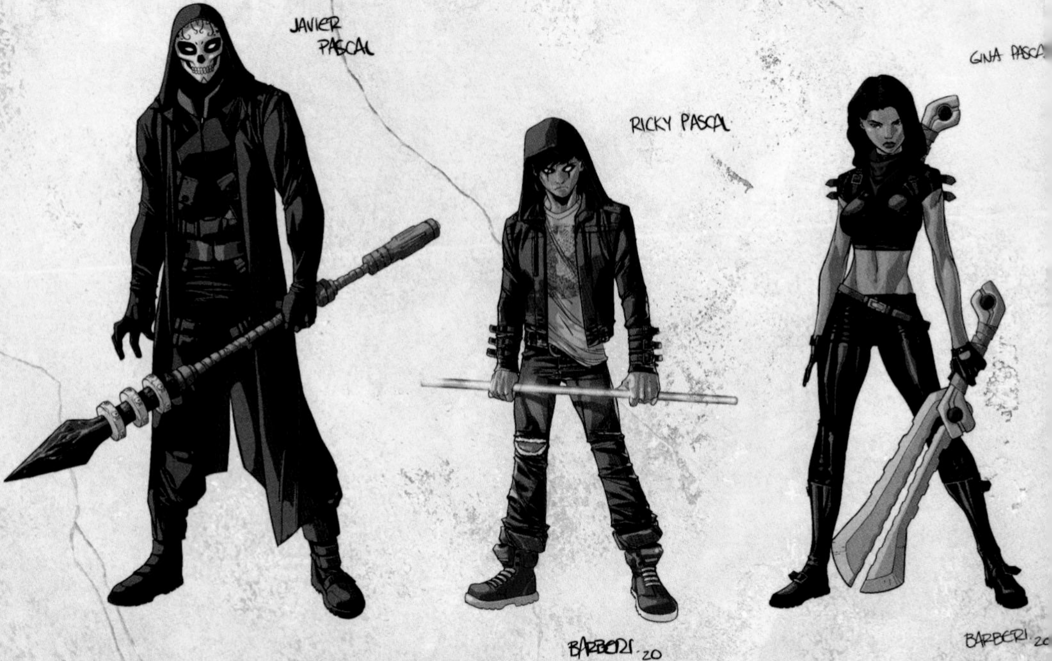
JAVIER PASCAL
RICKY PASCAL
GINA PASCA
BARBERI .20
BARBERI

ISSUE #1 PAGE 6

nel 1
:ky runs by a group of gangbangers (shaved heads, :oos, bandanas, Dickies), who heckle him.

ICKY CAP: I ran all the way home--not only because I ; late, but because it's the best way to avoid getting my kicked by some ese.

'OUGH GUY #1: Órale vato. What'choo running from?

TOUGH GUY #2: #!*@? Are #!*@ chasing you?

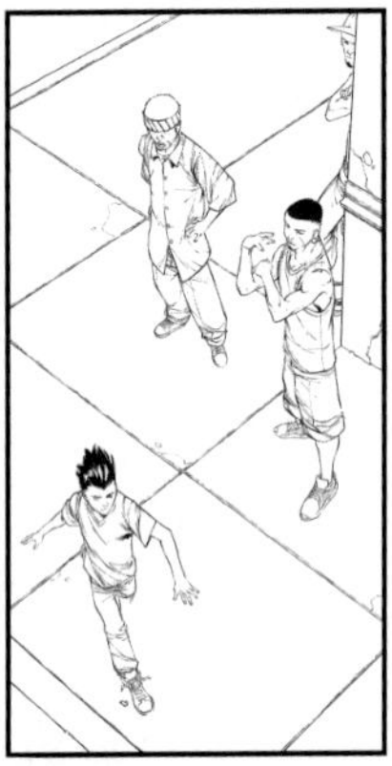

Panel 2
Ricky arrives at home. Lorenzo is there, arms crossed, disappointed, waiting for him.

4 LORENZO: Where were you…? I could have died!

RICKY CAP: Lorenzo is like an 85-year-old Jewish andma trapped in the body of an 11-year-old boy. Truth he should be babysitting me...

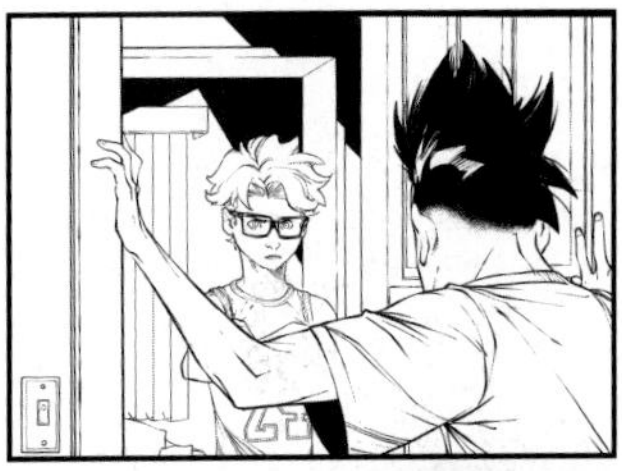

anel 3
cky stumbles through the house to his room.

RICKY: I'm fine…just don't tell Mom I was late, okay?

LORENZO: Only because if I told mom half the stuff you d, she'd murder you.

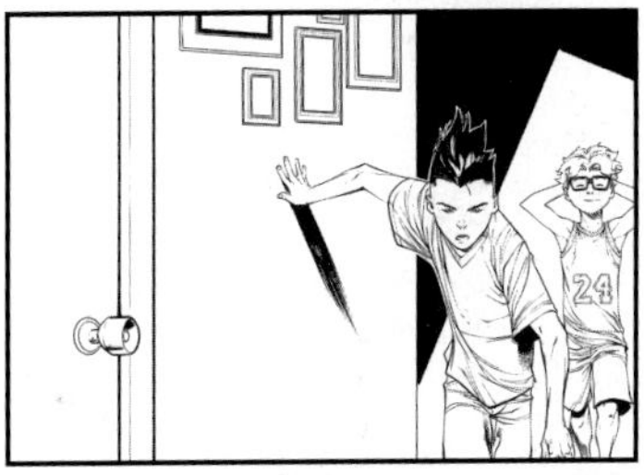

anel 4
ey lie on their bunk beds in silence. Suddenly, they ear something outside their bedroom door.

RICKY CAP: Luckily, he was too tired to blackmail me :e he usually does.

RICKY CAP: I was about to nod off when we heard the ound that changed everything.

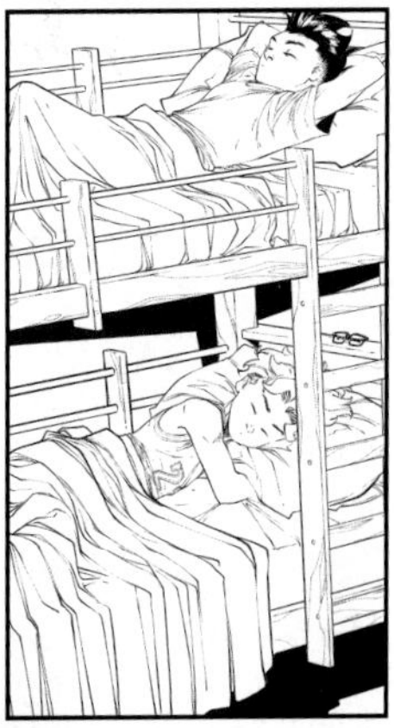

anel 5
orenzo sits up in his bed. Another sound emanates from ehind the bedroom door.

0 SFX: creak

1 LORENZO: Ricky, get up! I hear something!

2 RICKY CAP: And I mean everything.

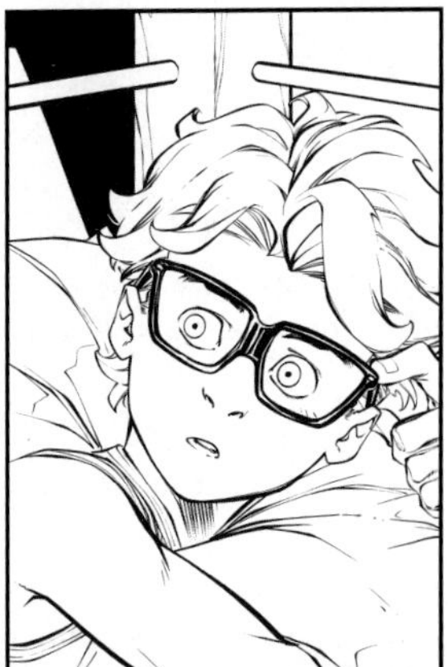

Panel 1
Is their house getting broken into?! Ricky slowly gets up, nervous

Panel 2
Ricky and Lorenzo move toward the door. Ricky holds a baseball bat, Lorenzo holds a chancla (a sandal).

Panel 3
They peek through the crack of the door, eyes wide, as if what they see before them is something unbelievable.

1 RICKY: Is that an old lady or a crackhead?

2 LORENZO: Maybe both?

Panel 4
From over their shoulders, we see what they see: an OLD SHAMAN WARRIOR stands in their living room. BIG PANEL

Panel 5
The boys slowly creep out of their room, weapons raised.

3 RICKY: You're gonna get your ass kicked, lady. I'm gonna beat you with a bat and my little brother's gonna slap you silly you with his chancla.

4 LORENZO: And I'm super-accurate!

Panel 6
The Warrior looks at them, unmoved and unphased.

5 WARRIOR: Ricky Pascal. Son of Gloria Pascal. Descendent of the great Pacal line of shamans...it is time.

Panel 7
Shot of Ricky and Lorenzo staring at each other wide-eyed.

6 RICKY CAP: Either that pill I took was starting to kick in to a whole 'nother level, or one of those pan-flute guys from CityWalk had snuck into my living room.

Panel 1

...ky stares at Lorenzo, runs at the shaman, brandish-
... their weapons. It's clear they don't know what they're
...ng.

...ICKY CAP: Of course, we did the dumb thing and
...rged his decorative ass.

Panel 2

The Warrior, GRIPPING AN ANCIENT STAFF, taps it
against the living floor.

2 SFX: Thump

WARRIOR: Siéntete!

Panel 3

...l of a sudden, Lorenzo and Ricky find themselves on
...e couch. The bat and chancla are on the floor behind
...e Warrior. They look at each other in shock. The Warrior
...ands in the middle of the room, wearing a trench coat
...ver his half naked body, and holding is a mysterious orb.
...IG PANEL

...RICKY CAP: Next thing I know, our asses are glued
... the couch, and dude's telling us he's a 1500-year-old
...ayan Emperor.

...JANAAB: Ricky Pascal, I am here to initiate you.

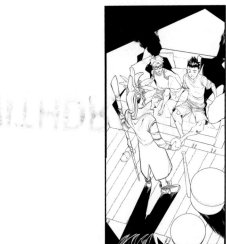

Panel 4

...he brothers, still on the couch, unsure of what to make
...f this.

...LORENZO: We should definitely call mom at work.

...RICKY: Um…

...RICKY: Not sure Mom's gonna be much help on this
...ne...

Panel 1
In addition to his Mayan plumage, Janaab wears a futuristic headset that translates his speech. He is holding up a hand, trying to calm them.

1 JANAAB: Ricky, you must listen. Time works against us.

2 JANAAB: We are of the same blood. Trust that I am you, and you are me.

Panel 2
Ricky freaks out, Lorenzo chides him. Janaab holds a out a hand to calm him.

3 RICKY (small): It's okay…This isn't real…Can't explain why my brother sees it, too…but it isn't real.

4 JANAAB: I can assure you this is no hallucination. Those visions you encountered tonight were prophecies.

5 JANAAB: Tell me, Ricky, have you not always had strange dreams that you could not explain?

Panel 3
Ricky and Lorenzo on the couch. Lorenzo's got eyes like saucers.

6 JANAAB: For the last 500 years, these powers--our powers--
have been suppressed. But no longer.
7 JANAAB: You are this world's most powerful sorcerer.

8 LORENZO: Hold on! Am I special, too?!

9 LORENZO: I'm his blood, which means I'm your blood. Our blood, right?

WITHDRAWN

Panel 4
Backs of Ricky and Lorenzo. Janaab faces them. An ominous mist surrounds them. (Implying a scene change is coming)

10 JANAAB: Beware of jealousy, young Lorenzo. Brothers must stick together, lest they sow destruction.

11 JANAAB: Allow me to share my story...